Writing Literature Reviews

A Guide for Students of the Social and Behavioral Sciences

Sixth Edition

Jose L. Galvan
California State University, Los Angeles

Routledge
Taylor & Francis Group
LONDON AND NEW YORK

First published 2002 by Pyrczak Publishing.

Published 2017 by Routledge
2 Park Square, Milton Park, Abingdon, Oxon OX14 4RN
711 Third Avenue, New York, NY 10017, USA

Routledge is an imprint of the Taylor & Francis Group, an informa business

Cover design by Ruben Hornillo.

ISBN-13: 978-1-936-52337-5 (pbk)

Contents

Continued →

Detailed Contents

Notes

Introduction to the Sixth Edition

This book provides students with practical guidelines for the complex process of writing literature reviews in the social and behavioral sciences. The primary focus is on reviewing original research published in academic journals and on its relationship to theoretical literature. However, most of the guidelines presented here can also be applied to reviews of other kinds of source materials.

Audience for This Book

This book was written for students required to write literature reviews as term papers in content-area classes in the social and behavioral sciences. Often, their previous training has not prepared them to search databases for reports of original research and related theoretical literature, analyze these particular types of literature, and synthesize them into a cohesive narrative. Instead, students are often taught how to use secondary sources such as encyclopedias, reports in the mass media, and books that synthesize the work of others. In addition, they are usually not taught the conventions for writing papers in the social and behavioral sciences. This book is designed to fill this gap by giving students detailed, step-by-step guidance on how to write comprehensive reviews of primary source materials.

Students beginning to work on their theses and dissertations will also benefit from this book if they have not previously received comprehensive instruction on how to prepare critical analyses of published research and the theories on which it is based. Undertaking a thesis or dissertation is stressful. This book serves as a source of calm and logic as students begin to work on their literature review chapter.

Finally, individuals preparing to write literature reviews for possible publication in journals as well as those who need to include literature reviews in grant proposals will find this book helpful.

Unique Features

The following features make this book unique among textbooks designed to teach analytical writing:

- The book's focus is on writing critical reviews of original research.
- It guides students through a systematic, multistep writing process.
- The steps and guidelines are organized sequentially and are illustrated with examples from a wide range of academic journals.
- Each chapter is designed to help students develop a set of specific products that will contribute to a competent literature review.

Notes to the Instructor

Many colleges and universities have adopted "writing across the curriculum" programs, in which students are required to write papers in all courses. While the goals of such programs are admirable, many instructors are pressed for time to cover just the traditional content of their courses, leaving them with little time to teach writing. Such instructors will find this book useful because the explicit steps in the writing process are illustrated with examples throughout, making it possible for students to use it largely on their own. In addition, many professors "naturally" write well but have given little thought to—and have no training in—*how to teach writing*. As a supplement, this book solves that dilemma by providing a detailed guide to the writing process.

Much of what most of us know about writing was learned through what Kamhi-Stein (1997) calls the "one-shot writing assignment" (p. 52).[1] This is where the instructor gives an assignment at the beginning of the term, using the prompt, "Write a paper about *<specific topic>*." Conceptually, we tend to view this type of assignment as a single task, even though students may go through several discrete steps in the process of completing it. In fact, when one is writing papers that involve library research, the quality of the finished product depends in large measure on the care with which one undertakes each of these steps.

In this book, the activities at the end of each chapter guide students through these various steps of the writing process. These activities can be recast as a series of tasks that can easily be incorporated into the syllabus of a survey course in a specific discipline as a multistep writing assignment. Thus, this book has two complementary audiences: (a) instructors who may want to incorporate this multistep writing approach into their course syllabus and (b) students, working independently, who may need help in planning and implementing the various stages involved in completing a major writing assignment, such as the literature review chapter of a thesis or dissertation.

Special Acknowledgment

I am indebted to my publisher, Dr. Fred Pyrczak, for suggesting the topic for this book, for his generous assistance with both the research design content of Chapters 1 and 5, and the updating of material throughout this book for the second through fifth editions. In addition, I am especially grateful to Dr. Pyrczak for writing and contributing Chapters 6 and 7 for inclusion in this book.

Acknowledgments

I would like to thank Jack Petit for updating the content on how to conduct electronic searches in Chapter 3 and for revising the entire chapter. In addition, I would like to thank Monica Lopez for her extensive revision of Chapter 9 and for providing new examples of published research throughout the book.

I would also like to thank Pyrczak Publishing for granting permission to include material from the third edition of *Preparing Literature Reviews: Qualitative and Quantitative Approaches* in Chapter 13 of this book.

---

[1] Kamhi-Stein, L. D. (1997). Redesigning the writing assignment in general education courses. *College ESL, 7,* 49–61.

In addition, I am indebted to my colleagues on the faculty of California State University, Los Angeles, especially Dr. Marguerite Ann Snow and Dr. Lia D. Kamhi-Stein, whose work on the multistep writing approach inspired this book's organization. Both of these individuals offered countless helpful suggestions, most of which are now part of the final manuscript. Errors and omissions, of course, remain my responsibility.

I would also like to thank my supervisor, Dr. Theodore J. Crovello, for allowing me to schedule days off when I need them and for encouraging me to find ways to pursue my professional and academic interests, even while working as an academic administrator.

DEDICATION

For my daughter, Melisa,
a wonderfully creative and independent writer.

Notes

Chapter 1

Writing Reviews of Academic Literature: An Overview

This book is a guide to the specialized requirements of writing a literature review in the social and behavioral sciences. In it, you will learn how to write a review of the literature using primary (original) sources of information in the social and behavioral sciences. By far, the most common primary sources are reports of empirical research published in academic journals. This chapter begins with a brief overview of this type of source. It is followed by brief descriptions of four other types of material found in journals: (1) theoretical articles, (2) literature review articles, (3) anecdotal reports, and (4) reports on professional practices and standards. These are followed by an overview of the writing process you will use as you write your review. This overview includes a brief summary of the rest of the book.

An Introduction to Reviewing Primary Sources

Why Focus on Empirical Research Reports?

The focus of this book is on *original* reports of research found in academic journals. They are original because they are the first published accounts of research. As such, they are *primary sources* of information, detailing the methodology used in the research and in-depth descriptions and discussions of the findings. In contrast, research summaries reported in textbooks, popular magazines, and newspapers, as well as on television and radio, are usually *secondary sources*, which typically provide only global descriptions of results with few details on the methodology used to obtain them. As scholars, you will want to emphasize primary sources when you review the literature on a particular topic. In fact, your instructor may require you to cite primary sources exclusively in your written reviews of literature.

Journals in the social and behavioral sciences abound with original reports of empirical research. The term *empirical* refers to *observation*, while the term *empirical research* refers to *systematic observation*. Research is systematic when researchers plan whom to observe, what characteristics to observe, how to observe, and so on. While empirical research is the foundation of any science, one could reasonably argue that all empirical research is inherently flawed. Hence, the results obtained through research should be interpreted with caution. For instance, the following is a list of three major issues that arise in almost all empirical studies and the problems they pose for reviewers of research.

- *Issue 1: Sampling.* Most researchers study only a sample of individuals and infer that the results apply to some larger group (often called the *population*). Furthermore, most researchers use samples with some kind of bias that makes them unrepresentative of the population of interest. For instance, suppose a professor conducted research using only students in his or her introductory psychology class, or suppose a researcher mailed a questionnaire and obtained only a 40% return from recipients. Clearly, these samples might not be representative of the population of interest.

> Problem: A reviewer needs to consider the possibility of errors in sampling when interpreting the results of a study. Deciding how much trust to put in the results of a study based on a flawed sample is a highly subjective judgment.

- *Issue 2: Measurement.* Almost all measures in empirical research should be presumed to be flawed to some extent. For instance, suppose a researcher uses a self-report questionnaire to measure the incidence of marijuana use on a campus. Even if respondents are assured that their responses are confidential and anonymous, some might not want to reveal their illegal behavior. On the other hand, others might be tempted to brag about doing something illegal even if they seldom or never do it. So what are the alternatives? One is to conduct personal interviews, but this measurement technique also calls for revelation of an illegal activity. Another alternative is covert observation, but this technique might be unethical. On the other hand, if the observation is not covert, participants might change their behavior because they know they are being observed. As you can see, there is no perfect solution.

> Problem: A reviewer needs to consider the possibility of measurement error. Ask yourself whether the method of measurement seems sound. Did the researcher use more than one method of measurement? If so, do the various methods yield consistent results?

- *Issue 3: Problem identification.* Researchers usually examine only part of a problem—often just a very small part. Here is an example: Suppose a researcher wants to study the use of rewards in the classroom and their effect on creativity. This sounds manageable as a research problem until one considers that there are many kinds of rewards—many kinds and levels of praise, many types of prized objects that might be given, and so on. Another issue is that there are many different ways in which creativity can be expressed. For instance, creativity is expressed differently in the visual arts, in dance, and in music. Creativity can be expressed in the physical sciences, in oral expression, in written communication, and so on. No researcher has the resources to examine all of these forms. Instead, he or she will probably have to select only one or two types of rewards and only one or two manifestations of creativity and examine them in a limited number of classrooms.

> Problem: A reviewer needs to synthesize the various research reports on narrowly defined problems in a given area, looking for consistencies and discrepancies from report to report while keeping in mind that each researcher defined his or her problem in a somewhat different way. Because empirical research provides only approximations and degrees of evidence on research problems that are necessarily limited in scope, creating a synthesis is like trying to put together a jigsaw puzzle for which most of the pieces are missing and with many of its available pieces not fully formed.

Considering the three issues presented, you might be tempted to conclude that reviewing original reports of empirical research is difficult. Undoubtedly, it sometimes is.

However, if you pick a topic of interest to you and thoroughly read the research on that topic, you will soon become immersed in a fascinating project. On the vast majority of topics in the social and behavioral sciences, there are at least minor disagreements about the interpretation of the available research data, and often there are major disagreements. Hence, you may soon find yourself acting like a juror, deliberating about which researchers have the most cohesive and logical arguments, which have the strongest evidence, and so on. This can be a fascinating activity.

You also might incorrectly conclude that only students who have intensively studied research methods and statistics can make sense of original research reports. While such a background is very helpful, this book was written with the assumption that any intelligent, careful reader can make sense of a body of empirical research if he or she reads extensively on the topic selected for review. Authors of reports of original research do not present statistics in isolation. Instead, they usually provide discussions of previous research on their topic, definitions of basic concepts, descriptions of relevant theories, their reasons for approaching their research in the way they did, and interpretations of the results that are moderated by acknowledgments of the limitations of their methodology. Thus, a skilled author of a report on original empirical research will guide you through the material and make it comprehensible to you even if you do not understand all the jargon and statistics included in the research report.

One final consideration: It is essential that you carefully and thoroughly read all the research articles that you cite in your literature review. Reading only the brief abstracts (summaries) at the beginning of research articles may mislead you because of their lack of detail and, therefore, cause you to mislead the readers of your literature review. Thus, it is your ethical responsibility to read each cited reference in its entirety.

Another Kind of Primary Source: Theoretical Articles

Not every journal article is a report of original research. For instance, some articles are written for the explicit purpose of critiquing an existing theory or to propose a new one. Remember, a *theory* is a general explanation of why variables work together, how they are related to each other, and especially how they influence each other. As a unified set of constructs, a theory helps to explain how seemingly unrelated empirical observations tie together and make sense. Here is a brief example:

> Consider the *relational theory of loneliness*.[1] Among other things, this theory distinguishes between *emotional loneliness* (utter loneliness created by the lack of a close emotional attachment to another person) and *social loneliness* (feelings of isolation and loneliness created by the absence of a close social network). This theory has important implications for many areas of social and behavioral research. For instance, this theory predicts that someone who is in bereavement due

---

[1] This example is based on material in Stroebe, W., Stroebe, M., Abakoumkin, G., & Schut, H. (1996). The role of loneliness and social support in adjustment to loss: A test of attachment versus stress theory. *Journal of Personality and Social Psychology, 70,* 1241–1249. The relational theory of loneliness is based on and is an extension of *attachment theory.* For a detailed discussion of attachment theory, see Milyavskaya, M., McClure, M. J., Ma, D., Koestner, R., & Lydon, J. (2011). Attachment moderates the effects of autonomy-supportive and controlling interpersonal primes on intrinsic motivation. *Canadian Journal of Behavioural Science.* Advance online publication. doi: 10.1037/a0025828

to the death of a spouse with whom he or she had a close *emotional* attachment will experience utter loneliness that cannot be moderated through *social* support.

Notice two things about the example given above. First, the prediction based on the theory runs counter to the commonsense notion that those who are lonely due to the loss of a significant other will feel less lonely with the social support of family and friends. The theory suggests that this notion is only partially true at best. Specifically, it suggests that family and friends will be able to lessen *social loneliness* but be ineffective in lessening the more deeply felt and potentially devastating *emotional loneliness*. Note that it is not uncommon for a theory to lead to predictions that run counter to common sense. In fact, this is a hallmark of theories that make important contributions to understanding human affairs and our physical world.

Second, the relational theory of loneliness can be tested with empirical research. A researcher can study those who have lost significant others, asking them about how lonely they feel and the types and strength of social support they receive. To be useful, a theory should be testable with empirical methods, which helps the scientific community to determine the extent of its validity.

Your job in reviewing literature will be made easier if you identify the major theories that apply to your topic of interest. Writers of empirical research reports often identify underlying theories and discuss whether their results are consistent with them. Following up on the leads they give you in their references to the theoretical literature will provide you with a framework for thinking about the bits and pieces of evidence you find in various reports about specific and often quite narrow research projects that are published in academic journals. In fact, you might choose to build your literature review around one or more theories. In other words, a topic for a literature review might be to review the research relating to a theory.

It is important to note that a literature review that contributes to a better understanding of one or more theories has the potential to make an important contribution to the writer's field because theories often have broad implications for many areas of concern in human affairs.

Literature Review Articles

Journals often carry literature review articles,[2] that is, articles that review the literature on specific topics—much like the literature review that you will write while using this book. Most journals that publish review articles set high standards for accepting such articles. Not only must they be well-written analytical narratives that bring readers up-to-date on what is known about a given topic, they must also provide fresh insights that advance knowledge. These insights may take many forms, including (a) resolving conflicts among studies that previously seemed to contradict each other, (b) identifying new ways to interpret research results on a topic, and (c) laying out a path for future research that has the potential to advance the field significantly. As a result, going through the process of preparing a literature review is not an easy way to get published in a journal. In fact, when you begin reviewing the literature on a topic, there is no guarantee that you will

---

[2] Some journals also carry book reviews, test reviews, and reviews of other products and services. These will not be considered in this book. Hence, the term *review article* in this book refers only to a *literature review* article.

arrive at the level of insight required to pass the scrutiny of a journal's editorial board. However, if you follow the guidelines outlined in this book, which emphasize analyzing and synthesizing literature (i.e., casting a critical eye on it; pulling it apart, sometimes into pieces; and putting the pieces back together in a new form), you stand a better chance than the average academic writer of producing a review suitable for publication.

It is worth noting that sometimes students are discouraged when they find that their topic has recently been reviewed in an academic journal. They may believe that if the topic was already reviewed, they should select a different topic. That is not necessarily a wise decision. Instead, these students should feel fortunate to have the advantage of considering someone else's labor and insights, that is, of having someone on whose work they can build or with whom they can agree or disagree. Writing is an individual process, so two individuals reviewing the same body of literature are likely to produce distinctly different but, potentially, equally worthy reviews.[3]

Anecdotal Reports

As you review the literature on a specific topic, you may encounter articles built on anecdotal accounts of personal experiences. An *anecdote* is a description of an experience that happened to be noticed (as opposed to an observation based on research, in which there was considerable planning regarding whom and what to observe as well as when to observe a particular phenomenon in order to gather the best information). Anecdotal accounts are most common in journals aimed at practicing professionals such as clinical psychologists, social workers, and teachers. For instance, a teacher might write a journal article describing his or her experiences with a severely underachieving student who bloomed academically while in that teacher's classroom. Other teachers may find this interesting and worth reading as a source of potential ideas. But as a contribution to science, such anecdotes are seriously deficient. Without control and comparison, we do not know to what extent this teacher has contributed to the student's progress, if at all. Perhaps the student would have bloomed without the teacher's efforts because of improved conditions at home or because of a drug for hyperactivity prescribed by a physician without the teacher's knowledge. Given these limitations, anecdotal reports should be used very sparingly in literature reviews, and when they are cited, they should be clearly labeled as anecdotal.

Reports on Professional Practices and Standards

Some journals aimed at practicing professionals publish reports on practices and standards, such as newly adopted curriculum standards for mathematics instruction in a state or proposed legislation to allow clinical psychologists to prescribe drugs. When these types of issues are relevant to a topic being reviewed, they may merit discussion in a literature review.

---

[3] Keep in mind that empirical knowledge is an ever-evolving process—not a set of facts. Nothing is proven by empirical research; rather, research is used to arrive at varying degrees of confidence. Thus, researchers may differ in their interpretations even if they review the same literature on a given topic.

The Writing Process

Now that we have considered the major types of materials you will be reviewing (i.e., reports of empirical research, theoretical articles, literature review articles, articles based on anecdotal evidence, and reports on professional practices and standards), we will briefly consider the process you will follow in this book.

An important but often overlooked distinction is made in this book between *conducting* a literature review (i.e., locating literature, reading it, and mentally analyzing it) and *writing* a literature review. Needless to say, one must first locate, read, and analyze literature before a review can be written. Furthermore, writing a literature review involves a series of steps. In the field of composition and rhetoric, these steps collectively are referred to as the writing process. They include (a) planning, (b) organizing, (c) drafting, (d) editing, and (e) redrafting. More specifically, the process involves defining a topic and selecting the literature for review (planning); analyzing, synthesizing, and evaluating the articles being reviewed (organizing); writing a first draft of the review (drafting); checking the draft for completeness, cohesion, and correctness (editing); and rewriting the draft (redrafting). The process is much like the one you may have followed in your freshman English class when you were asked to write an analytical essay. The organization of this book follows these steps in the writing process.

Writing for a Specific Purpose

The first order of business is to consider your reasons for writing a literature review. Reviews of empirical research can serve several purposes. They can constitute the essence of a research paper in a class, which can vary in length and complexity depending on the professor's criteria for the paper. In a research report in a journal, the literature review is often brief and to the point, usually focusing on providing the rationale for specific research questions or hypotheses explored in the research. In contrast, the literature review in a thesis or dissertation is usually meant to establish that the writer has a thorough command of the literature on the topic being studied, typically resulting in a relatively long literature review. Obviously, these different purposes will result in literature reviews that vary in length and style. Chapter 2 (Considerations in Writing Reviews for Specific Purposes) describes the differences in these three kinds of reviews.

Planning to Write

The first two tasks in planning to write a review of empirical research are defining the topic and locating relevant research articles. These steps are interrelated because the topic you specify will determine the specific literature you identify, and often the results of your literature search will guide you in defining the topic. Sometimes your instructor will assign a specific topic for a term paper. Other times, the choice will be left up to you. The process of defining the topic is the first step covered in Chapter 3 (Selecting a Topic and Identifying Literature for Review).

The remainder of Chapter 3 deals with the process of *selecting relevant journal articles*. Research libraries are not what they used to be. While searching the library's stacks may prove fruitful for you, it can be a hit-or-miss experience because a library's holdings will vary greatly depending on resources, availability, and even vandalism. A better option is to search computerized databases and Internet resources. Reference librarians can help you get started, or you can sign up for a workshop on how to use electronic resources. In this book, you will learn some of the basic steps involved in searching databases. However, keep in mind that each database has its own unique features. It is beyond the scope of this book to describe all these differences in detail.

After you have located an adequate collection of articles concerning your topic, you should read and analyze them. This step is called *analysis* and involves reading an article and taking notes. In other words, as you read, you separate the author's prose into its parts or elements. Because you will be analyzing a number of articles, you will need to prepare a systematic collection of notes. Part of the analysis process is sifting the elements on which you made notes, retaining the pertinent ones, and discarding those you do not need. This step is the subject of Chapter 4 (General Guidelines for Analyzing Literature).

It is sometimes necessary to read and analyze the literature from a more specialized perspective. For instance, if your literature review is part of a research study you are planning to conduct, you will want to pay special attention to Chapter 5 (Analyzing Quantitative Research Literature) and Chapter 6 (Analyzing Qualitative Research Literature). These chapters provide a brief overview of more technical issues in analyzing these types of research.

Organizing Your Notes and Your Thoughts

Having followed the aforementioned steps, you should begin creating a synthesis, which involves putting the parts from your notes back together into a new whole. Think of it like this: Each of the articles you will have read constitutes its own whole. In your research notes, you will have written down parts or elements from each article. Then, you will put these notes back together in a new organizational framework. After creating the new framework, you will evaluate the contents. In other words, you need to describe your evaluation of the quality and importance of the research you have cited. These steps are covered in Chapter 8 (Synthesizing Literature Prior to Writing a Review). At this point, you may want to build one or more tables to summarize the results of previous research. Chapter 7 (Building Tables to Summarize Literature) shows how to do this.

Drafting, Editing, and Redrafting

Next, you should write your first draft. With your audience in mind, decide whether you will write in a formal or less formal *voice*. An effective writer is aware of the reader's expectations. A term paper written for a professor who is knowledgeable in a particular field is different from a literature review in a thesis, which may be read by readers who are curious but not necessarily knowledgeable about a topic. A literature review in a thesis is different from a literature review in an article intended for publication in a journal or in a research paper written for a class. You should also identify the major subtopics and determine the patterns that have emerged from your notes, such as trends, similarities, contrasts, and generalizations. These steps are covered in Chapter 9 (Guidelines for Writing a First Draft).

Next, you should make sure that your argument is clear, logical, and well supported, and that your draft is free of errors. Chapter 10 (Guidelines for Developing a Coherent Essay) will help ensure that your argument makes sense to you and your readers.

Chapter 11 (Guidelines on Style, Mechanics, and Language Usage) describes the first steps in making sure that your review is free of errors.

The final three chapters of this book coincide with the last two steps in the writing process: editing and redrafting. These steps are iterative (i.e., they are meant to be repeated). It is not uncommon for a professional writer to rewrite a draft three or more times, each time producing a refined, new draft. Chapter 12 (Incorporating Feedback and Refining the First Draft) provides guidelines on how to approach this stage in the writing process. Chapter 13 (Preparing a Reference List) provides a detailed overview of how to prepare reference lists consistent with the principles in the *Publication Manual of the American Psychological Association* (APA), which is the most frequently used style manual in the social and behavioral sciences. Finally, Chapter 14 (Comprehensive Self-Editing Checklist for Refining the Final Draft) gives a detailed checklist for use in editing your own manuscript for style and correctness. Formal academic writing requires that you compose a manuscript that is as error-free as possible, and this checklist will help you to accomplish that goal.

Activities for Chapter 1

1. Locate an original report of empirical research in your field, read it, and respond to the following questions. (How to locate journal articles on specific topics is covered in considerable detail later in this book. At this point, simply locate one in your general field of study. Your reference librarian or instructor can help you to identify specific journals in your field that are available in your college library. Scan the tables of contents for a research article on a topic of interest and make a photocopy to bring to class with your answers.) Note that your instructor may want to assign a particular research article for this activity.

   A. Are there any obvious sampling problems? Explain. (Do not just read the section under the subheading "Sample" because researchers sometimes provide additional information about the sample throughout their reports, especially in the introduction, where they might point out how their sample is different from those used by other researchers, or near the end, where they might discuss the limitations of the sample in relation to the results.)

   B. Are there any obvious measurement problems? Explain.

   C. Has the researcher examined only a narrowly defined problem? Is it too narrow? Explain.

   D. Did you notice any other flaws? Explain.

   E. Overall, do you think the research makes an important contribution to advancing knowledge? Explain.

2. Read the first sample literature review (Review A) near the end of this book and respond to the following questions. Note that you will want to read this review again after you have learned more about the process of writing a literature review. The questions below ask only for your first, general impressions. Later, you will be able to critique the review in more detail.

  A. Have the reviewers clearly identified the topic of the review? Have they indicated its delimitations? (For instance, is it limited to a certain type of individual or certain period of time? Does it deal only with certain aspects of the problem?)

  B. Have the reviewers written a cohesive essay that guides you through the literature from subtopic to subtopic? Explain.

  C. Have the reviewers interpreted and critiqued the literature, *or* have they merely summarized it?

  D. Overall, do you think the reviewers make an important contribution to knowledge through their synthesis of the literature? Explain.

Notes

Chapter 2

Considerations in Writing Reviews for Specific Purposes

Although the guidelines given in this book apply to any literature review, you will want to vary your approach to the writing task depending on your purpose for writing a review. This chapter focuses on the three most common purposes for writing a critical review of research and on the audience for each type: (1) as a term paper for a class, (2) as a chapter for a thesis or dissertation, and (3) as part of an introduction to a journal article.

Writing a Literature Review As a Term Paper for a Class

Writing a literature review as a term paper assignment for a class can be somewhat frustrating because the task involves (a) selecting a topic in a field that may be new to you, (b) identifying and locating an appropriate number of research articles using databases that you may not be familiar with, and (c) writing and editing a well-developed essay, all in about three to four months. To compound matters, most instructors will expect you to prepare your review of literature outside of class time with minimal guidance from them. Of course, they will also expect your literature review to be thoroughly researched and well written. This book will help you to accomplish that.

With these difficulties in mind, it is necessary for you to plan your term paper project carefully. First, you should make sure you understand the assignment and know as much as possible about your instructor's expectations near the beginning of the semester. Thus, you should not hesitate to raise questions in class regarding the assignment. Keep in mind that if something is not clear to you, it may be unclear to other students and they will benefit by hearing the answers to your questions.[1] Second, you will need to pace yourself as you undertake the writing process. Make sure that you allow sufficient time to follow the steps outlined in this book, including selecting a topic; reading and evaluating the relevant research articles; synthesizing and organizing your notes; writing, revising, and redrafting your paper; and editing it for correctness and adherence to the required style manual.[2] It is helpful to map out the weeks of your school term and lay out a timeline. Following is a suggested timeline for a 15-week semester.

---

[1] Idiosyncratic questions that other students may not find of interest generally should be raised with the instructor outside of class, perhaps during office hours. Examples: You are planning to go to graduate school and want to write a more extensive paper than required by the professor, or you have written a literature review for a previous class and would prefer to expand on it rather than write a new review.

[2] The dominant style manual in the social and behavioral sciences is the *Publication Manual of the American Psychological Association*. It is available for purchase from most college and university bookstores, and it can be purchased online at www.apa.org.

Example 2.0.1

Stage 1	Preliminary library search and selection of topic
	Complete by the end of Week 3
Stage 2	Reading list and preliminary paper outline
	Complete by the end of Week 6
Stage 3	First draft of paper
	Complete by the end of Week 12
Stage 4	Revised final draft of paper
	Complete by the end of Week 15

Individual instructor's expectations regarding the length of a written review and the number of references cited may vary widely. For term papers written for introductory survey courses, instructors may require only a short review—perhaps as short as a few double-spaced typewritten pages with a minimum of 5 to 10 references. For such a review, you will need to be highly selective in identifying and citing references—usually choosing those that are the most important and/or most current. For upper-division courses, instructors may require longer reviews with more references. Finally, for graduate-level classes in your academic major, your instructor may place no restrictions on length or number of references, expecting you to review as many research reports as necessary to write a comprehensive literature review on your topic.

Given the limited time frame for writing a literature review as a term paper, your topic should usually be narrow. Look for an area that is well defined, especially if you are new to a field. A good way to select a topic is to examine the subheadings within the chapters in your textbook. For instance, an educational psychology textbook might have a chapter on creativity with subsections on definitions of creativity, the measurement of creativity, and fostering creativity in the classroom. As an example, suppose you are especially interested in fostering creativity in the classroom. Reading this section, you might find that your textbook author mentions that there is some controversy regarding the effects of competition on promoting creativity (i.e., Can teachers foster creativity by offering rewards for its expression?). This sounds like a fairly narrow topic that you might start with as a tentative subject. As you search for journal articles on this topic,[3] you may find that there are more articles on it than you need for the term project assignment. If so, you can narrow the topic further by specifying that your review will deal with competition and creativity only in (a) elementary school samples and (b) the fine arts.

If you are not given a choice of topics and are assigned a topic by your instructor, begin your search for literature as soon as possible and report to him or her any difficulties you encounter, such as finding that there is too little research on the assigned topic (perhaps the topic can be broadened or your instructor can point you toward additional sources your literature search did not identify), or that there is too much research (perhaps the topic can be narrowed or your instructor can help you to identify other delimiters, such as reviewing only recent articles).

One consequence of having a short time frame for preparing a literature review as a term paper is that opportunities for feedback on your early drafts will be limited, so you will be responsible for doing much of the editing yourself. When you lay out your time-

---

[3] Searching electronic databases with an emphasis on how to narrow the search is discussed in detail in the next chapter.

line, leave time to consult with your instructor about your first draft, even if this has to be done during an office visit. Finally, the self-editing checklist in Chapter 14 will help you eliminate some common problems before you turn in your paper.

Writing a Literature Review Chapter for a Thesis or Dissertation

The review chapter for a thesis or dissertation is the most complex of the literature review types covered in this book because you will be expected to prepare the initial literature review as part of your research proposal, well before you begin your actual research. Conducting a literature review is one of the steps you will follow in the process of defining the research questions for your study, so you will probably have to redefine your topic and revise your research questions several times along the way.

Students writing a literature review chapter frequently ask, "How many research articles must I cite?" In addition, they ask, "How long should I make the review?" Some students are frustrated when they learn that there is no minimum either on the number of research articles to review or on the length of a review chapter. Often, standards regarding this matter will vary, depending on the nature of the topic and the amount of literature on it.

You should establish two main goals for your literature review. First, attempt to provide a *comprehensive* and *up-to-date* review of the topic. Second, try to demonstrate that you have a thorough command of the field you are studying. Keep in mind that the literature review will provide the basic rationale for your research, and the extent to which you accomplish these goals will contribute in large measure to how well your project will be received. Note that these goals reflect the seriousness of the task you have undertaken, which is to contribute to the body of knowledge in your field. Several traditions that have evolved through the years reflect how seriously academic departments view the writing of a thesis or dissertation. These include the defense of the research proposal, the defense of the finished thesis or dissertation, and the careful scrutiny of the final document by the university's librarian prior to its acceptance as a permanent addition to the library's holdings.

Some students procrastinate when it comes to writing a literature review chapter for a thesis or dissertation. After all, usually there are no set timelines. Therefore, it is important for you to set deadlines for yourself. Some students find it useful to plan an informal timeline in collaboration with the committee chair, perhaps by setting deadlines for completing the various steps involved in the overall process. The guidelines described in this book will be helpful in this regard. You should adopt a regular pattern of consulting with the professors on your committee to ensure that you remain focused and on track.

Finally, the level of accuracy expected in a thesis or dissertation project is quite high. This will require that you edit your writing to a level that far exceeds what may be expected in a term paper assignment. Not only must your writing conform to the particular style manual used in your field, but it should also be free of mechanical errors. The guidelines in Chapter 11 and the self-editing checklist in Chapter 14 will help you accomplish this. Make sure that you allow enough time to set your draft aside for at least a few days before editing your writing, and expect to use the self-editing guide several times before you give your adviser a draft of the review.

Writing a Literature Review for a Research Article

The literature review section of a research article published in a journal is the most straightforward of the three types of reviews covered in this book. These literature reviews are usually shorter and more focused than other types because their major purpose is to provide the background and rationale for specific and often very narrow research projects.

On the other hand, these reviews undergo a level of scrutiny that may exceed even that of a review for a thesis or dissertation. Research article submissions for refereed journals are routinely evaluated by two or three of the leading scholars in the area in which the research was conducted. This means that the literature review should not only reflect the current state of research on the topic, but it should also be error-free. Again, the self-editing checklist in Chapter 14 should be carefully applied.

Frequently, an author will write a journal article a year or more after the research was conducted. This often happens when students decide to write shorter, article-length versions of their theses or dissertations. If this applies to you, search the latest issues of the journals in your field to make sure that your literature review cites the latest work published on your topic.

Although there is some variation among journals, the literature review in a research article for a journal is usually expected to be combined with the introduction. In other words, the introduction to the research is an essay that introduces readers to both the topic and the purpose of the research while providing an overview of the relevant literature. Therefore, the emphasis of the review should be on establishing the scientific context in which a particular study was conducted and on how it contributes to the field. It should help to demonstrate the rationale for the original research reported in the article. As such, it is typically much more narrow and focused than a literature review chapter for a thesis or dissertation.

Activities for Chapter 2

1. What is your purpose in writing a literature review?
   A. As a term paper for a class.
   B. As a chapter for a thesis or dissertation.
   C. As part of the introduction to a research article.
   D. Other: _____

2. If you are writing a literature review as a term paper, has your instructor assigned a specific topic for review? If yes, write the topic here. Also, write any questions you need to ask your instructor.

3. If you are writing a literature review as a term paper and your instructor has not assigned a specific topic, briefly describe two or three possible topics here. (If you are at a loss, examine your textbooks for ideas.)

4. If you are writing a literature review for a thesis or dissertation, write the topic here.

5. If you are writing a literature review for a thesis or dissertation, what is your timeline for completing the first draft? Share your timeline with your instructor for feedback.

6. If you are writing a literature review for a research article that might be published in a journal, name your research purpose or hypothesis. After you have read the literature on your topic, revise your purpose or hypothesis, if necessary, in light of the literature. (Remember that a research purpose or hypothesis should flow directly and logically from the literature reviewed.)

7. If you are writing a literature review for a thesis or dissertation, read the literature review chapters in at least three of the theses or dissertations approved by your committee chair. These are usually housed in the university library. Then, make an appointment with your committee chair to discuss his or her expectations for your review. Make notes here on what you learned about your chair's expectations for your literature review chapter.

Notes

Chapter 3

Selecting a Topic and Identifying Literature for Review

"Where should I begin?" This may be the question most commonly asked by students preparing to write a literature review. While there is no easy answer, this chapter was designed to illustrate the process used by many professional writers and researchers in getting started. Keep in mind that writing is an individual process, so the procedures described here are intended as a roadmap rather than a prescription. By working through this chapter, you will be able to develop two important products that will help you to begin writing an effective literature review: a written description of your topic and a working draft of your reading list.

Obviously, the first step in any kind of academic writing is to decide what you will write about, but the specific path you follow in working through this step will vary depending on your purpose for writing a literature review. The previous chapter described the three most common reasons for writing literature reviews.

In any of these types of literature reviews, you usually should narrowly define your topic. Example 3.0.1 presents a topic that is much too general. In fact, it is the title of a survey course taught at many major universities and represents a very extensive body of literature.

Example 3.0.1

General Topic: Child Language Acquisition

Obviously, the topic in Example 3.0.1 will have to be narrowed down considerably before it can be used as the basis for a literature review of manageable length. The steps that follow will guide you through a process that will result in better alternatives to this example.

✔ Step 1: Search an appropriate database.

Before you select a database and search it, you need to at least select a general topic. Suppose you select the topic in Example 3.0.1, Child Language Acquisition, which is very general. This topic will yield more references than you can possibly use (as you will see in Example 3.1.1). It is usually suitable to start with a general topic, see how much literature exists on it, and then narrow the topic to a more manageable one—a process that you will learn about in this chapter.

A general search using the topic in Example 3.0.1 will yield many thousands of records. Therefore, you should specify a set of parameters that will give you a focused result. For instance, you can limit your search to journal articles, which is recommended, or you can specify a limited range of publication dates, perhaps going back only 5 to 7 years. A sample search conducted in the *Educational Resource Information Center (ERIC)* database using the general topic in Example 3.0.1, Child Language Acquisition, yielded the results in Example 3.1.1, presented here in order of the steps followed:

Example 3.1.1

Step	Number of Records
Search with descriptor "*language acquisition*"[1]:	**17,853**
Limit search to journal articles AND to publication dates of 2006 to present:	**2,725**
Further limit the search to "*language acquisition*" AND "*child language*":	**387**
Further limit the search to "*language acquisition*" AND "*child language*" AND "*speech*"	**137**

How the search in Example 3.1.1 was conducted:

1. Accessed the *ERIC* database at www.eric.ed.gov.
2. Clicked on "Advanced Search."
3. In the first field for "Keywords (all fields)," entered "*language acquisition*" (quotation marks, as shown, are essential).
4. For "Publication Date," accepted default dates of "pre-1966" in the "From" field and "2012" in the "to" field.
5. Clicked on "Search," which yielded **17,853 records** as shown in Example 3.1.1.
6. Clicked on "Back to Search."
7. Changed "Publication Date" default of "pre-1966" in the "From" field to *2006*.
8. For "Publication Type(s)," de-selected "Any Publication Type" by checking the box for "Journal Articles."
9. Clicked on "Search," which yielded **2,725 records** for journal articles since 2006 as shown in Example 3.1.1.
10. Clicked on "Back to Search."
11. Left "*language acquisition*" in the first field for Keywords, and added "*child language*" in the second field for Keywords.
12. Clicked on "Search," which yielded **387 records** for journal articles as shown in Example 3.1.1.
13. Clicked on "Back to Search."
14. Left "*language acquisition*" and "*child language*" in the first and second fields for Keywords and added "*speech*" in the third Keyword field.
15. Clicked on "Search," which yielded **137 records** for journal articles as shown in Example 3.1.1.

---

[1] By enclosing the two-word phrase *language acquisition* in quotations, *ERIC* will search for the complete phrase only—not for the individual words *language* and *acquisition*, which would produce far more results.

Note that for each article identified by the database, you will be given an excerpt of the abstract (i.e., brief summary). Appendix A in this book contains the 137 titles and excerpted abstracts obtained by using the procedures described. Note that the *ERIC* database was used in this example because its holdings are comprehensive and encompass several disciplines with an emphasis on education. Other databases, such as *PsycINFO* and *Sociological Abstracts*, would produce results that focus on other disciplines.[2]

✔ Step 2: Shorten your reference list if it is too long.

Example 3.2.1 presents five possible revised topics based on the sample *ERIC* search. In this example, the articles in Appendix A have been reclassified according to major areas of study that can be discerned from a review of the titles and abstracts of the articles. Having done this, you could then choose from one of the five resulting topic areas, according to your interest and relevance to your course of study.

Example 3.2.1
Possible topic areas, with reference numbers from Appendix A: Sample ERIC Search. Article numbers in bold deal with vocalization.

Disorders Affecting Language Acquisition
> *Sample reference numbers*: 3, 6, 54, 65, 81, 100, 105, 131

Role of Parents in Child Language Acquisition
> *Sample reference numbers*: 4, 12, 15, 16, 20, 25, 34, 44, 52, 67, 73, 77, 89, 97, 103, 114, 116

Language Acquisition Specifically Limited to Spanish-Speaking Children
> *Sample reference numbers*: 57, 59, 68, 91, 92, 119

Acquisition of Grammatical Structures and Categories
> *Sample reference numbers*: 2, 28, 31, 50, 54, 59, 82, 92, 96, 102, 106, 108, 111, 127, 128, 130

Language Acquisition in Infancy
> *Sample reference numbers*: 11, 27, 29, 32, 35, 36, 37, **42**, 43, 46, **72**, 74, 80, 82, **85**, 86, 88, 109, 113, **120**, 126, **132**, 136

These classifications are given merely to illustrate the process. In fact, Appendix A could be reclassified into numerous other categories, but it is not necessary to subcategorize them all. The objective here is to get a feel for the topics of interest or for methods of study represented within the broader spectrum of research articles suggested by your initial database search. Also, you will note that some of the articles appear in more than one category. For instance, reference number 54 has been classified as belonging to two categories: (1) Disorders Affecting Language Acquisition and (2) Acquisition of Grammatical Structures and Categories.

After classifying the records for journal articles as shown in Example 3.2.1, examine them carefully for subsets that might serve as a topic for your literature review. For instance, five of the articles for Language Acquisition in Infancy deal specifically with

---

[2] Unlike *ERIC*, the *PsycINFO* and *Sociological Abstracts* databases are available by subscription only. Most academic libraries maintain subscriptions that grant students and faculty free access.

infant vocalization. These article numbers are shown in bold in Example 3.2.1. If five articles are not sufficient for your purposes, go to Step 3 below.

✓ Step 3: Increase the size of your reference list, if necessary.

If you do not have enough references for your literature review, you can, of course, search further back than 2006. Searching for historical literature is discussed in Step 14.

If you are using *ERIC*, you might also find additional references by clicking on the link (i.e., underlined words) that contains the author(s) name(s). For instance, for the first *ERIC* record in Appendix A, clicking on the second co-author's name provided 13 additional references written by the same author, including research reports and journal articles. Because academic scholars tend to conduct research and write on a given topic over an extended period, these references are often quite relevant to the topic at hand (i.e., Language Acquisition and Speech Development in Young Children).

In addition, when examining an *ERIC* journal article record, you can examine the list of "Descriptors" for that article. The descriptors for record Number 1 in Appendix A are shown in Example 3.3.1. These are related topics. By clicking on one, you will conduct a search of articles on these topics, potentially increasing the size of your reference list by identifying additional related articles.

Example 3.3.1
Descriptors associated with the record for the first article in Appendix A:

Video Technology; Language Acquisition; Discourse Analysis; Case Studies; Speech Impairments; Peer Relationship; Interpersonal Competence; Males; Young Children; Friendship; Sociolinguistics; Foreign Countries

It is also possible to search *ERIC* for documents such as papers presented at conventions, curriculum guides, and theses and dissertations, which can be used to supplement the journal articles already identified. To locate these sources that might provide additional references, near the beginning of the *ERIC* search, leave "Any Publication Type" checked (see the box on page 18 in this book), then conduct another search. Note that for a report to be published in a journal, it usually must pass the scrutiny of one or more editors and editorial consultants or reviewers with special knowledge of the area. This is *not* the case, however, for many of the other types of documents included in the *ERIC* database. Also, note that *ERIC* does not attempt to judge the soundness or quality of the information in the documents. Thus, some nonjournal documents may be less valid than journal articles as sources of information.

✓ Step 4: Consider searching for unpublished studies.

Searching for unpublished studies is another way to increase the size of your reference list (see Step 3). In addition, you may want to search for studies not published in journals[3] because some of these unpublished studies may be important. A potentially important study may not be published in a journal for the following reasons:

1. Some studies of potential importance are never even submitted to journals for possible publication. For instance, theses and dissertations tend to be too long to publish in an academic journal and must undergo extensive rewriting for publication. Many authors of theses and dissertations do not undertake this rewriting process. In addition, some researchers may become discouraged when the results of their studies are not consistent with their hypotheses. Instead of writing up such studies for submission to a journal, they may move on to conduct research in what they consider more fruitful areas using alternative research methods.

2. Some journal editors and expert reviewers may be biased against studies that show no significant difference or that fail to confirm the research hypotheses posed by the researchers.

One way to locate unpublished studies is to contact authors of published studies to ask them if they are aware of any unpublished studies on your topic.[4] For instance, they may have conducted studies that they decided not to submit for publication, or they may know of students or colleagues who have done this. A second way is to search electronic databases via the Internet. How this was done by one team of researchers is described in Example 3.4.1 (italics and bold are added for emphasis).

Example 3.4.1[5]

Description of how a search for unpublished studies was conducted (italics and bold were added for emphasis):

The sample of studies was generated via three methods: (a) a computerized search of social scientific databases (via Web of Knowledge, PsycINFO, and ***Dissertation Abstracts International***) for articles published before January 1, 2010, using the search terms *mood* emotion** AND *reapprais suppress distract* ruminat mindful acceptance** (articles had to include respective terms in either the title, abstract or keywords); (b) reference lists in each article were evaluated for inclusion (ancestry approach; Johnson, 1993); and (c) ***authors of unpublished theses were contacted and requests were made for data***. The literature search identified 12,740 articles and theses.

✓ Step 5: Write the first draft of your topic statement.

Now that you have identified appropriate references, you can reexamine the list of articles you have generated and choose a more specific topic for your literature review.[6] The first draft of your topic statement should attempt to name the area you will investi-

---

[3] Studies not published in journals are commonly referred to as "unpublished studies" even though they may be available in print form in certain academic libraries.

[4] Contact information such as a physical address or e-mail address is usually provided either as a footnote on the first page of a research article or near the end of an article—just before or after the reference list.

[5] Webb, T. L., Miles, E., & Sheeran, P. (2012). Dealing with feeling: A meta-analysis of the effectiveness of strategies derived from the process model of emotion regulation. *Psychological Bulletin*, 138, 775–808.

[6] At this point, it is premature for you to decide on a *final topic*. You should do this only after reading some of the articles you have located.

gate. Think of this statement as a descriptive phrase rather than as a paper or chapter title. Example 3.5.1 presents two statements: one for a literature review topic in the area of psychology and the other in linguistics. Note that these first drafts are still very general.

Example 3.5.1

Psychology:
Language Acquisition by Children With Speech Disorders

Linguistics:
Acquisition of Grammatical Structures and Categories

Both of the topics in Example 3.5.1 could be further narrowed by restricting it to a particular group, such as very young children (e.g., Language Acquisition by *Very Young Children* With Speech Disorders).

✔ Step 6:   Familiarize yourself with online databases—especially Google Scholar.

All university libraries now subscribe to electronic databases. The manual searches of the past have given way to computerized searches. Therefore, it is important to familiarize yourself with your campus library's computer resources. If you are new to online databases, you should attend a workshop or class to learn how to use these services as well as carefully read any handouts concerning your university's database resources. As noted earlier, this book shows you only some general approaches to databases—not all the specific features of any of them.

Most students will find Google Scholar (http://scholar.google.com/) very helpful. The journal database coverage is immense. Moreover, when on a campus network, Google Scholar links students to whatever library database includes the full text. Finally, each entry includes a "cited by" link, which allows students to view other related articles that cite the reference.

✔ Step 7:   Identify the relevant databases in your field of study.

Every academic field has developed its own database services, which are used by its students and scholars. Early in your search, you should identify the databases specific to your field of study. In addition to the information you receive in the library, you should ask your adviser or instructor about the preferred databases in your major. Then, you can find out where they are available and whether they can be accessed from your home or dormitory.

Table 1 illustrates the range of database resources available through the California State University, Los Angeles (CSU, Los Angeles) library, as an example. This list is by no means exhaustive. In fact, larger research libraries will have many more research services than are listed in this table. If you are a student at a small university, it is recommended that you investigate whether your university's library maintains cooperative arrangements with larger institutions in your area.

Table 1
Summary of Selected Library Databases

Database	Subject Areas	Database Statistics
Basic Biosis	Life science	350,000+ records from 350 journals 1926–present, updated monthly
CINAHL	Nursing, allied health, biomedical, and consumer health	2,600,000+ records from 3,000 journals 1981–present, updated quarterly
CSA Sociological Abstracts	Sociology, social work, and other social sciences	636,000+ records from 3,000 journals 1963–present, updated bimonthly
Dissertation Abstracts	Complete range of academic subjects	2,274,000+ records 1861–present, updated monthly
ERIC	Education and related fields	1,440,000+ records from journals, books, theses, and unpublished reports 1966–present, updated monthly
LLBA	Linguistics and language behavior abstracts	479,505+ records from journals, books, dissertations, book reviews, and other media 1973–present, updated quarterly
Medline	Nursing, public health, pharmacy, sports medicine, psychiatry, dentistry, and veterinary medicine	19,000,000+ records, including articles from 5,600 journals published internationally 1946–present, updated monthly
MLA	Literature, language, linguistics, and folklore	1,308,000+ records from 8,800 journals and books 1926–present, updated monthly
NCJRS	Corrections, drugs and crime, juvenile justice, law enforcement, statistics, and victims	210,000+ publications, including journal articles, government documents, and unpublished reports 1960s–present, updated periodically
PAIS International	Social sciences, emphasis on contemporary social, economic, and political issues, and on public policy	670,678+ records from journals 1972–present, updated monthly
PsycINFO	Psychology and related fields. For full-text articles, use *PsycARTICLES.*	3,244,205+ records from 2,500 journals 1806–present, updated weekly
Social Sciences Abstracts	Sociology, psychology, anthropology, geography, economics, political science, and law	562,000 records from 620 journals 1983–present, updated monthly
Social Work Abstracts	Social work and related fields	30,000 records from over 850 journals 1965–present, updated quarterly
Sport Discus	Sports medicine, physical education, exercise, physiology, biomechanics, psychology, training, coaching, and nutrition	1,700,000+ records 1800–present, updated quarterly

✔ Step 8:   Familiarize yourself with the organization of the database.

The online databases described in Table 1 contain abstracts of several kinds of documents, including journal articles, books, conference presentations, project reports, and government documents. As you know from Chapter 1, this book focuses on reviewing articles in academic journals. For each of the thousands of journal articles in these databases, there is a single *record* with specific information about the article. In other words, each item on the list of titles you derive from your search of a database will be linked to an expanded description organized according to a set of categories of information. For instance, each of these records contains a number of *fields*, which include the article's title, author, source journal, publication date, abstract, and list of descriptors (i.e., terms and phrases that describe the article's contents). You can narrow the scope of a search by manipulating one or more of these fields. Publication date, source journal, and author are often used to narrow a search, but the most common method of searching a database is by specifying one or more descriptors. This method is covered next.

✔ Step 9:   Begin with a general descriptor, then limit the output.

Unless you have previous knowledge of a particular topic, you should begin a search with a general descriptor from the database's thesaurus. If a thesaurus is not available, use a label or phrase that describes the topic you are investigating. If this procedure results in too many references, you can limit the search by adding additional descriptors using AND. For instance, if you search for *social* AND *phobia*, you will get only those articles that mention *both* of these terms. Here is an example: Searching one major database in psychology, *APA PsycNET*, from 2006 to the present yields 101 documents (mainly journal articles) relating to phobia. A search for *social* AND *phobia* for the same time yields 75 documents. Finally, a search for *children* AND *social* AND *phobia* yields only 16 documents.

Another effective technique for limiting the number of documents retrieved from an electronic database is to limit the search to descriptors that appear in only the title and/or abstract (summary of the article), restrictions that are permitted in *APA PsycNET* and some other databases. Using these restrictions will help to eliminate articles in which the descriptor is mentioned only in passing in the body of the article because an article dealing primarily with phobias would almost certainly mention the term in one of these important places. (Note that in an unrestricted search, the contents of entire documents are searched.) A search of *APA PsycNET* restricting the search for *phobia* to only the titles OR the abstracts from 2006 to the present yields a total of 56 documents, which is just over one-half the 101 retrieved in an unrestricted search. With the additional restriction that *phobia* appears in *both* the title AND the abstract, 21 articles were obtained, which is about one-fourth the original 101.

✔ Step 10:   Redefine your topic more narrowly.

Selecting a reasonably narrow topic is essential if you are to defend your selection of a topic and write an effective review on it. Topics that are too broad will stretch the limits of your energy and time—especially if you are writing a review for a term project in a single-semester class. A review of a topic that is too broad very likely will lead to a review that is superficial, jumps from area to area within the topic, and fails to demonstrate to your reader that you have thoroughly mastered the literature on the topic. Thus, at this point, you should consider redefining your topic more narrowly.

Example 3.10.1 presents a topic that is problematic in that it is much too broadly defined. Even though the writer has limited the review to English-speaking children as old as 4 years of age, it is still quite broad. Apparently, the writer has chosen to consider studies of children acquiring both the sound and the grammatical systems. If so, the finished review will either be a book-length manuscript (or two) or a shorter manuscript that presents a superficial treatment of the literature on this broad topic.

Example 3.10.1
A topic that is too broad for most purposes:

This paper deals with child language acquisition. I will review the literature that deals with how children learn to speak in a naturalistic setting, starting with the earliest sounds and progressing to fully formed sentences. I will limit myself to English-speaking children, from birth to 4 years old.

Example 3.10.2 is an improved version of the topic in Example 3.10.1. Note that the writer has narrowed the focus of the review to a specific aspect of language. The writer has stated clearly that the review has two main goals: (1) to catalog the range of verbal features that have been studied and (2) to describe what is known about the route children follow in acquiring them. Even though it is very likely that this topic will be modified several more times based on a careful reading of the studies found, it is sufficiently focused to provide the writer with a suitable initial statement of the topic for his or her literature review.

Example 3.10.2
An improved, more specific version of Example 3.10.1:

This paper describes what is known about how children acquire the ability to describe time and to make references to time, including the use of verbs and other features contained in the verb phrase. I will attempt, first, to describe the range of verb-phrase features that have been studied, and second, to describe the path children follow as they develop greater linguistic competence with reference to time.

✓ Step 11: Start with the most current research, and work backward.

The most effective way to begin a search in a field that is new to you is to start with the most current journal articles. If you judge a recently published article to be relevant to your topic, the article's reference list or bibliography will provide useful clues about how to pursue your review of the literature. For Appendix A, for instance, a good strategy would be to obtain articles relevant to your research topic, photocopy the reference lists at the end of each one, compare those lists with the contents of Appendix A, and make strategic decisions about rounding out your reading list. Keep in mind two important criteria for developing your reading list: The reading list should (1) represent the extent of knowledge about the topic and (2) provide a proper context for your own research if you are writing a literature review as part of an introduction to a research study you will be conducting.

✔ Step 12: Search for theoretical articles on your topic.

As you learned in Chapter 1, theoretical articles that relate directly to your topic should be included in your literature review. However, a typical search of the literature in the social and behavioral sciences will yield primarily original reports of empirical research because these types of documents dominate academic journals. If you have difficulty locating theoretical articles on your topic, include *theory* as one of your descriptors. A search of the *APA PsycNET* database from 2006 to 2012 using the descriptors *social* AND *phobia* AND *theory* in any field yielded six documents, including the one in Example 3.12.1, which would clearly be useful for someone planning to write about theories relating to social phobia.

> **Example 3.12.1**[7]
> *An abstract of an article using the term* theory *in the search*:
>
> According to social rank theory, involuntary subordination may be adaptive in species that compete for resources as a mechanism to switch off fighting behaviors when loss is imminent (thus saving an organism from injury). In humans, major depression is thought to occur when involuntary subordination becomes prolonged. The present study sought to operationalize involuntary subordination. Study 1 involved a reanalysis of a Gilbert and Allan (1998) study, with the hypothesis that social comparison (i.e., perceived status), submissive behavior, feelings of defeat, and entrapment would load on a common factor (interpreted as involuntary subordination). Exploratory and confirmatory factor analysis supported this model. In Study 2, measures of these same variables were administered to a group of undergraduate students. Eight items were selected from each measure (on the basis of item-total correlations) to form the Involuntary Subordination Questionnaire (ISQ). In Study 3, scores on the ISQ showed high levels of internal consistency and test-retest reliability in a sample of undergraduate students....

It is important to note that writers of empirical research reports will often discuss the relationship of their studies to theoretical literature and, of course, provide references to this literature. You should follow these leads by looking up the references.

✔ Step 13: Look for "review" articles.

A corollary to the search technique described in the previous step is to use the descriptor "review" as a search term when searching for review articles. Previously published review articles are very useful in planning a new literature review because they are helpful in identifying the breadth and scope of the literature in a field of study. They usually will include a much more comprehensive reference list than is typical in a research article.

---

[7] Sturman, E. D. (2011). Involuntary subordination and its relation to personality, mood, and submissive behavior. *Psychological Assessment, 23,* 262–276.

Note that some journals publish only literature reviews, some emphasize original reports of empirical research but occasionally will publish literature review articles by leading researchers in a field, and other journals have editorial policies that prohibit publishing reviews. If you know the names of journals in your field that publish reviews, you might specify their names in a database search.[8] Because this will restrict your search to just those journals, this should be a separate search from your main one.

A search of *APA PsycNET* using the phrase *"substance abuse"* (include quotation marks) AND *treatment* as keywords (descriptor) in any field AND *review* as a descriptor in the "Title" field identified eight potentially useful articles that contain reviews on the treatment of substance abusers. Two are shown in Example 3.13.1.

Example 3.13.1

Two articles obtained through using review *in the search*:

Fortune, E. E.; Goodie, A. S. (2012). Cognitive distortions as a component and treatment focus of pathological gambling: A review. *Psychology of Addictive Behaviors*, *26*, 298–310.

Seto, M. C.; Lalumière, M. L. (2010). What is so special about male adolescent sexual offending? A review and test of explanations through meta-analysis. *Psychological Bulletin*, *136*, 526–575.

✓ Step 14:   Identify the landmark or classic studies and theorists.

Finally, it is important to identify the landmark studies and theorists on your topic (i.e., those of *historical importance* in developing an understanding of a topic or problem). Unfortunately, some students believe that this is an optional nicety. However, without at least a passing knowledge of landmark studies, you will not understand the present context for your chosen topic. If you are writing a thesis or dissertation, in which fairly exhaustive reviews are expected, a failure to reference the landmark studies might be regarded as a serious flaw.

It is not always easy to identify historically important studies at the very beginning of a literature search. However, authors of some journal articles explicitly note these, as is done in Example 3.14.1.

Example 3.14.1[9]

Excerpt from a research article that identifies a landmark theorist and related studies:

A significant contribution of Rogers is that he was the first to attempt to demystify the nature of psychotherapy by making sessions open to public scrutiny. In the 1940s, he published verbatim transcripts of therapeutic encounters. For more than 50 years, investigators such as Porter (1943), Snyder (1945), and, more recently, Brodley (1994), using these transcripts, have measured how therapists ac-

---

[8] In psychology, for instance, *Psychological Bulletin* is an important journal devoted to literature reviews. A premier review journal in education is the *Review of Educational Research*.
[9] Kahn, E., & Rachman, A. W. (2000). Carl Rogers and Heinz Kohut: A historical perspective. *Psychoanalytic Psychology*, *17*, 294–312.

tually behave with clients. Regarding this issue, Gill (personal communication, August 28, 1991) wrote, "I also think Rogers deserves a great deal of credit for being the first person to present verbatim sessions. Since him, a number of people have plucked up the courage to do so but he was the first." (p. 311)

While reading the articles you selected, you will often notice that certain authors' names are mentioned repeatedly. For instance, if you read extensively on how social factors affect learning, you will find that Albert Bandura's social-learning theory is cited by numerous authors of research articles. At this point, you would want to search the database again using Bandura's first and last names as one of the descriptors for two reasons: (1) to locate material he has written on his theory (keep in mind that you want it from the *original source* and not just someone else's paraphrasing of the theory) and (2) to try to locate any early studies that he may have conducted that led him to the theory or that he originally presented to lend credence to the theory. Keep in mind that individuals who present theories very often conduct research and publish it in support of their theories. Their early studies that helped establish their theories are the ones that are most likely to be considered "landmark" or "classic." Note that when you conduct such a search of the database for this purpose, you should *not* restrict the search to only articles published in recent years. Searching all years of the *APA PsycNET* database while restricting the search to articles with the name *Albert Bandura*[10] as the author of the article, AND *social* in the title of the article, AND *learning* in all fields yields relevant documents, including an early one, which is shown in Example 3.14.2.

Example 3.14.2
An early study by a leading researcher and theoretician:

Bandura, A. (1969). Social learning of moral judgments. *Journal of Personality and Social Psychology, 11*, 275–279.

Finally, consult the relevant college textbooks. Textbook authors often briefly trace the history of thought on important topics and may well mention what they believe to be the classic studies.

---

[10] When specifying an author's name, use both first and last names but do not enclose the full name with quotation marks, as this would exclude instances where the last name is listed first.

Activities for Chapter 3

1. First, become familiar with the electronic databases in your field. (See Table 1 earlier in this chapter for a partial list of available databases.) You can do so either by attending a workshop in your university library or by reading the documentation and practicing on your own. Note that many libraries now allow you to search their databases online from your home, but you will probably need to use a university computer account to do so. Once you are familiar with the databases, select one database to complete the rest of this exercise.

2. If your instructor has assigned a term paper on a specific topic, search the database using a simple phrase that describes this topic. If you are working on your own, select an area that interests you, and search the database using a simple phrase that describes your area of interest. How many citations for the literature did the search produce?

3. Retrieve two or three records from your search and locate the lists of descriptors. Compare the lists and note the areas of commonality as well as differences.
   - Write down the exact wording of three descriptors that relate to your intended topic. Choose descriptors that reflect your personal interest in the topic.
   - Compared to the simple phrase you used when you started, do you think these descriptors are more specific *or* more general? Why?

4. Now use the descriptors you just located to modify the search.
   - First, modify the search to select more records.
   - Then, modify the search to select fewer records.
   - If you used the connector AND, did it result in more *or* fewer sources? Why do you think this happened?
   - If you used the connector OR, did it result in more *or* fewer sources? Why do you think this happened?

5. If necessary, narrow the search further until you have between 50 and 150 sources, and print out the search results.
   - Carefully scan the printed list to identify several possible subcategories.
   - Compare the new categories to your original topic.
   - Redefine your topic more narrowly, and identify the articles that pertain to your new topic. Prepare a list of the references for these articles.

Notes

Chapter 4

General Guidelines for Analyzing Literature

Now that you have identified the preliminary set of articles for your review, you should begin the process of analyzing them *prior to* writing your review. This chapter is designed to help you through this process. The end result will be two important products: (1) a working draft of your reference list and (2) a set of note cards that will contain specific, detailed information about each article, both of which you will need before you begin to write.

✔ Guideline 1: Scan the articles to get an overview of each one.

Obviously, you read the titles of the articles when you selected them, and you probably also read the abstracts (i.e., summaries) that most journals include near the beginning of each article. Next, you should read the first few paragraphs of each article, where the author usually provides a general introduction to his or her problem area. This will give you a feel for the author's writing style as well as his or her general perspectives on the research problem. Then, jump to the last paragraph before the heading "Method," which is usually the first major heading in the text of a research article. This is the paragraph in which it is traditional for researchers to state their specific hypotheses, research questions, or research purposes. Next, scan the rest of the article, noting all headings and subheadings. Scan the text in each subsection, but do not allow yourself to get caught up in the details or any points that seem difficult or confusing. Your purpose at this point is to get an overview.

Note that by following this guideline, you will be *prereading*, which is a technique widely recommended by reading specialists as the first step in reading a technical report. Because prereading gives you an overview of the purpose and contents of a report, it helps you keep your eye on the big picture as you subsequently work through the details of a research report from beginning to end. The information you gain by prereading will also help you group the articles into categories, as suggested in the next guideline.

Example 4.1.1 shows in bold a typical set of major headings for a short research report in a journal.

Example 4.1.1

Title [followed by researchers' names and their institutional affiliations]
Abstract [a summary of the complete report]
[An introduction in which related literature is reviewed follows the abstract; typically, there is *no* heading called "Introduction."]

31

Method
    Participants [or Subjects]
    Measures [or Instrumentation]
Results
Discussion

Longer articles will often contain additional headings, such as *Assumptions*, *Definitions*, *Experimental Treatments*, *Limitations*, and so on. Scanning each of these sections will help prepare you to navigate when you begin to read the article in detail from beginning to end.

The last heading in a research article is usually "Discussion." Researchers often reiterate or summarize their research purposes, research methods, and major findings in the first few paragraphs under this heading. Reading this section of a report on research will help you when you read the results section in detail, which can be difficult if it contains numerous statistics.

✓ Guideline 2: Based on your overview (see Guideline 1), group the articles by category.

Sort the articles you have amassed into stacks that correspond roughly to the categories of studies you will describe. You may choose to organize them in any number of ways, but the most common practice is to first organize them by topic and subtopic and then in chronological order within each subtopic. Example 4.2.1 shows a possible grouping of articles into categories and subcategories for a review of research literature on the psychological effects of meditation.

Example 4.2.1[1]

I. Theoretical Considerations About the Effects of Meditation
    A. What Is Meditation?
    B. Meditation as a Means to Transformed Consciousness:
    Indian Theoretical Approaches
        1. Hindu approaches to meditation
        2. Buddhist approaches to meditation
    C. Meditation as a Means to Self-Regulation:
    Western Theoretical Approaches
        1. Cultivating mental balance
        2. Specific effects of mindfulness practice
            a. Effects via attention control
            b. Effects via a shift in perspective
    D. What Could Have Been Predicted?
        1. Predictions of the Indian theoretical approaches

---

[1] Based on Sedlmeier, P., Eberth, J., Schwarz, M., Zimmermann, D., Haarig, F., Jaeger, S., & Kunze, S. (2012). The psychological effects of meditation: A meta-analysis. *Psychological Bulletin*. Advance online publication.

         2. Predictions of the Western theoretical approaches
         3. Common predictions
    II. Studies, Dependent Measures, and Moderator Variables
       A. Selection of Studies
       B. Categorization of Studies
         1. Classification of dependent measures
         2. Potential moderating variables
            a. Kind of control group
            b. Design of studies
            c. Randomization
            d. Publication outlet
            e. Year of publication
            f. Kind of meditation
            g. Amount of meditation practice

Example 4.2.2 shows a possible grouping of articles into categories and subcategories for a review of research literature on smoking cessation and menopause.

Example 4.2.2[2]

I. Smoking, the Menopausal Transition, and Health
    A. Hormone Therapy
II. Weight Gain and Weight Concern in Peri- and Postmenopausal Women
    A. Weight Gain During the Menopausal Transition
    B. Smoking Cessation-Related Weight Gain in Peri- and Postmenopausal Women
    C. Weight Concern in Peri- and Postmenopausal Women
    D. Interventions Targeting Weight Gain or Overconcern About Weight Gain
III. Menopausal Symptoms and Smoking Cessation
    A. Negative Affect
    B. Other Menopausal Symptoms
IV. Estrogen Level, Nicotine Metabolism, and Nicotine Reinforcement
V. Smoking Cessation Outcomes in Peri- and Postmenopausal Women

Organizing the articles into categories will facilitate your analysis if you read all the articles in each category or subcategory at about the same time. For instance, it will be easier to synthesize the literature on the effects of weight gain during the menopausal transition (see point II.A in Example 4.2.2) if all the articles on this topic are read together, starting with the most recent one.

✓ Guideline 3:   Organize yourself before reading the articles.

It is important to organize yourself prior to beginning a detailed reading of the ar-

---

[2] Based on McVay, M. A., & Copeland, A. L. (2011). Smoking cessation in peri- and postmenopausal women: A review. *Experimental and Clinical Psychopharmacology, 19*, 192–202.

ticles. You will need a computer, a pack of note cards to write your comments on, and several packs of self-adhesive flags that you can use to identify noteworthy comments. You can use different-colored self-stick flags to mark different subtopics, different research methods, a review article or landmark study, or anything else that should be noted or might help you organize your review. If you are using a computer, you can use different colors of highlighting (available on word-processing programs) instead of colored flags on note cards.

✓ Guideline 4: Use a consistent format in your notes.

After you have organized the articles, you should begin to read them. As you read, summarize the important points and write them on the note cards. Develop a format for recording your notes about the articles you will be reading, and use this same format consistently. Building consistency into your notes at this stage in the process will pay off later when you start to write the review. As has been noted, you will encounter considerable variation across studies, and your notes should be consistent and detailed enough for you to be able to describe both differences and similarities across them. Example 4.4.1 illustrates the recommended format for recording your notes. Remember to note the page numbers whenever you copy an author's words verbatim. Direct quotations should always be accompanied by page numbers, and it will save you considerable time later in the process if you already have the page numbers noted. Make sure to double-check your quotes for accuracy.

Example 4.4.1

Author's(s') Last Name(s), Initial(s)
Title of Article
Publication Year
Name of Journal/Volume Number/Page Numbers

Notes (*responding to the following questions*):
1. What is the main point of this article?
2. Describe the methodology used. (Include numbers of participants, controls, treatments, etc.)
3. Describe the findings.
4. What, if anything, is notable about this article? (Is it a landmark study? Does it have flaws? Is it an experimental study? Is it qualitative *or* quantitative? and so on.)
5. Note specific details you find especially relevant to the topic of your review. (Make this as long as necessary.)

The points in Example 4.4.1 are given as examples to guide you through this process. In an actual case, you may choose to disregard one or more of them, or you may decide that others are more appropriate. You may need to create several note cards per source. For instance, you might have a card for each article on the main point of the article, another one on the research methodology used, and so on.

It may also be helpful to use a separate card to make notes of questions or concerns you have as you read a particular article, or to note any conclusions you may reach about the validity of the research. These notes can later be incorporated into your paper, perhaps in your discussion or conclusion, and using a separate card for this will save you valuable time later. These cards will also be quite helpful if you decide to build tables that summarize groups of studies for presentation in your literature review. Guidelines for building such tables are presented in Chapter 7.

For each article, one card should contain the complete bibliographic details, while the other cards on the article should be coded with just part of the bibliographic information, such as the first author's last name, a key word from the title of the article, and the year of publication.

✓ Guideline 5: Look for explicit definitions of key terms in the literature.

It should not surprise you that different researchers sometimes define key terms in different ways. If there are major differences of opinion on how the variables you will be writing about should be defined, you will want to make notes on the definitions. In fact, if several different definitions are offered, you might find it helpful to prepare a separate set of cards containing just the definitions.

To see the importance of how a term is defined, consider definitions of *justice programs* and *entertainment-based justice programs* in Example 4.5.1. It excludes programs that are more than one hour long and ones that are based on real events from the study. Another researcher who uses a definition without these exclusions might obtain different results. As a reviewer, you will want to note such differences in definitions because they may help to explain discrepant results from study to study.

Example 4.5.1[3]

Considered a particular "genre," or general category of TV entertainment (Gitlin, 1979), "justice" programs (sometimes called police dramas, crime dramas, legal shows, or lawyer shows) were defined as half-hour or one-hour television programs that focus on some aspect of the criminal justice system, such as law enforcement, criminal prosecution, courts, or corrections. Furthermore, entertainment-based justice programs were defined as fictional; that is, characters and events are fictional, they do not portray real-life characters or actual events. Using these…definitions, the researcher discovered 13 entertainment-based justice programs being broadcast…which included: *NYPD Blue*…. (p. 18)

Make special note of authoritative definitions (i.e., definitions offered by experts), which you can quote or summarize. For instance, the author of Example 4.5.2 cites a definition used by a professional association in the literature review.

---

[3] Soulliere, D. M. (2003). Prime-time murder: Presentations of murder on popular television justice programs. *Journal of Criminal Justice and Popular Culture, 10*, 12–38.

Example 4.5.2[4]

Throughout the article, I adopt the definition of *terrorism* used by the Department of Defense (2010a): "The calculated use of unlawful violence or threat of unlawful violence to inculcate fear, intended to coerce or to intimidate governments or societies in the pursuit of goals that are generally political, religious, or ideological."

Keep separate note cards with definitions of related terms. For instance, consider Example 4.5.3, in which the term *sex differences* is defined separately from the term *gender differences*.

Example 4.5.3[5]

Although terminology in the field is not standardized, *sex differences* generally refers to biological differences or psychological differences stemming from biological origins, whereas *gender differences* generally refers to social-cultural differences, socially constructed differences, or differences in which the origin is unknown. In this meta-analysis, we are unable to make claims about the causal origins of differences in self-conscious emotional experience between men and women. Thus, insofar as the origin of such differences remains unknown, we use the term *gender differences* to refer to differences in the emotional experience between men and women.

Note that it is usually a good idea to present definitions of key terms near the beginning of a literature review.

Consider pointing out contrasting terms when citing a definition, which is done in Example 4.5.4.

Example 4.5.4[6]

Collectivism, a concept that "emphasizes close, nurturing, and supportive interpersonal relationships," is valued in most Latino cultures over *individualism*, which is a more prominent value in mainstream U.S. culture (Mason et al., 1995, p. 7). Collectivism points to Latinos' tendency to think of collective well-being (that is, that of the family) over one's individual needs.

✓ Guideline 6:   Look for key statistics to use near the beginning of your literature review.

Keep a separate set of note cards with key statistics that you might want to cite near the beginning of your literature review. Example 4.6.1 shows the first sentence of a

---

[4] Monahan, J. (2012). The individual risk assessment of terrorism. *Psychology, Public Policy, and Law, 18,* 167–205.

[5] Else-Quest, N. M., Higgins, A., Allison, C., & Morton, L. C. (2012). Gender differences in self-conscious emotional experience: A meta-analysis. *Psychological Bulletin.* Advance online publication.

[6] Acevedo, V. (2008). Cultural competence in a group intervention designed for Latino patients living with HIV/AIDS. *Health & Social Work, 33,* 111–120.

literature review on intimate-partner violence. Note that citing a specific percentage is a much stronger beginning than a general statement, such as "Many individuals in the United States are victimized by their partners," would be.

Example 4.6.1[7]

Over 10% of women and men in a nationally representative United States sample have reported victimization by their partners within the prior 12 months (Straus & Gelles, 1990), reflecting the high prevalence of intimate partner violence in this country.

Citing statistics at the beginning of a literature review is optional, with some topics lending themselves more to the technique than others. However, if you plan to start with a reference to quantities (e.g., *Some* adolescents....; *Frequently*, voters prefer....), it is desirable to provide a specific estimate if it is available. For many topics in the social and behavioral sciences, relevant statistics can be found online at www.census.gov.

✓ Guideline 7: Pay special attention to review articles on your topic.

If you find literature review articles (i.e., articles that consist solely of a literature review that is not just an introduction to a report of original research) on your topic or a closely related topic, read them carefully and make notes that will allow you to summarize them in your literature review. This was done by the authors of Examples 4.7.1 and 4.7.2, in which they briefly summarized a previous review in their review.

Example 4.7.1[8]

A recent review of studies on the psychological health of cancer survivors reported that the prevalence of anxiety ranges by study from 6% to 23%, and the prevalence of depression from 0% to 58% (Andrykowski et al., 2008). The variance in these estimates can be explained by the diversity of the cancer survivor samples from which these prevalence estimates have been derived; samples differed with respect to time since diagnosis, type of cancer, stage of disease, and cancer treatment.

Example 4.7.2[9]

For example, a recent review on adolescents' religiosity and mental health revealed that religious adolescents showed fewer internalizing and externalizing problems and had higher psychological well-being (Wong, Rew, & Slaikeu, 2006).

---

[7] Jose, A., Olino, T. M., & O'Leary, K. D. (2012). Item response theory analysis of intimate-partner violence in a community sample. *Journal of Family Psychology, 26,* 198–205.

[8] Boehmer, U., Glickman, M., & Winter, M. (2012). Anxiety and depression in breast cancer survivors of different sexual orientations. *Journal of Consulting and Clinical Psychology, 80,* 382–395.

[9] Seol, K. O., & Lee, R. M. (2012). The effects of religious socialization and religious identity on psychosocial functioning in Korean American adolescents from immigrant families. *Journal of Family Psychology, 26,* 371–380.

✓ Guideline 8: Prepare note cards with short notable quotations that might be used very sparingly in your review.

Direct quotations should be used very sparingly in literature reviews. This is because the use of too many quotations can interrupt the flow of the narrative. In addition, the writer of a review is usually able to summarize and paraphrase points more succinctly than the original author, who is obligated to provide more details on the research than the reviewer is. Nevertheless, there are instances in which an especially apt statement might be worthy of being quoted in a literature review. For instance, in Example 4.8.1, the writers are reviewing literature on attachment and parenting. The quoted material succinctly defines the term *attachment* in their review.

Example 4.8.1[10]

Bowlby (1969) described attachment as a "lasting psychological connectedness between human beings" (p. 194), defining it as an emotional bond established with someone who is perceived as a source of security and who provides a safe base from which individuals explore the world (Bowlby, 1988).

Another appropriate use of quotations is when citing legal matters, where the exact wording is important and even a small change in wording might change its legal meaning. Example 4.8.2 shows such a quotation of a federal law.

Example 4.8.2[11]

Almost a decade into the reform, [No Child Left Behind] is a large and complex piece of legislation that elicits a focus on public school education. However, the language of the federal NCLB is fairly straightforward. Section 111(b)(2)(K) of the Elementary and Secondary Education Act of 1965, as amended by NCLB, states:

> Accountability for Charter Schools—The accountability provisions under this Act shall be overseen for charter schools in accordance with State charter school law.

Note that the quotations in Examples 4.8.1 and 4.8.2 are quite short. It is almost always inappropriate to include long quotations (i.e., longer than a few sentences) in a literature review. After all, a review should be an original synthesis, not a repeat of already published materials.

✓ Guideline 9: Look for methodological strengths.

It is unlikely that you will find a single research article with definitive results about any aspect of the human condition. Inevitably, some studies will be stronger than others, and these strengths should be noted in your review. Ask yourself how strong the

---

[10] Vieira, J. M., Ávila, M., & Matos, P. M. (2012). Attachment and parenting: The mediating role of work-family balance in Portuguese parents of preschool children. *Family Relations, 61,* 31–50.
[11] Gawlik, M. A. (2012). Moving beyond the rhetoric: Charter school reform and accountability. *The Journal of Educational Research, 105,* 210–219.

evidence is, and keep in mind that in your role as the reviewer, you have the right and the responsibility to make these subjective evaluations.

The strength of a research article may come from the research methodology used. Do the research methods of one study improve on the data-gathering techniques of earlier studies? Does the article's strength derive from the size and generalizability of its subject pool? Does a set of studies demonstrate that the same conclusion can be reached through use of a variety of methods? These and other similar questions will guide you in determining the strengths of particular studies. Identifying methodological strengths is considered in more detail in Chapters 5 and 6. The authors of Example 4.9.1 discuss the strength of one particular study on school-aged children.

Example 4.9.1[12]

The Health Behavior in School-aged Children Study (HBSC) is perhaps the single best source of data on younger adolescents in multiple countries. Involving 42 countries in Europe and North America, the HBSC conducts school-based surveys every 4 years with national probability samples of youth with mean ages of 11.5, 13.5, and 15.5 years.

✓ Guideline 10: Look for methodological weaknesses.

Remember that you should note any major weaknesses you encounter when reviewing research literature. The same process you used in identifying strengths should be used when you are identifying weaknesses. For instance, you should determine whether the author's research method has provided new insights into the research topic. Particularly, if an innovative methodology is used, does it seem appropriate, or does it raise the possibility of alternative explanations? Has an appropriate sample been used? Are the findings consistent with those of similar studies? Is enough evidence presented in the article for a reasonable person to judge whether the researcher's conclusions are valid?

Here again, it may be preferable to critique groups of studies together, especially if their flaws are similar. Generally, it is *inappropriate* to note each and every flaw in every study you review. Instead, note major weaknesses of individual studies, and keep your eye out for patterns of weaknesses across groups of studies. For instance, if all the research reports on a subtopic you are reviewing are based on very small samples, you might note this fact on a separate card that relates to the collection of articles on that subtopic.

The authors of Example 4.10.1 point out a weakness in the studies conducted on tobacco screening in college student health centers.

Example 4.10.1[13]

Few studies have focused on the tobacco screening and interventions practices in

---

[12] Farhat, T., Simons-Morton, B. G., Kokkevi, A., Van der Sluijs, W., Fotiou, A., & Kuntsche, E. (2012). Early adolescent and peer drinking homogeneity: Similarities and differences among European and North American Countries. *Journal of Early Adolescence, 32,* 81–103.

[13] Sutfin, E. L., McNamara, R. S., Blocker, J. N., Ip, E. H., O'Brien, M. C., & Wolfson, M. (2012). Screening and brief intervention for tobacco use by student health providers on college campuses. *Journal of American College Health, 60,* 66–73.

college student health centers specifically, but more importantly, the literature that has been presented is primarily self-reported data by health care providers themselves, not students.

✓ Guideline 11: Distinguish between assertion and evidence.

A common mistake made in literature reviews is to report an author's assertions as though they were findings. To avoid this mistake, make sure you have understood the author's evidence and its interpretation. A finding derives from the empirical evidence presented. An assertion is the author's opinion.

In Example 4.11.1, readers can easily distinguish between the assertions in the body of the paragraph and the evidence-based statements in the last sentence. Bold italics have been added for emphasis.

Example 4.11.1[14]

The risk factor for binge eating that has received the most attention is dieting (Lowe, 1994). Dieting *is thought to* increase the risk that an individual will over-eat to counteract the effects of caloric deprivation. Dieting *may* also promote binge eating because violating strict dietary rules can result in disinhibited eating (the abstinence–violation effect). Moreover, dieting entails a shift from a reliance on physiological cues to cognitive control over eating behaviors, which leaves the individual vulnerable to disinhibited eating when these cognitive processes are disrupted. In support of *these assertions*, dieting predicted binge eating onset in adolescent girls (Stice & Agras, 1998; Stice, Killen, Hayward, & Taylor, 1998), and acute caloric deprivation resulted in elevated binge eating in adult women (Agras & Telch, 1998; Telch & Agras, 1996). (p. 132)

✓ Guideline 12: Identify the major trends or patterns in the results of previous studies.

When you write your literature review, you will be responsible for pointing out major trends or patterns in the results reported in the research articles you review. This is done in Example 4.12.1.

Example 4.12.1[15]

Points out major trends in research:

A plethora of randomized clinical trials (RCTs) and recent meta analyses have indicated that cognitive behavioral therapy (CBT) is an efficacious treatment for youth with anxiety disorders (e.g., Bodden, Bögels, et al., 2008; Bodden, Dirksen, et al., 2008; Kendall, Hudson, Gosch, Flannery-Schroeder, & Suveg, 2008;

---

[14] Stice, E., Presnell, K., & Spangler, D. (2002). Risk factors for binge eating onset in adolescent girls: A 2-year prospective investigation. *Health Psychology, 21,* 131–138.
[15] Walker, J. V. III (2012). Parental factors that detract from the effectiveness of cognitive-behavioral treatment for childhood anxiety: Recommendations for practitioners. *Child & Family Behavior Therapy, 34,* 20–32.

Spielmans, Pasek, & McFall, 2007). While the earliest therapeutic interventions for childhood anxiety were merely downward extensions of adult treatment protocols, current interventions have since been appropriately modified to take into account relevant considerations in treating the child population—including such factors as developmental level, familial factors, and autonomy (Kendall et al., 2008).

Of course, you may not be as fortunate as the reviewer who wrote Example 4.12.1. There may be considerable inconsistencies in results from one research article to another. When this is the case, you should try to make sense of them for your readers. For instance, you might state a generalization based on a *majority* of the articles, or you might state a generalization based only on those articles you think have the strongest research methodology. Either option is acceptable as long as you clearly describe to your reader the basis for your generalization. Once again, careful note taking during the analysis stage will help you in this process.

✔ Guideline 13: Identify gaps in the literature.

It is every graduate student's dream to discover a significant gap in the literature, especially one that can form the crux of the student's thesis or dissertation study. In fact, gaps often exist because research in these areas presents considerable obstacles for researchers. These gaps should be noted in a literature review, along with discussions of why they exist. If you identify a gap that you believe should be addressed, make note of it, and take it into consideration as you plan the organization of your review.

You will often find gaps mentioned in previous literature reviews, as in Example 4.13.1.

Example 4.13.1[16]
Points out gaps in the literature:

The research discussed previously was mainly based on findings from Western literature conducted in the area of adolescent coping and the gender differences that existed in their coping styles. In comparison, there is a dearth of research in adolescent coping and the role of gender in predicting their choice of coping styles in Asian countries. Therefore, the aim of this study was to examine the coping behaviors of a sample of academically advanced students in an Asian context....

✔ Guideline 14: Identify relationships among studies.

As you read additional articles on your list, make note of any relationships that may exist among studies. For instance, a landmark research article may have spawned a new approach subsequently explored in studies conducted by others, or two articles may explore the same or a similar question but with different age groups or language groups.

---

[16] Huan, V. S., Yeo, L. S., Ang, R. P., & Chong, W. H. (2012). Concerns and coping in Asian adolescents—gender as a moderator. *The Journal of Educational Research, 105,* 151–160.

It is important to point out these relationships in your review. When you write, you probably will want to discuss related ones together.

✓ Guideline 15: Note how closely each article relates to your topic.

Try to keep your review focused on the topic you have chosen. It is inappropriate to include studies that have no relationship to the area of study in your literature review. Therefore, your notes should include explicit references to the specific aspects of a study that relate to your topic.

If you determine that there is no literature with a direct bearing on one or more aspects of your research topic, it is permissible to review peripheral research, but this should be done cautiously. Pyrczak and Bruce (2011) cite the example of year-round school schedules, implemented in Los Angeles as a curricular innovation, as shown in Example 4.15.1.

Example 4.15.1[17]

When Los Angeles first started implementing year-round school schedules, for example, there was no published research on the topic. There was research, however, on traditional school-year programs in which children attended school in shifts, on the effects of the length of the school year on achievement, and on the effectiveness of summer school programs. Students who were writing theses and dissertations on the Los Angeles program had to cite such peripheral literature in order to demonstrate their ability to conduct a search of the literature and write a comprehensive, well-organized review of literature.

Such examples are rare, and you are advised to consult your instructor before you reach the conclusion that no studies have dealt with your specific research topic.

✓ Guideline 16: Evaluate your reference list for currency and for coverage.

When you have finished reading the articles you have collected, you should re-evaluate your entire reference list to ensure that it is complete and up-to-date. A literature review should demonstrate that it represents the latest work done in the subject area. As a rule of thumb, use a 5-year span from the present as a tentative limit of coverage, keeping in mind that you will extend your research further back when it is warranted. If your review is intended to present a historical overview of your topic, for instance, you may have to reach well beyond the 5-year span. However, remember that the reader of a literature review expects that you have reported on the most current research available. Thus, you should make explicit your reasons for including articles that are not current (e.g., Is it a landmark study? Does it present the only evidence available on a given topic? Does it help you to understand the evolution of a research technique?).

---

[17] Pyrczak, F., & Bruce, R. R. (2011). *Writing empirical research reports: A basic guide for students of the social and behavioral sciences* (7th ed.). Glendale, CA: Pyrczak Publishing.

The question of how much literature is enough to include in a review is difficult to answer. In general, your first priority should be to establish that you have read the most current research available. Then, you should try to cover your topic as completely as necessary, not as completely as possible. Your instructor or faculty adviser can help you determine how much is enough.

Activities for Chapter 4

Directions: Refer to the printed list of sources you developed in Activity 5 at the end of Chapter 3.

1. Obtain copies of two articles from this list, and look over each of the articles.

   - Did the authors include a summary of the contents of the literature review at or near the beginning? If so, highlight or mark this summary for future reference.
   - Did the authors use subheadings?
   - Scan the paragraph(s) immediately preceding the heading "Method." Did the authors describe their hypotheses, research questions, or research purposes?
   - Without rereading any of the text of the article, write a brief statement describing what each article is about.

2. Based on your overview of all the articles on your list, make predictions of some of the likely categories and subcategories for your review. Reread the printed list of sources and try to group them by these categories and subcategories. Then, using these categories and subcategories, create an outline for describing your topic.

3. Carefully review your outline and select the articles you will read first. Within each category, start with the most recent studies. You now have your initial reading list.

Notes

Chapter 5

Analyzing Quantitative Research Literature

In the previous chapter, you were advised to make notes on important methodological strengths and weaknesses of the research articles you are reading prior to writing your literature review. This chapter will provide you with information on some points you may want to note regarding research methodology in quantitative studies. Those of you who have taken a course in research methods will recognize that this chapter contains only a very brief overview of some of the important issues.

✓ Guideline 1: Note whether the research is quantitative or qualitative.

Because quantitative researchers reduce information to statistics such as averages, percentages, and so on, their research articles are easy to spot. If an article has a results section devoted mainly to the presentation of statistical data, it is a safe bet that it is quantitative. The quantitative approach to research has dominated the social and behavioral sciences throughout the 1900s and into the 2000s, so for most topics, you are likely to locate many more articles reporting quantitative than qualitative research.

The literature on how to conduct quantitative research emphasizes the following:

1. Start with one (or more) explicitly stated hypothesis that will remain unchanged throughout the study.[1] The validity of the hypothesis is evaluated only after the data have been analyzed (i.e., the hypothesis is not subject to change while the data are being collected).

2. Select an unbiased sample (such as a simple random sample obtained by drawing names out of a hat) from a particular population.

3. Use a relatively large sample of participants (typically at least 30 for an experiment and sometimes as many as 1,500 for a national survey).

4. Use measures that can be scored objectively, such as multiple-choice achievement tests and forced-choice questionnaires or attitude scales and personality scales with choices that participants mark.

5. Present results using statistics and make inferences to the population from which the sample was drawn (i.e., infer that what the researchers found by studying a sample is similar to what they would have found if they had studied the whole population from which the sample was drawn).

---

[1] Quantitative researchers sometimes start with specific research questions or purposes instead of a hypothesis. As with hypotheses, the research questions or purposes remain unchanged throughout the study.

Qualitative research has a long tradition in the social and behavioral sciences, but it has gained a large following in many applied fields only in recent decades. It is sometimes easy to spot because the titles of the articles in this field often contain the word qualitative. In addition, qualitative researchers usually identify their research as qualitative in their introductions as well as in other parts of their reports.[2] You can also identify qualitative research because the results sections will be presented in a narrative describing themes and trends—often accompanied by quotations from the participants.

The literature on how to conduct qualitative research emphasizes the following:

1. Start with a general problem without imposing rigid, specific purposes and hypotheses to guide the study. As data are collected on the problem, hypotheses may emerge, but they are subject to change during the course of a study as additional data are collected.

2. Select a purposive sample—not a random one. For instance, a qualitative researcher may have access to some heroin addicts who attend a particular methadone clinic, and he or she may believe that the clients of this clinic might provide useful insights into the problems of recovering addicts. In other words, qualitative researchers use their *judgment* in selecting a sample instead of a mechanical, objective process such as drawing names from a hat at random.

3. Use a relatively small sample—sometimes as small as one exemplary case, such as a mathematics teacher who has received a national teaching award (once again, a purposive sample—selecting someone judged to be a potential source of important information).

4. Use relatively unstructured measures, such as semistructured interviews with open-ended questions (i.e., without "choices" for selection by participants), unstructured observations of behavior in natural contexts, and so on.

5. Measure intensively (e.g., spend extended periods of time with the participants to gain in-depth insights into the phenomena of interest).

6. Present results mainly or exclusively in words, with an emphasis on understanding the particular purposive sample studied and usually de-emphasizing or ignoring generalizations to larger populations.

As you can see by comparing the previous two lists, the distinction between quantitative and qualitative research will be important when you evaluate studies for their strengths and weaknesses. This chapter presents major guidelines for evaluating quantitative research, which you should consider when evaluating and synthesizing research in order to prepare a literature review. Guidelines for evaluating qualitative research are presented in the next chapter.

✓ Guideline 2:   Note whether a study is experimental or nonexperimental.

An *experimental* study is one in which treatments are administered to participants *for the purposes of the study* and their effects are assessed. For instance, in an experi-

---

[2] Note that quantitative researchers rarely explicitly state that their research is quantitative.

ment, some hyperactive students might be given Ritalin® while others are given behavior therapy (such as a systematic application of one or another type of reward system) so that the relative effectiveness of the two treatments in reducing the number of classroom discipline problems may be assessed. (Note that almost all experiments are quantitative.) More generally, the purpose of an experimental study is to identify cause-and-effect relationships.

A *nonexperimental* study is one in which participants' traits are measured without attempting to change them. For instance, hyperactive students might be interviewed for an understanding of their perceptions of their own disruptive classroom behaviors without any attempt by the researcher to treat the students. Such a study might be quantitative (if the researcher uses highly structured interview questions with choices for students to select from and summarizes the results statistically) or qualitative (if a researcher uses semistructured or unstructured interview questions[3] and uses words to summarize the results in terms of themes, models, or theories).[4]

Here is an important caveat: Do not fall into the habit of referring to all research studies as experiments. For instance, if you are reviewing nonexperimental studies, refer to them as *studies*—not *experiments*. Use the term *experiment* only if treatments were administered to participants in order that the effects of the treatments could be observed.

✔ Guideline 3: In an experiment, note whether the participants were assigned at random to treatment conditions.

An experiment in which participants are assigned at random to treatments is known as a *true experiment*. Random assignment to treatments guarantees that there is no bias in the assignment (e.g., with random assignment, there is no bias that would systematically assign the more disruptive students to the behavior therapy treatment while assigning the rest to treatment with Ritalin™). Other things being equal, more weight should be given to true experiments than to experiments employing other methods of assignment, such as designating the students in one school as the experimental group and the students in another school as the control group. Note that students are not normally assigned to schools at random. Hence, there may be important preexisting differences between the students in the two schools that may confound the interpretation of the results of such an experiment (e.g., socioeconomic status, language background, or self-selection, as occurs in magnet schools for the arts, the sciences, etc.).

✔ Guideline 4: Note attempts to examine cause-and-effect issues in nonexperimental studies.

The experimental method (with random assignment to treatment conditions) is widely regarded as the best quantitative method for investigating cause-and-effect issues. However, it is sometimes infeasible or impossible to treat participants in certain ways. For instance, if a researcher was exploring a possible causal link between the divorce of

---

[3] In addition, a qualitative researcher would be likely to conduct significantly longer interviews and possibly more than one interview.
[4] Obviously, then, nonexperimental research can be quantitative or qualitative, while experimental research is almost always quantitative.

parents and their children dropping out of high school, it would obviously be impossible to force some parents to get divorced while forcing others to remain married for the purposes of an experiment. For this research problem, the best that can be done is to select some students who have dropped out and some who have not dropped out but who are very similar in other important respects (such as socioeconomic status, the quality of the schools they attended, and so on), and then investigate whether their parents' divorce rates differ in the hypothesized direction.[5] Suppose that the children of the divorced parents exhibited somewhat higher dropout rates than those of the children of nondivorced parents. Does this mean that divorce causes higher dropout rates? Not necessarily. The conclusion is debatable because the researchers may have overlooked a number of other possible causal variables. Here is just one: Perhaps parents who tend to get divorced have poorer interpersonal skills and relate less well to their children. It may be this deficit in the children's upbringing (and not the divorce *per se*) that contributed to their dropping out.[6]

The study we are considering is an example of a causal-comparative (or *ex post facto*) study. When using it, a researcher observes a current condition or outcome (such as dropping out) and searches the past for possible causal variables (such as divorce). Because causal-comparative studies are considered more prone to error than true experiments for examining causality, you should note when a conclusion is based on the causal-comparative method. In addition, you should consider whether there are other plausible causal interpretations the researcher may have overlooked.

✓ Guideline 5: Consider the test-retest reliability of the measure.

Quantitative researchers refer to the tools they use (such as tests and questionnaires) as *measures*. Thus, the term *measurement* refers to the process by which quantitative researchers measure key variables.

Reliability refers to consistency of results. Here is an example: Suppose we administered a college admissions test one week and then readministered it to the same examinees the following week. The test would be considered reliable if the examinees who scored high the first week also tended to score high the second week.[7] By calculating a correlation coefficient, one can quantify the reliability of a test. Correlation coefficients can range from 0.00 to 1.00, with 1.00 indicating perfect reliability. Quantitative re-

---

[5] If the researcher had considerable resources and a long time frame, a study could be conducted in which children are tracked from the day they begin school until they graduate or drop out, noting which students drop out and which ones do not, as well as which students' parents get divorced. This longitudinal method is also inferior to the experimental method for identifying cause-and-effect relationships because of possible confounding variables (i.e., many variables other than divorce may be responsible for the student's decision to drop out and the researchers may fail to control for all of them).

[6] If this limitation is still not clear, consider the example further. Suppose that, based on the study in question, a dictatorial government made it illegal for parents to divorce in order to reduce the dropout rate. If the real cause of dropping out were parents' poor interpersonal skills, preventing divorce would not have the predicted effect because it was misidentified as a causal agent. Instead, the government should have mounted programs to assist parents in improving their interpersonal skills, especially in their dealings with their children.

[7] Likewise, for high reliability, those examinees who scored low the first week would also score low the second week.

searchers generally regard a coefficient of 0.75 or higher to indicate adequate reliability. The type of reliability we are considering here is called *test-retest reliability*.[8]

When you analyze a quantitative study, examine the section on measurement to see if the researchers provide information on the reliability of the measures they used in their research. Typically, this information is very briefly presented, as in Example 5.5.1.

Example 5.5.1

A brief statement in a research report on test-retest reliability:

The test-retest reliability of the measure with a 2-week interval between administrations was reported to be 0.81, which indicates adequate reliability (Doe, 2011).

While the statement in Example 5.5.1 is very brief, it assures you that the researcher whose research you are analyzing has considered the important issue of reliability. In addition, it provides you with a reference (i.e., Doe, 2011) that you could consult for more information on how reliability was determined.

✓ Guideline 6: Consider the internal consistency reliability of the measure.

While test-retest reliability concerns the consistency of results over time (see Guideline 5), *internal consistency reliability* refers to consistency of results at one point in time. To understand this concept, consider a multiple-choice test with only two algebra test items. Suppose an examinee marked one item correctly and the other item incorrectly. This would indicate a *lack* of internal consistency because what we learned about the examinee's algebra knowledge varied from one item to the next (i.e., on one test item, the examinee earned one point, while on the other test item, the examinee earned zero points, which is the lowest possible score on a single item). Extending this concept to a test with a larger number of items and examinees, if those examinees who mark any one test item correctly *tend* to mark the other test items correctly (and if those examinees who mark any one test item *in*correctly *tend* to mark the other test items *in*correctly), the test would be said to have good internal consistency reliability. Put more generally, internal consistency refers to the idea that what is learned about an examinee's ability by examining responses to some of the items is similar to what is learned by examining responses to other items.[9]

Failure to have internal consistency indicates that some of the items are not operating as indicated. There may be many reasons for this. One obvious reason is that some items may be ambiguous, causing examinees with much knowledge to mark incorrect answers. Of course, this would be undesirable.

Internal consistency reliability is almost universally examined by computing a statistic known as *Cronbach's alpha* (whose symbol is α). Like a correlation coefficient, α can range from 0.00 to 1.00, with values above 0.75 usually considered to indicate ade-

---

[8] Other methods for determining reliability are beyond the scope of this book.
[9] In other words, a measure with high internal consistency may be viewed as consisting of a set of homogenous items (i.e., all items tend to tap similar skills, attitudes, and so on).

quate internal consistency reliability for research purposes.[10] Example 5.6.1 shows how alpha might be reported in a research report.

Example 5.6.1[11]
A brief statement in a research report on internal consistency reliability:

One point was given for each correctly answered item. Points were summed, to obtain a score reflecting declarative emotion knowledge, ranging from 0 to 25. Internal consistency (Cronbach's alpha) of this measure was $\alpha = .82$.

While the statement in Example 5.6.1 is brief, it assures you that the researchers have considered internal consistency reliability.

✓ Guideline 7: Consider the validity of the measure.

A measure (such as a college admissions test) is said to be *valid* to the extent that it measures what it is supposed to measure. For instance, to the extent that a college admissions test correctly predicts who will and who will not succeed in college, the test is said to be valid. In practice, it is safe to assume that no measure is perfectly valid. For instance, college admissions tests are at best only modestly valid.

In a *criterion-related validity* study, scores earned by examinees on a measure (such as a college admissions test) are correlated with scores earned on some other measure (such as freshmen GPAs earned in college). The extent of criterion-related validity is determined by calculating a correlation coefficient to describe the relationship. When this is done, the resulting correlation coefficient is called a *validity coefficient*.[12] Generally, coefficients above 0.30 indicate adequate validity for research purposes. Example 5.7.1 shows a brief statement regarding the *predictive criterion-related validity* of a college admissions test. It is called *predictive* because the admissions test was administered at one point in time, while the outcome (GPAs) was measured later, with the purpose being to determine how well the scores predict GPAs.

Example 5.7.1
A brief statement in a research report on predictive criterion-related validity:

Using a sample of 240 examinees admitted to a small liberal arts college, Doe (2012) correlated scores on the XYZ College Admissions test with freshmen grades. The test was found to have adequate criterion-related validity ($r = .49$).

---

[10] If you have studied statistics, you know that correlation coefficients can also have negative values. In practice, however, when estimating reliability and internal consistency, they are always positive in value.
[11] Beck, L., Kumschick, I. R., Eid, M., & Klann-Delius, G. (2012). Relationship between language competence and emotional competence in middle childhood. *Emotion, 12*, 503–514.
[12] A *validity coefficient* is a correlation coefficient whose symbol is *r*.

Example 5.7.2 shows a brief statement regarding *concurrent criterion-related validity*. The adjective *concurrent* refers to the fact that the two measures were administered at about the same time.

Example 5.7.2
A brief statement in a research report on concurrent criterion-related validity (predictive):

In a previous study, Doe (2011) correlated scores on the Smoking Cessation Questionnaire with data regarding smoking cessation gathered by trained and experienced interviewers. The questionnaire was administered to the participants on the same day that the participants were interviewed. Using the interview data as the criterion for judging the validity of the questionnaire, the questionnaire was found to have good criterion-related validity ($r = .68$). Thus, the Smoking Cessation Questionnaire is a reasonably valid substitute for the more expensive interview process for measuring smoking-cessation behaviors.

Another major type of validity is *construct validity*. This term refers to any type of data-based study that sheds light on the validity of a measure. Construct validity studies can take many forms, most of which are beyond the scope of this book. However, to illustrate how such a study might be conducted, consider Example 5.7.3.

Example 5.7.3
A brief statement in a research report on construct validity:

Scores on the new ABC Anxiety Scale were correlated with scores on the well-established Beck Depression Inventory, resulting in a correlation of .45. This result is consistent with major theories as well as previous studies (e.g., Doe, 2011) that indicate that individuals who are anxious have a moderate tendency to also be depressed. Thus, the correlation provides indirect evidence on the validity of the new anxiety scale.

The last major type of validity is *content validity*. Content validity is determined by having one or more experts evaluate the contents of a measure. It is especially important to determine the content validity of achievement tests. For instance, experts can be asked to compare the instructional objectives with the material covered by an achievement test in order to determine the extent to which they match. Content validity can also be determined for other types of measures, as illustrated in Example 5.7.4.

Example 5.7.4
A brief statement in a research report on content validity:

The Infant Development Checklist was used as the measure of the outcome in this experiment. In a previous study, Doe (2012) reported that it had adequate content validity, as judged by three professors whose specialty is developmental psychology.

✔ Guideline 8: Consider whether a measure is valid for a particular research purpose.

A measure that has been shown to be reasonably valid in previous research may not be especially valid for use in all other studies. For instance, an attitude scale that has been shown to be valid for use with adolescents may have some unknown amount of validity for use with younger children in another study. Thus, if the purpose of the study is to study attitudes of younger children, the validity of the measure might be unknown. Put in more general terms, the validity of a measure is *relative* to the purposes of a study. It may be more valid in a study with one purpose (e.g., to determine attitudes of adolescents) than in another study with a different purpose (e.g., to determine attitudes of young children).

✔ Guideline 9: Note differences in how a variable is measured across studies.

When you examine various published studies in which a variable of interest to you has been measured, you will often find that different researchers used different tools to measure the variable. For instance, one researcher may have measured attitude toward school with a forced-choice questionnaire (e.g., items for which participants respond to choices from "Strongly Agree" to "Strongly Disagree"), while another researcher might have used an observational checklist for classroom behaviors that indicate positive or negative attitudes (e.g., children working cooperatively on classroom projects). If similarities are found in results across studies using different measures, this lends support to the results. Obviously, differences in results among studies could be attributable to differences in the measurement.

Note that part of the measurement process is to determine the sources from which to collect data. For instance, to study violent juvenile delinquent behavior, one researcher might seek data from the participants' peers, while another might seek it from the participants themselves using essentially the same questions.[13] Differences in the sources with which the measure is used could also account for differences in results.

In light of the above, you should look for patterns across studies that might be attributable to measurement. For instance, do all the studies that support a certain conclusion use one method or type of measure while those that support a different conclusion use a different method? If your notes reveal this, you might consider making a statement such as the one in Example 5.9.1.

Example 5.9.1
A statement from a literature review that points out differences in measurement techniques (desirable):

While the two studies that used mailed questionnaires support the finding that inhalant use among adolescents is extremely rare (less than one-half of 1%), the three studies that used face-to-face interviews reported an incidence of more than 5%.

---

[13] Peers might be asked, "Has your friend John told you about any fights he has had in the past week?" while the participant might be asked, "Have you had any fights in the past week?"

Note that Example 5.9.1 is much more informative than Example 5.9.2.

Example 5.9.2
A statement from a literature review that fails to point out differences in measurement techniques (undesirable):

The research on the incidence of adolescent inhalant use has yielded mixed results, with two studies reporting that it is extremely rare and three others reporting an incidence of more than 5%.

✔ Guideline 10: Note how the participants were sampled.

Most quantitative researchers study only samples from which they make inferences about the populations sampled. You should make notes on whether the samples studied seem likely to be representative of the populations to which one might wish to generalize. From a quantitative researcher's point of view, drawing a sample at random is best.

Unfortunately, most researchers cannot use random samples (at least not in their purest form). This is true for two reasons. First, many researchers work with limited funds and have limited cooperative contacts, which might be required for access to random samples. Because most researchers in the social and behavioral sciences are professors, it is not surprising that they often draw their samples from the student populations at the colleges or universities where they teach. Of course, what is true of college students might not generalize to other groups of individuals.

Second, even if a random sample of names is drawn, almost invariably, some of the individuals selected refuse to participate. This is especially problematic in mailed surveys, for which response rates are notoriously low. It would not be surprising, for instance, to receive only a 25% response rate in a national survey that was mailed to a random sample of members of a professional association (e.g., an association of public school teachers).

Studies without random sampling and with low response rates should be interpreted with considerable caution. Such studies usually should be regarded as *suggestive* because they do not offer firm evidence.

✔ Guideline 11: Make notes on the demographics of the participants.

Making notes on the demographics[14] of the participants can also help you to identify patterns in the literature. For instance, have the researchers who studied the transition from welfare to work using urban samples obtained different results from researchers who have studied rural samples? Could the differences in the urban-rural status of the participants (a demographic characteristic) help to explain the differences in the findings? Note that you cannot answer such a question with certainty, but you could raise the possibility in your literature review. Other demographic characteristics often reported in research reports are gender, race, ethnicity, age, and socioeconomic status.

---

[14] *Demographics* are background characteristics of the participants.

Research reports in which demographics are not reported in detail are generally less useful than ones in which demographics are reported in detail.

✔ Guideline 12:   Note how large a difference is—not just whether it is statistically significant.

When a researcher says a difference is statistically significant, he or she is reporting that a statistical test has indicated that the difference is greater than might be created by chance alone. This does *not* mean that the difference is necessarily large. It would take several chapters of a statistics textbook to explain why this is true. However, the following analogy may help you to understand this point: Suppose there is a very tight race for the United States Senate, and Candidate A wins over Candidate B by 10 votes. This is indeed a very small difference, but it is quite significant (i.e., by counting all the votes systematically and carefully, we have identified a very small, nonchance, "real" difference).

Given that even a small difference is often statistically significant, you will want to make note of the sizes of the differences you find in the literature.[15] Suppose you read several studies that showed that computer-assisted instruction in English composition led to very slight but statistically significant increases in students' achievement. In fairness to your reader, you should point out the size of the differences, as illustrated in Example 5.12.1. You will be prepared to write such statements if you make appropriate notes as you read and analyze the literature.

Example 5.12.1

In a series of true experiments at various colleges throughout the United States, the experimental groups receiving computer-assisted instruction in English composition consistently made very small but statistically significant gains as compared to the control groups in mathematics achievement. On average, the gains were only about one percentage point on multiple-choice tests. Despite their statistical significance, these very small gains make the use of the experimental treatment on a widespread basis problematic because of the greatly increased cost of using it instead of the conventional (control) treatment.

✔ Guideline 13:   Presume that all quantitative studies are flawed.

All quantitative studies are subject to errors of various kinds, so no one study should be taken as providing the definitive answer(s) to a given research problem. In fact, that is why you are combing through the evidence contained in original reports of research—to weigh the various pieces of evidence, all of which are subject to error—in order to arrive at some reasonable conclusions based on a body of literature. This brings us to an important point: Never use the word *prove* when discussing the results of empirical

---

[15] Increasingly, quantitative researchers are reporting a relatively new statistic called *effect size*, which measures the size of differences between groups of participants relative to the differences among individual participants. While a discussion of this statistic is beyond the scope of this book, if you encounter this statistic while reviewing literature, use this rough guideline: Effect sizes of less than about .25 indicate a small difference, while effect sizes above .50 indicate a large difference.

research. Empirical studies do not offer proof. Instead, they offer *degrees of evidence*, with some studies offering stronger evidence than others. While analyzing research articles, make notes on how convincing the evidence is in each article. Other things being equal, you should emphasize in your literature review the research articles that present the strongest evidence.

This guideline leads to another important principle. Namely, you will not be expected to dissect and discuss every flaw of every study you cite because flaws abound in studies. Instead, you should make notes on major flaws, especially in studies that you plan to emphasize in your review. In addition, you should critique the methodology of studies in groups whenever possible. For instance, you might point out that all studies in a group you are reviewing have common weaknesses. Good note-taking while you are reading the articles will help you to identify such commonalities.

Concluding Comment

This chapter briefly covers only some of the major methodological issues you might consider when you make notes on reports of quantitative research in preparation for writing a review of literature. As you read the articles you have selected for your review, you will find additional information on these and other issues because researchers often critique their own research as well as that of others in their journal articles. Reading these critiques carefully will help you to comprehend more fully the research articles you will be reviewing.

Activities for Chapter 5

Directions: Locate an original report of quantitative research, preferably on a topic you are reviewing, and answer the following questions. For learning purposes, your instructor may choose to assign an article for all students in your class to read.

1. What characteristics of the report you located led you to believe that it is an example of quantitative research?

2. Is the study experimental *or* nonexperimental? On what basis did you decide?

3. If the study is experimental, were the participants assigned at random to treatment conditions? If not, how were they assigned?

4. If the study is nonexperimental, was the researcher attempting to examine cause-and-effect issues? If yes, did he or she use the causal-comparative method? Explain.

5. What types of measures (i.e., instruments) were used? Did the researcher provide enough information about them to allow you to make judgments on their adequacy for use in the research? If yes, do you believe they were adequate in light of the information provided? If no, what types of additional information about the measures should have been reported?

6. How did the researcher obtain a sample of participants? Was it at random from a population? If the study is a mailed survey, what was the response rate?

7. Has the researcher described the demographics of the participants in sufficient detail? Explain.

8. If the researcher reported statistically significant differences, did he or she discuss whether they were large differences? In your opinion, are the differences large enough to be of practical importance? Explain.

9. Did the researcher critique his or her own research by describing its limitations? Explain.

10. Briefly describe any major flaws in the research that you did not cover in your answers to Questions 1 through 9.

Chapter 6

Analyzing Qualitative
Research Literature

The major differences between qualitative and quantitative research are described in Guideline 1 in Chapter 5. Chapter 6 was written with the assumption that you have already carefully considered the material in that guideline. While Chapter 5 emphasizes the analysis of quantitative research before the writing of a literature review, this chapter explores criteria for analyzing qualitative research.

✓ Guideline 1: Note whether the research was conducted by an individual or by a research team.

While both published quantitative and published qualitative research are frequently conducted by teams of researchers, the use of a team is more important in qualitative research than in quantitative research. For instance, if a quantitative researcher administers an objective attitude scale, scores it, and analyzes the data using a statistical software package, it is reasonable to expect that anyone else who uses care in scoring and entering the data would obtain the same results that the original researcher obtained. However, if a qualitative researcher conducts open-ended, semistructured interviews, the resulting raw data typically consist of many pages of transcripts of what the participants said in the interviews. It is possible that different researchers might analyze and interpret such data differently, calling into question the validity of the analysis of the data. However, if a team of researchers analyzes a set of qualitative data and arrives at a consensus on its meaning, consumers of research can have more confidence in the results of the research than if it were conducted by an individual.

It is not necessary for research to be conducted by a team. In fact, other qualified researchers may not be available to work with a researcher, or the requirements for a thesis or a dissertation might stipulate that the researcher work as an individual. When this is the case, it is especially important for consumers of qualitative research to ensure that the individual who conducted the qualitative research used at least one of the techniques described in Guidelines 3 and 4 in this chapter.

✓ Guideline 2: When there is a research team, note whether analysis of the data was initially conducted independently.

Researchers who analyze a set of qualitative data should first analyze it independently (i.e., without consulting each other) in order to prevent one or more researchers from unduly influencing the others in the interpretation of the data. After the initial analysis, researchers then resolve any discrepancies, usually by discussing them until a consensus is reached. This process is described in Example 6.2.1.

Example 6.2.1[1]

Description of independent analysis followed by reaching a consensus:

In identifying and coding domains, each of the four research team members read the transcripts and developed a list of domains independently, which were then revised and continued to be modified until a consensus was reached by the team.

Other things being equal, qualitative research in which a team of researchers first analyze the data independently and then discuss their analyses to reach a consensus is stronger than research in which this is not done.

✓ Guideline 3: Note whether outside experts were consulted.

Consultation with one or more outside experts increases the confidence consumers of research can have in a qualitative study's research results. Consultation is especially important if an individual (and not a team) has conducted the research (see Guideline 1).

Qualitative researchers usually refer to input on the adequacy of the results of data analysis from outside experts as a *peer review* process. When the expert reviews the entire process of conducting the research as well as reviewing the results of the data analysis, the expert is usually referred to as an *auditor*, as is done in Example 6.3.1.

Example 6.3.1[2]

Description of independent analysis followed by reaching a consensus:

The auditor was an African American female doctoral student with expertise in counseling African immigrants and international college students. The audit process entailed checking to ensure that raw data were appropriately sorted into domains and abstracted into accurate and complete core summaries. The auditor made several written suggestions for changes, and the researchers who originally constructed the domains and core ideas evaluated the auditor's comments and made changes by consensus judgment.

✓ Guideline 4: Note whether the participants were consulted on the interpretation of the data.

The literature on how to conduct qualitative research emphasizes conducting research in such a way that the results reflect the realities *as perceived by the participants*. In other words, the goal of qualitative research is to understand how participants perceive their own reality—not to establish a so-called objective reality. Thus, it is appropriate for qualitative researchers to write up a tentative report of results and ask the participants (or a sample of them) to review the report and provide feedback on how well it reflects their

---

[1] Tuason, M. T. G., Güss, C. D., & Carroll, L. (2012). The disaster continues: A qualitative study on the experiences of displaced Hurricane Katrina survivors. *Professional Psychology: Research and Practice.* Advanced online publication. doi: 10.1037/a0028054
[2] Modified from Friedman, M. L., Friedlander, M. L., & Blustein, D. L. (2005). Toward an understanding of Jewish identity: A phenomenological study. *Journal of Counseling Psychology, 52,* 77–83.

perceptions. Qualitative researchers call this process *member checking*. This term has its origins in the idea that the participants in qualitative research are in fact *members* of the research team who are *checking* the results for accuracy. Example 6.4.1 illustrates how this might be described in a research report.

Example 6.4.1[3]
Description of the use of member checking:

Member checking is particularly important because it helps ensure that the meaning-making processes of the participants were represented well. It is critical in a constructivist study to stay as true to the participants' perceptions as possible (Crotty, 2003). The former students all indicated that the data analysis results fit with their experiences. For example, it was reported that learning to set limits and use child-centered attending skills as a unique way to relate to children were most relevant in the study findings. Members also agreed that their confidence in practicing and adherence to play therapy increased throughout their experiences.

While member checking is not essential for qualitative research to be judged adequate, it is especially helpful to an individual who is conducting research alone (as opposed to a research team, whose members can reflect with each other on the accuracy of results).

✔ Guideline 5:   Note whether the researchers used a purposive sample or a sample of convenience.

As you know from the material in Guideline 1 in Chapter 5, qualitative researchers strive to use *purposive samples*. These are samples of individuals who are selected on purpose based on the careful judgment of the researchers regarding what types of individuals would be especially good sources of data for a particular research topic. For instance, a qualitative researcher evaluating a clinical program might select for interviews several individuals who are just beginning the program and several who have been attending the program for more than a certain length of time. Selection criteria might also include gender (for instance, selecting some men and some women), age, and attendance (for instance, selecting only those who have attended regularly).

The authors of Example 6.5.1 indicate the criteria for their purposive sample.

Example 6.5.1[4]
Description of the use of purposive sampling:

A nonprobabilistic purposive sampling strategy was used to recruit one-parent families, where fathers had been nonresident from early in the child's life and mothers had not entered into cohabiting relationships with subsequent partners.

---

[3] Smith-Adcock, S., Davis, E., Pereira, J., Allen, C., Socarras, K., Bodurtha, K., & Smith-Bonahue, T. (2012). Preparing to play: A qualitative study of graduate students' reflections on learning play therapy in an elementary school. *International Journal of Play Therapy, 21*, 100–115.
[4] Nixon, E., Greene, S., & Hogan, D. (2012). "Like an uncle but more, but less than a father"—Irish children's relationships with nonresident fathers. *Journal of Family Psychology, 26*, 381–390.

We sampled on the basis of the age of the child at which their father left the family home, rather than marital status of parents per se, as it has been suggested that living arrangements may be a better indicator of family structure than parental marital status (Bumpass & Raley, 1995; Sigle-Rushton & McLanahan, 2004). Families were excluded if fathers had left the home after the child was 2.5 years of age, in line with Weinraub and Wolf (1983) who used a similar cutoff age in their study of solo mother families. Families in which mothers had entered into cohabiting relationships with subsequent partners were also excluded, to avoid the confounding influence of substitute father figures on children's relationship with their nonresident father, as has been demonstrated by previous research (Amato et al., 2009; Juby, Billette, Laplante, & Le Bourdais, 2007). Finally, children who had no memory of contact with their fathers or did not know his identity were excluded.

In contrast, a *sample of convenience* is one in which the participants are selected solely or primarily on the basis that they are readily available (i.e., convenient to work with), as illustrated in Example 6.5.2.

Example 6.5.2[5]

Description of the use of a sample of convenience:

We collected data from a convenience sample of 258 female and 190 male college students (M = 21.0 years old, SD = 4.67 years) enrolled in introductory undergraduate psychology courses at a large southeastern university. Students self-selected to participate in this study in exchange for partial fulfillment of a course research requirement.

Note that both qualitative and quantitative researchers regard samples of convenience as undesirable, although sometimes such a sample is the only type available to a researcher with limited contacts and resources. Nevertheless, research employing samples of convenience yields results that should be interpreted very cautiously.

✓ Guideline 6: Note whether the demographics of the participants are described.

As you know from Guideline 11 in Chapter 5, it is a good idea to make notes on the demographics of participants in preparation for analyzing research for inclusion in your literature review. By providing demographics relevant to the research topic, consumers of research can "see" the participants and make judgments on the adequacy of the sample. For instance, the researchers who wrote the description of demographics in Example 6.6.1 were studying racial hierarchy in biracial individuals. As you can see, the demographics they reported are relevant to the topic of their research.

---

[5] Anthony, E. R., & Cook, S. L. (2012). Assessing the impact of gender-neutral language on disclosure of sexual violence. *Psychology of Violence*, 2, 297–307.

Example 6.6.1[6]

Description of demographics in a qualitative study:

Two hundred and seventeen participants were recruited around the campus of a university in New England and received candy in return for participation in the study. The ethnic makeup consisted of 116 Caucasian/Whites, 43 Asian/Asian American/Pacific Islanders, six African American/Blacks, eight Latino/Hispanics, three Middle Eastern, one Native American, 25 biracial/mixed race, nine "other," and six who did not report their ethnicity. Six participants did not indicate their race. Of the sample, 119 were female, 91 were male, and seven did not report their gender. The average age was 23.3 years ($SD = 9.86$), excluding six participants who did not indicate their age. Because these data were not collected through a research study pool and were collected during the summer, the sample is not composed exclusively of students from the university.

✓ Guideline 7:   Consider whether the method of qualitative analysis is described in sufficient detail.

To qualify as *research*, the method used to analyze the data must be carefully planned and systematic. In contrast, casual observation followed by a purely subjective discussion of it does not qualify as research.

To help consumers of research to determine whether a given report qualifies as *qualitative research*, qualitative researchers should describe in some detail how they analyzed the data. Note that it is insufficient for a researcher to say only that "the grounded-theory approach was used" or that "the analysis was based on a phenomenological approach." In Example 6.7.1, the researchers begin by naming *consensual qualitative research* (CQR) as the method of analysis and provide references where more information on the approach can be obtained. They follow this by summarizing the steps in CQR that they applied in the analysis.

Example 6.7.1[7]

Description of the use of Consensual Qualitative Research Methodology:

Analyses consisted of using consensual qualitative research (CQR) methodology (Bogdan & Biklen, 1992; Henwood & Pidgeon, 1992; Hill, Thompson, & Williams, 1997; Stiles, 1993). CQR is a highly reliable and cost-effective method of analyzing qualitative data, making use of multiple researchers, the process of reaching consensus, and a systematic way of examining representativeness of results across cases. Once the responses to the open-ended questions are transcribed, CQR involves three steps: developing and coding domains, constructing core ideas, and developing categories to describe consistencies across cases (cross-analysis).

Development and Coding into Domains

Two independent research psychologists developed a list of *domains* or *topic areas* based on the content of the discussions and the focus group questions used to organize information into

---

[6] Ho, A. K., Sidanius, J., Levin, D. T., & Banaji, M. R. (2011). Evidence for hypodescent and racial hierarchy in the categorization and perception of biracial individuals. *Journal of Personality and Social Psychology, 100,* 492–506.
[7] Williams, J. K., Wyatt, G. E., Resell, J., Peterson, J., & Asuan-O'Brien, A. (2004). Psychosocial issues among gay- and non-gay-identifying HIV-seropositive African American and Latino MSM. *Cultural Diversity and Ethnic Minority Psychology, 10,* 268–286.

similar topics. Once each reviewer had independently identified their domains, the two reviewers compared their separate lists of domains until consensus was reached. The final seven domains were: (1) sex with men, (2) sex with women, (3) the importance of family, including having children, (4) gender roles and social expectations, (5) sex or "partying" with drugs and alcohol, (6) church and religion, and (7) living with HIV. Each reviewer, along with all the investigators, independently read through the transcripts and assigned sentences or paragraphs to a domain. Attempts were made to avoid double coding the data by careful review of domains. Reviewers compared their coding, differences were discussed, and consensus was obtained.

Constructing Core Ideas

The two independent reviewers along with the investigators reread all the raw data and attempted to summarize the data into core ideas. This process, called *boiling down* or *abstracting*, summarizes the content and accurately reflects the participants' statements in fewer words while avoiding inferences. Once the team members developed the core ideas independently, the reviewers and the investigators met again as a team to discuss their ideas until consensus was achieved.

Cross-Analyses

While in the first and second steps of CQR the investigators examined the statements of individuals, the purpose of cross-analyses was to determine whether there were similarities among the cases in the sample. The team in this step attempted to look across cases to determine whether there were similarities among the cases. The independent reviewers and the investigators identified all of the core ideas for each domain across cases and determined how these core ideas clustered into *categories*. Individual team members reviewed the core ideas within a single domain and assigned them to relevant categories. The team compared categories again and determined which ones were significant on the basis of the self-report of participants. Consensus by the independent reviewers and the investigators was obtained. After consensus, the team reviewed the cross-analysis, ensuring that each core idea fit and the category label adequately described the core ideas listed.

✓ Guideline 8:   Note whether quantities are provided when qualitative researchers discuss quantitative matters.

Just because research is qualitative does not mean that no quantities should be reported. For instance, it is appropriate to use statistics when describing demographics of participants in qualitative research, as in Example 6.6.1, in which the average age as well as a large number of percentages were provided.

When describing the results, it is usually undesirable to make statements such as "a few of the participants raised the issue of…" or "many of the participants perceived the issue as…."

One approach to quantifying qualitative results is to use what qualitative researchers call *literal enumeration*, which merely means reporting specific numbers of participants for each statement of results. However, reporting many numbers can clutter up a report of qualitative research results. An alternative is to establish quantitative categories for otherwise vague terms such as *many*. This is illustrated in Example 6.8.1. Such a statement near the beginning of the results section helps to clarify how the terms were defined and used by the researchers.

Example 6.8.1[8]
Definitions of otherwise vague terms that refer to quantities:

Enumeration data were used in the results section that follows. Specifically, the word *many* indicates that more than 50% of the participants gave a particular type of response, the term *some* indicates that between 25% and 50% did so, while the term *a few* indicates that less than 25% did so.

Other things being equal, qualitative reports that provide guidance on quantities are more useful to consumers of research than those that do not.

Concluding Comment

This chapter briefly covers only some major methodological issues you might consider when you make notes on reports of qualitative research in preparation for writing a review of literature. As you read the articles you have selected for your review, make notes on any other methodological issues and decisions made by the researchers that might affect the validity of the research results.

Activities for Chapter 6

Directions: Locate an original report of qualitative research, preferably on a topic you are reviewing, and answer the following questions. For learning purposes, your instructor may choose to assign an article for all students in your class to read.

1. What characteristics of the report you located led you to believe that it is an example of qualitative research?

2. Was the study conducted by an individual *or* by a research team?

3. Was the initial analysis of the results conducted *independently* by more than one researcher?

4. Were outside experts consulted for peer review? For an audit? If yes, does this increase your confidence in the validity of the results?

---

[8] This example is drawn from Orcher, L. T. (2005). *Conducting research: Social and behavioral science methods*, p. 72. Glendale, CA: Pyrczak Publishing.

5. Did researchers use *member checking*? If yes, does this increase your confidence in the validity of the results?

6. Is it clear whether a purposive *or* a convenience sample was used? Explain.

7. Has the researcher described the demographics of the participants in sufficient detail? Explain.

8. Did the researcher name a specific method of qualitative data analysis (e.g., consensual qualitative research)? Is it described in sufficient detail? Explain.

9. Did the researcher provide sufficiently specific qualitative information in the results section? Explain.

10. Briefly describe any major flaws in the research that you did not cover in your answers to Questions 1 through 9.

Chapter 7

Building Tables to Summarize Literature

The guidelines in the previous chapters have helped you to select a topic, identify literature, and conduct a preliminary analysis. Building tables that summarize literature is an effective way to help you get an overview of the literature you have considered. In addition, you may want to include in your literature review one or more of the tables you build, which will also help to provide an overview for the readers of your review.

✓ Guideline 1: Consider building a table of definitions.

Each of the variables you are considering should be defined early in your review. Building a table of definitions helps you and your readers under two circumstances. First, if there are a number of definitions of closely related variables, a table of definitions, such as the one in Example 7.1.1, makes it easy to scan the definitions in order to identify similarities and differences.

Example 7.1.1[1]

Table 7.1.1
Definitions of Psychological Empowerment Relevant to Tobacco Control Initiatives

Domain	Attributes	Definitions
Intrapersonal	Domain-specific efficacy	Beliefs in one's capabilities to organize and execute the courses of action required to produce specific changes related to tobacco control.
	Perceived sociopolitical control	Beliefs about one's capabilities and efficacy in social and political systems.
	Participatory competence	Perceived ability to participate in and contribute to the operations of the group or organization, through talking at meetings, working as a team member, and so on.
Interactional	Knowledge of resources	Awareness of whether resources exist to support the group and how to acquire them.
	Assertiveness	Ability to express your feelings, opinions, beliefs, and needs directly, openly, and honestly while not violating the personal rights of others.
	Advocacy	Pursuit of influencing outcomes, including public policy and resource allocation decisions within political, economic, and social systems and institutions that directly affect people's lives.

Second, a table of definitions can be helpful if there are diverse definitions of a given variable. Consider arranging them chronologically by year to see if there are historical trends in how the variable has been defined across time. Example 7.1.2 illustrates the organization of such a table.

---

[1] Holden, D. J., Evans, W. D., Hinnant, L. W., & Messeri, P. (2005). Modeling psychological empowerment among youth involved in local tobacco control efforts. *Health Education & Behavior, 32*, 264–278. Reprinted with permission.

Example 7.1.2

Table 7.1.2
Definitions of Child Abuse Over Time (1945 to 2012)

Author	Definition	Notes
Doe (1945)	Defined as...	First published definition. Does not include psychological abuse.
Smith (1952)	Defined as...	
Jones (1966)	Defined as...	First definition to mention sexual abuse.
Lock (1978)	Defined as...	
Black & Clark (1989)	Defined as...	
Solis (2000)	Defined as...	Legal definition in Texas.
Ty (2003)	Defined as...	Most widely cited definition in recent literature.
Bart (2012)	Defined as...	

✔ Guideline 2: Consider building a table of research methods.

Because different research methods can cause differences in the outcomes of studies, it is helpful to build a table summarizing the methods employed, such as the one in Example 7.2.1. In addition to the methods described in Table 7.2.1, for experiments (see Guidelines 2 and 3 in Chapter 5), it is desirable to include a row indicating the type of experimental design that was used (e.g., randomized control group design) in each study.

Example 7.2.1[2]

Table 7.2.1
Primary Study Characteristics (Methods)

	Pope (1994)	Preyde (2000)	Cherkin (2001)
Sample size	$n = 164$	$n = 98$	$n = 267$
Recruitment of participants	Those attending clinic	University e-mail & advertisements in newspaper	Mailed letters to HMO
Presenting condition	Nonspecific low back pain	Subacute low back pain	Persistent low back pain
Type of massage	Massage	Comprehensive massage	Therapeutic massage
Duration of study	Not indicated	1 year	6 months
Outcome measure	Visual Analog Scale	Roland Disability Questionnaire	Symptom Bothersomeness Scale

✔ Guideline 3: Consider including a summary of research results in the methods table.

Results can be summarized in a table showing the research methods (see Guideline 2) by adding an additional row or column to the table.

Instead of authors' names featured at the top of the columns, as in Example 7.2.1, they can be placed at the beginning of the rows, as in Example 7.3.1. In this example, the results of the studies are briefly summarized.

---

[2] Loosely based on Dryden, T., Baskwil, A., & Preyde, M. (2004). Massage therapy for the orthopaedic patient: A review. *Orthopaedic Nursing, 23*, 327–332.

Example 7.3.1[3]

Table 7.3.1
Longitudinal Studies Linking Religion and Adolescent Sexual Behavior

Publication date, authors	Location, year, SES; sample N	Age or grade; gender; ethnicity	Religiosity measures	Sexual behavior measures	Impact of religion on sex behavior
(1975) Jessor & Jessor	Small city in Rocky Mountain region, 1969 to 1971, middle class; N = 424	High school; M and F; White	Religiosity; church attendance	Ever had sexual intercourse at Time 1	High school females who initiated sexual intercourse between Time 1 and Time 2 were less religious and attended church less frequently.
(1983) Jessor, Costa, Jessor, & Donovan	Rocky Mountains, 1969 to 1972 and 1979; N = 346 virgins	Grades 7, 8, and 9 in 1969; M and F; White	Church attendance; religiosity[a]	Age at first coitus	Religiosity and more frequent attendance predicted later initiation of first coitus.
(1991) Beck, Cole, & Hammond[b]	United States, 1979, 1983; N = 2,072	14 to 17 years old; M and F; White virgins in 1979	Religious affiliation of adolescents and parents (Catholic, Baptist, mainline Protestant, institutional sect, Fundamentalist)	Coital experience (yes or no)	White adolescent females and males with institutionalized sect affiliation (e.g., Pentecostal, Mormon, Jehovah's Witness) were less likely than were mainline Protestants (e.g., Episcopalian, Lutheran, Methodist) to engage in first coitus between 1979 and 1983. Even when controlling for attendance, females with Baptist affiliation and males with Fundamentalist affiliation were less likely than were mainline Protestants to experience first coitus.
(1996) Crockett, Bingham, Chopack, & Vicary	Single rural school district in eastern United States, 1985, lower SES; N = 289	7th to 9th grades; M and F; White	Attendance	Age at first coitus	Females (but not males) who attended more frequently were more likely to be older (more than age 17) at first coitus.
(1996) Mott, Fondell, Hu, Kowaleski-Jones, & Menaghan[c]	United States, 1988, 1990, and 1992; N = 451	At least 14 years old in 1992; M and F; White (Black and Hispanic over-sampled)	Attendance; do friends attend same church?	Early initiation of first coitus (using age 14 as criterion for *early*)	Frequent attendees who also had peers attending the same church were less likely to be engaging in sexual intercourse at age 14.
(1996) Pleck, Sonenstein, Ku, & Burbridge[d]	United States, 1988 (Wave I, N = 1,880) 1990 to 1991 (Wave II, N = 1,676)	15 to 19 years old in 1988; males; 37% Black, 21% Hispanic, 3% other	Importance of religion; frequency of church attendance	Number of coital acts in past 12 months that did not include use of a condom	Males who attended church more frequently in mid-adolescence showed a decline (relative to predicted levels) in the frequency of unprotected sex in late adolescence.
(1997) Miller, Norton, Curtis, Hill, Schvaneveldt, & Young[e]	United States, 1976, 1981, and 1987; N = 759	7 to 11 years old in 1976; M and F; White and Black	Attendance (parent report); attitudes toward attending	Age at first coitus (reported retrospectively in Wave III)	Families who reported positive attitudes toward attending religious services were more likely to delay sexual debut.
(1999) Bearman & Bruckner[f]	United States, 1994 to 1996; N = 5,070	7th to 12th grades; females only; White, Black, Asian, Hispanic	Religious affiliation	First sexual intercourse (yes or no); age of first coitus; pregnancy risk (yes or no)	Beyond the effects of age on sexual debut, conservative Protestants and Catholics were less likely than were mainstream Protestants to experience first intercourse (sexual debut) between Time 1 and Time 2.
(1999) Whitbek, Yoder, Hoyt, & Conger	Midwestern state, 1989 to 1993, rural; N = 457	8th to 10th grades; M and F; White	Composite: attendance, importance (mother and adolescent)	Sexual intercourse (yes or no)	Mother's religiosity decreased likelihood of adolescent's sexual debut in 9th and 10th grades. Adolescent religiosity had strong negative effects on sexual debut.
(2001) Bearman & Bruckner	United States, 1994 to 1995 (Wave I), 1996 (Wave II); N = 14,787	7th to 12th grades; M and F; White, Hispanic, Asian, Black	Composite of attendance, perceived importance, and frequency of praying	Age at first coitus; contraceptive use at first coitus (yes or no); virginity pledger (yes or no)	Higher religiosity decreased the risk of sexual debut for White, Asian, and Hispanic adolescents of both genders. For Black adolescents, no relation between religiosity and risk of sexual debut was found. Religiosity delayed sexual debut in middle and late, but not early, adolescence. (Analyses conducted with non-Black respondents only.) Religiosity and contraceptive use at first coitus were unrelated.

Note: M = male; F = female.
a. The religiosity measure is not described for this article.
b. Data are from the National Longitudinal Survey of Youth (NLSY).
c. Data are from the National Longitudinal Survey of Youth (NLSY).
d. Data are from the National Survey of Adolescent Males (NSAM).
e. Data are from all three waves of the National Survey of Children (NSC).
f. Data are from Waves I and II of the National Longitudinal Study of Adolescent Health (Add Health).

[3] Rostosky, S. S., Wilcox, B. L., Wright, M. L. C., & Randall, B. A. (2004). The impact of religiosity on adolescent sexual behavior: A review of the evidence. *Journal of Adolescent Research, 19,* 677–697. Reprinted with permission.

Note that the summaries of results of the various studies in Example 7.3.1 are in words (not statistics). Often, this is the best way to present the summaries of results. It is acceptable to present statistics, however, if they are straightforward and are comparable from study to study. For instance, if there are five studies that estimate the prevalence of inhalant use by high school students, and they all present results in terms of percentages, including the percentages would be appropriate in the summaries of results. On the other hand, if the statistics reported on a topic are diverse from study to study, it would be less desirable to present them because they are not directly comparable from one study to another (e.g., one study presents percentages, one presents means and medians, another presents a frequency distribution, and so on). This is true because a reader should be able to scan columns and rows to note differences among studies. Scanning and comparing mixed statistics in a column can be confusing.

✓ Guideline 4:   When there is much literature on a topic, establish criteria for determining which literature to summarize in a table.

Summary tables that will be inserted into a literature review do not necessarily need to include all studies on the topic of the review. However, if only some are included, you should describe the criteria for inclusion. Examples 7.4.1 and 7.4.2 show sample statements that inform readers of such criteria.

Example 7.4.1
Description of criterion (i.e., only true experiments) for inclusion in a table:

Table 1 summarizes characteristics of the participants, the treatments applied, and the outcome measures. This table includes only *true experiments* (i.e., experiments in which participants were assigned at random to experimental and control groups).

Example 7.4.2
Description of criterion (i.e., only recent surveys) for inclusion in a table:

Table 2 summarizes the research methods and results of the five most recent surveys on the topic. Because the literature indicates that opinions on the issue vary over time, the most recent surveys provide the best indication of current public opinion on this issue.

✓ Guideline 5:   When there is much literature on a topic, consider building two or more tables to summarize it.

Even after establishing criteria for inclusion of studies in a table (see Guideline 4), there may be too many studies to include in a single table. When this is the case, consider how the literature might be divided into groups so a different table may be built for each group of studies. For instance, one table might summarize the theories relevant to the topic, another might summarize the quantitative studies on a topic, and a third table might summarize the qualitative studies.

✔ Guideline 6: Present tables in a literature review only for complex material.

During the early stages of synthesizing literature, there is no limit to how many tables you may create to get an overview of the literature. However, you should include in your literature review only tables that deal with complex matters that might be difficult for your readers to follow in the text (i.e., difficult to follow in the narrative of the literature review).

A literature review should *not* be a collection of tables. Instead, it should be primarily a narrative in which you summarize, synthesize, and interpret the literature on a topic, with only a small number of tables inserted to assist readers in comprehending complex material.

✔ Guideline 7: Discuss each table included in a literature review.

All tables in a literature review should be introduced and discussed in the narrative of the literature review. Example 7.7.1 illustrates how this might be done.

Example 7.7.1
Discussion of a table:

Table 1 summarizes the five studies in which the effectiveness of cognitive/behavioral therapy was examined using the Beck Depression Inventory as the outcome measure. Overall, the sample sizes were quite small, ranging from $n = 4$ to $n = 16$. Despite this limitation, the results show promise for use of cognitive/behavioral therapy because all the treated groups (i.e., experimental groups) showed statistically significant decreases in depression in comparison with the control groups.

While you should discuss each table, it is not necessary to describe every element in it. For instance, Example 7.7.1 discusses a table that summarizes five studies, yet the sample sizes used in only two of the studies ($n = 4$ and $n = 16$) are mentioned in the narrative.

✔ Guideline 8: Give each table a number and descriptive title.

All tables should have a number (e.g., Table 1, Table 2, and so on) as well as a descriptive title (i.e., a caption). Note that all tables in this chapter have table numbers and titles.

✔ Guideline 9: Master table-building using your word processor.

Word-processing programs have features that facilitate the building of tables with columns and rows. For instance, in Microsoft Word®, clicking on "Table"[4] near the top of the screen will give you the option to "Insert" a table. After clicking on "Insert," click on "Table" in the drop-down list. Doing this will produce a dialog box in which you can indicate the number of columns and rows you need. Doing this for a table with five columns and four rows will produce a raw table such as the table on the next page.

---

[4] An underlined letter such as the a in Table indicates a keyboard shortcut for touch typists who are more efficient when they do not use the mouse. For instance, holding down the "Alt" key on the keyboard while typing the letter *a* will produce the drop-down list that will permit building a table without using the mouse.

To refine the table, you need to bring up the "Tables and Borders" toolbar. To do this, click on "View," then click on "Toolbars" from the drop-down list, then click on "Tables and Borders." The toolbar will appear on your screen. Scrolling the cursor across the toolbar (with a slight pause on each icon) will produce pop-up boxes that indicate the function of each icon. For instance, you will find one that reads "Merge Cells." This can be used to merge the cells in the first row of the table to provide room for the table number and title. Specifically, to do this, highlight the first row of the table by dragging the cursor across it. (It will become black.) Then, click on the "Merge Cells" icon, and the table will look like this:

The table number is placed here. No italics (e.g., "Table 1"). The title is placed here (italicize title; cap the first letter of each word; no period).[5]			

It is beyond the scope of this book to provide comprehensive directions for using a word processor to build tables. In programs such as Word®, with only a little experimentation while paying attention to the pop-up boxes in the "Tables and Borders" toolbar, it is quite easy to learn how to modify tables.

✓ **Guideline 10: Insert *continued* when tables split across pages.**

While it is desirable to fit each table on a single page, it is not always possible. When a table splits across pages, put (*continued*) at the bottom of the table so that readers know to turn the page and continue reading the table. At the top of the second part of the table on the next page, repeat the table number followed by (*continued*).

Activities for Chapter 7

Directions: It is assumed that you have already read many of the articles that you will be evaluating and synthesizing in your literature review. Answer the following questions to the extent that you can based on your preliminary reading of the literature.

1. Do you plan to build a table of definitions? Explain.

---

[5] This table format is consistent with guidelines outlined in the *Publication Manual of the American Psychological Association.*

2. Do you plan to build a table of research methods? Will it also include a row or column that summarizes the results of the studies?

3. Will you apply criteria to select among studies for inclusion in a table? Explain.

4. Do you anticipate inserting more than one table in your literature review? Explain.

5. Have you considered how you will discuss the literature that you plan to summarize in one or more tables?

6. Have you explored table-building using your word processor? How easy is it to use? Have you experienced any difficulties in using it? If so, have you consulted with others (e.g., other students) to resolve your difficulties? Explain.

Notes

Chapter 8

Synthesizing Literature Prior to Writing a Review

At this point, you should have read and analyzed a collection of research articles and prepared detailed notes, possibly including summary tables (see Chapter 7). You should now begin to synthesize these notes and tabled materials into a new whole, the sum of which will become your literature review. In other words, you are now ready to begin the process of *writing* a literature review. This chapter will help you to develop an important product: a detailed writing outline.

✔ **Guideline 1: Consider your purpose and voice before beginning to write.**

Begin by asking yourself what your purpose is in writing a literature review. Are you trying to convince your professor that you have expended sufficient effort in preparing a term paper for your class? Are you trying to demonstrate your command of a field of study in a thesis or dissertation? Or is your purpose to establish a context for a study you hope will be published in a journal? Each of these scenarios will result in a different type of final product, in part because of the differences in the writer's purpose, but also because of differences in readers' expectations. Review the descriptions of three types of literature reviews in Chapter 2.

After you establish your purpose and have considered your audience, decide on an appropriate *voice* (or style of writing) for your manuscript. A writer's voice in a literature review should be formal because that is what the academic context dictates. The traditional voice in scientific writing requires that the writer de-emphasize himself or herself in order to focus readers' attention on the content. In Example 8.1.1, the writer's *self* is too much in evidence. It distracts the reader from the content of the statement. Example 8.1.2 is superior because it focuses on the content.

Example 8.1.1[1]
Improper voice for academic writing:

In this review, I will show that groups are often indispensable to many important life activities and have the potential for enhancing performance and productivity. However, I believe this potential is seldom fully realized. One well-documented limitation of groups I observed in the literature is the tendency for individuals to exert less effort when working in a group than when working individually, a phenomenon known as social loafing (Latané, Williams, & Harkins, 1979).

---

[1] This is a hypothetical example based on Example 8.1.2.

Example 8.1.2[2]

Suitable voice for academic writing:

Groups are often indispensable to many important life activities and have the potential for enhancing performance and productivity. However, this potential is seldom fully realized. One well-documented limitation of groups is the tendency for individuals to exert less effort when working in a group than when working individually, a phenomenon known as social loafing (Latané, Williams, & Harkins, 1979).

Notice that academic writers tend to avoid using the first person. Instead, they let the material, including statistics and theories, speak for itself. This is not to say that the first person should never be used. However, it is traditional to use it exceedingly sparingly.

✔ Guideline 2: Consider how to reassemble your notes.

Now that you have established the purpose for writing your review, identified your audience, and established your voice, you should reevaluate your notes to determine how the pieces you have described will be reassembled. At the outset, you should recognize that it is almost always unacceptable in writing a literature review to present only a series of annotations of research studies. In essence, that would be like describing individual trees when you really should be describing the forest. In a literature review, you are creating a unique new forest, which you will build by using the trees you found in the literature you read. In order to build this new whole, you should consider how the pieces relate to one another while preparing a topic outline, which is described in more detail in the next guideline.

✔ Guideline 3: Create a topic outline that traces your argument.

Like any other kind of essay, the review should *first* establish for the reader the line of argumentation you will follow (this is called the *thesis*). This can be stated in the form of an assertion, a contention, or a proposition. *Then*, you should develop a traceable narrative that demonstrates that the line of argumentation is worthwhile and justified. This means that you should have formed judgments about the topic based on the analysis and synthesis of the literature you are reviewing.

The topic outline should be designed as a road map of the argument, which is illustrated in Example 8.3.1. Notice that it starts with an assertion (that there is a severe shortage of donor organs, which will be substantiated with statistics, and that the review will be delimited to the psychological components of the decision to donate). This introduction is followed by a systematic review of the relevant areas of the research literature (points II and III in the outline), followed by a discussion of methodological issues in the relevant research (point IV). It ends with a summary, implications, and a discussion of suggestions for future research and conclusions that refer back to the introduction (point I).

---

[2] Smrt, D. L., & Karau, S. J. (2011). Protestant work ethic moderates social loafing. *Group Dynamics: Theory, Research, and Practice, 15*, 267–274.

Note that the authors of Example 8.3.1 have chosen to discuss weaknesses in research methodology in a separate section (point IV in the outline). Using a separate section for such a discussion is especially appropriate when all or many of the studies suffer from the same weaknesses. If different studies have different weaknesses, it is usually best to refer to the weaknesses when each study is cited (as opposed to discussing them in a separate section of the literature review).

Because the following outline will be referred to at various points throughout the rest of this chapter, please take a moment to examine it carefully. Place a flag on this page or bookmark it for easy reference to the outline when you are referred to it later.

Example 8.3.1[3]

Sample topic outline:

Topic: Psychological Aspects of Organ Donation: Individual and Next-of-Kin
       Donation Decisions

I. Introduction
    A. Establish importance of the topic (cite statistics on scarcity of organs).
    B. Delimit the review to psychological components of decisions.
    C. Describe organization of the paper, indicating that the remaining topics in the outline will be discussed.
II. Individual decisions regarding posthumous organ donation
    A. Beliefs about organ donation.
    B. Attitudes toward donating.
    C. Stated willingness to donate.
    D. Summary of research on individual decisions.
III. Next-of-kin consent decisions
    A. Beliefs about donating others' organs.
    B. Attitudes toward next-of-kin donations.
    C. Summary of research on next-of-kin consent decisions.
IV. Methodological issues and directions for future research
    A. Improvement in attitude measures and measurement strategy.
    B. Greater differentiation by type of donation.
    C. Stronger theoretical emphasis.
    D. Greater interdisciplinary focus.
V. Summary, Implications, and Discussion
    A. Summary of points I–IV.
    B. Need well-developed theoretical models of attitudes and decision making.
    C. Current survey data limited in scope and application points to the need for more sophisticated research in the future.
    D. Need more use of sophisticated data-analysis techniques.
    E. Conclusions: Psychology can draw from various subdisciplines for an understanding of donation decisions so that intervention strategies can be identified. Desperately need to increase the supply of donor organs.

---

[3] The outline is based on the work of Radicki, C. M., & Jaccard, J. (1997). Psychological aspects of organ donation: A critical review and synthesis of individual and next-of-kin donation decisions. *Health Psychology, 16*, 183–195.

✓ Guideline 4: Reorganize your notes according to the path of your argument.

The topic outline described in the previous guideline describes the path of the authors' argument. The next step is to reorganize the notes according to the outline. Begin by coding the notes with references to the appropriate places in the outline. For instance, on the actual note cards, write a "I." beside notations that cite statistics on the scarcity of donated organs, a "II." beside notations that deal with individual decisions about organ donations, a "III." beside notations that deal with next-of-kin decisions, and a "IV" beside notations that pertain to methodological issues. Then, return to the topic outline and indicate the specific references to particular studies. For instance, if Doe and Smith (2012) cite statistics on the scarcity of donated organs, write their names on the outline to the right of Topic I.

✓ Guideline 5: Within each topic heading, note differences among studies.

The next step is to note on your topic outline the differences in content among studies. Based on any differences, you may want to consider whether it is possible to group the articles into subtopics. For instance, for "Beliefs about organ donation" (point II.A. in Example 8.3.1), the literature can be grouped into the five subcategories shown in Example 8.5.1.

Example 8.5.1
Additional subtopics for point II.A. in Example 8.3.1:

1. Religious beliefs
2. Cultural beliefs
3. Knowledge (i.e., beliefs based on "facts" individuals have gathered from a variety of sources)
4. Altruistic beliefs
5. Normative beliefs (i.e., beliefs based on perceptions of what is acceptable within a particular social group)

These would become subtopics under point II.A. ("Beliefs about organ donation") in the topic outline. In other words, your outline will become more detailed as you identify additional subtopics.

The other type of difference you will want to consider is the consistency of results from study to study. For instance, the reviewers on whose work Example 8.3.1 is based found three articles suggesting that there are cultural obstacles that reduce the number of organ donations among Hispanics, while one other article indicated a willingness to donate and a high level of awareness about transplantation issues among this group. When you discuss such discrepancies, assist your reader by providing relevant information about the research, with an eye to identifying possible explanations for the differences. Were the first three articles older and the last one more current? Did the first three use a different methodology for collecting the data (e.g., did those with the negative results examine hospital records while the one with a positive result used self-report questionnaires)? Noting differences such as these may provide you with important issues to discuss when you are writing your literature review.

✓ Guideline 6: Within each topic heading, look for obvious gaps or areas needing more research.

In the full review based on the topic outline in Example 8.3.1, the reviewers noted that whereas much cross-cultural research has been conducted on African Americans, Asian Americans, and Hispanics, only a few studies have focused on Native Americans. Thus, any conclusions may not apply to the latter group. In addition, this points to an area that might be recommended for consideration in the planning of future research.

✓ Guideline 7: Plan to briefly describe relevant theories.

The importance of theoretical literature is discussed in Chapter 1. You should plan to briefly describe each theory that is relevant to the topic of your literature review. Example 8.7.1 illustrates this guideline with a description of objectification theory. Note that the authors start with a summary of the original theory and then summarize research that supports the theory. Finally, they note that the theory has not been tested with men.

Example 8.7.1[4]
Definition of a relevant theory:

Originally grounded in the experiences of women, objectification theory (Fredrickson & Roberts, 1997) posits that sexual objectification of women's bodies is omnipresent and can be internalized. Internalization of cultural standards of attractiveness occurs through constant exposure to socialization messages that promote compliance and identification with those messages. Such internalization can promote the adoption of an observer's perspective on one's own body, or self-objectification, which is manifested as persistent body surveillance. Body surveillance involves habitual monitoring and comparison of one's body against the internalized standard of attractiveness with a focus on how one's body looks rather than how it feels or functions. Body surveillance can, in turn, result in feelings of body shame for not meeting the (generally unattainable) cultural standards of attractiveness.

Research using cross-sectional and longitudinal data has supported a model of relations among these three objectification theory variables, such that internalization is related positively to body surveillance and body shame and body surveillance also has a unique positive relation with body shame. Body shame often mediates relations among objectification theory variables with outcomes variables, although both internalization and body surveillance often have unique additional relations with outcomes (for a review, see Moradi & Huang, 2008). This chain of relations is posited to underlie unhealthy efforts to alter one's appearance to comply with the internalized ideal; such efforts could include excessive dieting and

---

[4] Parent, M. C., & Moradi, B. (2011). His biceps become him: A test of objectification theory's application to drive for muscularity and propensity for steroid use in college men. *Journal of Counseling Psychology*, *58*, 246–256.

exercise, eating disorders, and body-modifying surgery or drug use. An extensive body of literature has tested this model and extended its application to women of diverse racial and ethnic backgrounds, ability statuses, and sexual orientation identities, and aspects of the model are also gaining support in emerging research with men (Moradi & Huang, 2008). However, evaluation of the model's applicability to men's body image concerns is still needed.

✓ Guideline 8: Plan to discuss how individual studies relate to and advance theory.

You should consider how individual studies, which are often narrow, help to define, illustrate, or advance theoretical notions. Often, researchers will point out how their studies relate to theory, which will help you in your considerations of this matter. In your topic outline, specify that one or more theories will be discussed in your literature review, as was done in point V.B. in Example 8.3.1, which indicates that the reviewer will discuss the need for well-developed theoretical models.

If there are competing theories in your area, plan to discuss the extent to which the literature you have reviewed supports each of them, keeping in mind that an inconsistency between the results of a study and a prediction based on theory may result from *either* imperfections in the theoretical model *or* imperfections in the research methodology used in the study.

✓ Guideline 9: Plan to summarize periodically and again near the end of the review.

It is helpful to summarize the inferences, generalizations, and/or conclusions you have drawn from your review of the literature in stages. For instance, the outline in Example 8.3.1 calls for summaries at two intermediate points in the literature review (i.e., points II.D. and III.C.). Long, complex topics within a literature review often deserve their own separate summaries. These summaries help readers to understand the direction the author is taking and invite readers to pause, think about, and internalize difficult material.

You have probably already noticed that the last main topic (Topic V.) in Example 8.3.1 calls for a summary of all the material that preceded it. It is usually appropriate to start the last section of a long review with a summary of the main points already covered. This shows readers what the writer views as the major points and sets the stage for a discussion of the writer's conclusions and any implications he or she has drawn. In a very short literature review, a summary may not be needed.

✓ Guideline 10: Plan to present conclusions and implications.

Note that a *conclusion* is a statement about the state of the knowledge on a topic. Example 8.10.1 illustrates a conclusion. Note that it does not say that there is "proof." Reviewers should hedge and talk about degrees of evidence (e.g., "It seems safe to conclude that…," "One conclusion might be that…," "There is strong evidence that…," or "The evidence overwhelmingly supports the conclusion that…").

Example 8.10.1

Statement of a conclusion:

In light of the research on cultural differences in attitudes toward organ donation, *it seems safe to conclude that* (emphasis added) cultural groups differ substantially in their attitudes toward organ donation and that effective intervention strategies need to take account of these differences. Specifically….

If the weight of the evidence on a topic does not clearly favor one conclusion over the other, be prepared to say so. Example 8.10.2 illustrates this technique.

Example 8.10.2

Statement that a conclusion cannot be made:

Although the majority of the studies indicate Method A is superior, several methodologically strong studies point to the superiority of Method B. In the absence of additional evidence, *it is difficult to conclude that* (emphasis added)….

An *implication* is usually a statement of what individuals or organizations should do in light of existing research. In other words, a reviewer usually should make suggestions as to what actions seem promising based on the review of the research. Thus, it is usually desirable to include the heading "Implications" near the end of a topic outline. Example 8.10.3 is an implication because it suggests that a particular intervention might be effectively used with a particular group.

Example 8.10.3

Statement of an implication:

The body of evidence reviewed in this paper suggests that when working with Asian Americans, Intervention A seems most promising for increasing the number of organ donations made by this group.

At first, some novice writers believe that they should describe only "facts" from the published research and not venture to offer their own conclusions and related implications. Keep in mind, however, that an individual who thoroughly and carefully reviewed the literature on a topic has, in fact, become an expert on it. For advice on the state of a knowledge base (conclusions) and what we should do to be more effective (implications), whom else should we look to than an expert who has up-to-date knowledge of the research on a topic? Thus, it is appropriate to express your conclusions regarding the state of knowledge on a topic and the implications that follow from them.

✓ Guideline 11: Plan to suggest specific directions for future research near the end of the review.

As you plan what to say, keep in mind that it is inadequate to simply suggest that "more research is needed in the future." Instead, make specific suggestions. For instance, if all (or almost all) the researchers have used self-report questionnaires, you might call for future research using other means of data collection, such as direct observation of physical behavior and an examination of records kept by agencies that coordinate donations. If there are understudied groups such as Native Americans, you might call for more research on them. If almost all the studies are quantitative, you might call for additional qualitative studies. The list of possibilities is almost endless. Your job is to suggest those that you think are most promising for advancing knowledge in the area you are reviewing.

✓ Guideline 12: Flesh out your outline with details from your analysis.

The final step before you begin to write your first draft is to review the topic outline and flesh it out with specific details from your analysis of the research literature. Make every effort, as you expand the outline, to include enough details to be able to write clearly about the studies you are including. Make sure to note the strengths and weaknesses of studies as well as the gaps, relationships, and major trends or patterns that emerge in the literature. At the end of this step, your outline should be several pages long, and you will be ready to write your first draft.

Example 8.12.1 illustrates how a small portion of the topic outline in Example 8.3.1 (specifically, point II.A.1.) would look if it were fleshed out with additional details.

Example 8.12.1
Part of a fleshed-out outline:

II. Individual decisions regarding posthumous organ donation
    A. Beliefs about organ donation (research can be categorized into five major groupings)
        1. Religious beliefs
           a. Define the term *religious beliefs*
           b. Religions that support organ donation
               (1) Buddhism, Hinduism (Ulshafer, 1988; Woo, 2002)
               (2) Catholicism (Ulshafer, 1988)
               (3) Judaism (Bulka, 1990; Cohen, 1988; Pearl, 1990; Weiss, 1988)
               (4) Protestantism (Walters, 1988)
               (5) Islam (Gatrad, 1994; Rispler-Chaim, 1989; Sachedina, 2003)
           c. Religions that do not support it
               (1) Jehovah's Witnesses (Corlett, 2003; Pearl, 2004)
               (2) Orthodox Judaism (Corlett, 2003; Pearl, 2004)
           d. Other sources that have commented on religion as a barrier (Basu et al., 1989; Gallup Organization, 1993; Moore et al., 2004)

Notice that several of the references in Example 8.12.1 appear in more than one place. For instance, Corlett's 2003 report will be referred to under a discussion of both Jehovah's Witnesses and Orthodox Judaism. This is appropriate because a reviewer should *not* be writing a series of summaries in which Corlett's study is summarized in one place and then dropped from the discussion. Instead, it should be cited as many times as needed, depending on how many specific points it bears on in the outline.

Activities for Chapter 8

Directions: For each of the model literature reviews that your instructor assigns, answer the following questions. The model literature reviews are near the end of this book.

1. Did the author use an appropriate academic voice? Did the author write in the first person? Explain.

2. Does the author's argument move logically from one topic to another? Explain.

3. Has the author pointed out areas needing more research? Explain.

4. Has the author discussed how the individual studies help to define, illustrate, and/or advance theory? Explain.

5. If the review is a long one, does it include a summary? Explain.

6. Has the author clearly discussed conclusions and implications?

7. Has the author suggested specific directions for future research?

Notes

Chapter 9

Guidelines for Writing a First Draft

Up to this point, you have searched for literature on the topic of your review, made careful notes on specific details of the literature, and analyzed these details to identify patterns, relationships among studies, and gaps in the body of literature, as well as strengths and weaknesses in particular research studies. Then, in Chapter 8, you reorganized your notes and developed a detailed writing outline as you prepared to write your literature review.

In other words, you have already completed the most difficult steps in the writing process: the analysis and synthesis of the literature and the charting of the course of your argument. These preliminary steps constitute the intellectual process of preparing a literature review. The remaining steps—drafting, editing, and redrafting—will now require you to translate the results of your intellectual labor into a narrative account of what you have found.

The guidelines in this chapter will help you to produce a first draft of your literature review. The guidelines in Chapter 10 will help you to develop a coherent essay and avoid producing a series of annotations, and Chapter 11 presents additional guidelines that relate to style, mechanics, and language usage.

✓ Guideline 1: Begin by identifying the broad problem area, but avoid global statements.

Usually, the introduction of a literature review should begin with the identification of the broad problem area under review. The rule of thumb is, "Go from the general to the specific." However, there are limits on how general to be in the beginning. Consider Example 9.1.1. As the beginning of a literature review on a topic in higher education, it is much too broad. It fails to identify any particular area or topic. You should avoid starting your review with such global statements.

Example 9.1.1
Beginning of a literature review in education that is too broad:

Higher education is important to both the economy of the United States and to the rest of the world. Without a college education, students will be unprepared for the many advances that will take place in this millennium.

Contrast Example 9.1.1 with Example 9.1.2, which is also on a topic in education but clearly relates to the specific topic that will be reviewed: bullying in schools.

Example 9.1.2[1]

Beginning of a literature review on a topic in education that is sufficiently specific:

A significant proportion of children are involved in bullying across their school years. Children who are bullied report a range of problems, including anxiety and depression (Nansel, Overpeck, Pilla, Ruan, Simons-Morton, & Scheidt, 2001), low self-esteem (Egan & Perry, 1998), reduced academic performance (Juvonen, Nishina, & Graham, 2000), and school absenteeism (Eisenberg, Neumark-Sztainer, & Perry, 2003). Bullying may also be a significant stressor associated with suicidal behavior (Klomek, Marrocco, Kleinman, Schonfeld, & Gould, 2007).

✓ **Guideline 2:   Early in the review, indicate why the topic being reviewed is important.**

As early as the first paragraph in a literature review, it is desirable to indicate why the topic is important. The authors of Example 9.2.1 have done this by pointing out that their topic deals with a serious health issue.

Example 9.2.1[2]

Beginning of a literature review indicating the importance of the topic:

Vitamin D insufficiency is increasing across all age groups (Looker et al., 2008). Recent research implicates vitamin D insufficiency as a risk factor for a variety of chronic diseases, including type 1 and 2 diabetes, osteoporosis, cardiovascular disease, hypertension, metabolic syndrome, and cancer (Heaney, 2008; Holick, 2006).

Of course, not all issues are of as much universal importance as the one in Example 9.2.1. Nevertheless, the topic of the review should be of importance to some group(s), and this should be pointed out, as in Example 9.2.2, which points at the high incidence of minority students enrolled in low-track mathematics courses.

Example 9.2.2[3]

Beginning of a literature review indicating the importance of the topic:

National educational data prove that minority students are much more likely than White students to be enrolled in low-track mathematics courses by the 10th grade (Kelly, 2009). Several research studies emphasized that Black students are found disproportionately in lower-ability groups and academic courses as early as the first grade (Entwisle, Alexander, and Olson, 1997).

---

[1] Hunt, C., Peters, L., & Rapee, R. M. (2012). Development of a measure of the experience of being bullied in youth. *Psychological Assessment, 24*, 156–165.

[2] Lukaszuk, J. M., Prawitz, A. D., Johnson, K. N., Umoren, J., & Bugno, T. J. (2012). Development of a noninvasive vitamin D screening tool. *Family & Consumer Sciences Research Journal, 40*, 229–240.

[3] Faitar, G. M., & Faitar, S. L. (2012). The influence of ability tracking on the performances of minority learners. *Journal of Instructional Pedagogies, 7*, 1–9.

✓ Guideline 3: Distinguish between research findings and other sources of information.

If you describe points of view that are based on anecdotal evidence or personal opinions rather than on research, indicate the nature of the source. For instance, the three statements in Example 9.3.1 contain key words (e.g., *speculated*), which indicate that the material is based on personal points of view (not research).

Example 9.3.1
Beginnings of statements that indicate that the material that follows is based on personal points of view (not research):

"Doe (2012) speculated that…."

"It has been suggested that…. (Smith, 2011)."

"Black (2011) related a personal experience, which indicated that…."

Contrast the statements in Example 9.3.1 with those in Example 9.3.2, which are for introducing research-based findings in a literature review.

Example 9.3.2
Beginnings of statements that indicate that the material that follows is based on research:

"In a statewide survey, Jones (2012) found that…."

"Hill's (2011) research in urban classrooms indicates that…."

"Recent findings indicate that… (Barnes, 2011; Hanks, 2012)."

If there is little research on a topic, you may find it necessary to review primarily literature that expresses only opinions (without a research base). When this is the case, consider making a general statement to indicate this situation before discussing the literature in more detail in your review. This technique is indicated in Example 9.3.3.

Example 9.3.3
Statement indicating a lack of research:

This database contains more than 50 documents, journal articles, and monographs devoted to the topic. However, none are reports of original research. Instead, they present anecdotal evidence, such as information on individual clients who have received therapeutic treatment.

✓ Guideline 4: Indicate why certain studies are important.

If a particular study has methodological strengths, mention them to indicate their importance, as was done in Example 9.4.1.

Example 9.4.1[4]

Indicates why a study is important (in this case, "a national survey" and "randomly selected"):

The Pew Research Center (2007) recently conducted a national survey of 2,020 randomly selected adults and found that 21% of employed mothers preferred full-time work, 60% preferred part-time work, and 19% preferred no employment.

A study may also be important because it represents a pivotal point in the development of an area of research, such as a research article that indicates a reversal of a prominent researcher's position or one that launched a new methodology. These and other characteristics of a study may justify its status as important. When a study is especially important, make sure your review makes this clear to the reader.

✓ Guideline 5: If you are commenting on the timeliness of a topic, be specific in describing the time frame.

Avoid beginning your review with unspecific references to the timeliness of a topic, as in, "In recent years, there has been an increased interest in…." This beginning would leave many questions unanswered for the reader, such as the following: What years are being referenced? How did the writer determine that the "interest" is increasing? Who has become more interested: the writer or others in the field? Is it possible that the writer became interested in the topic recently while others have been losing interest?

Likewise, an increase in a problem or an increase in the size of a population of interest should be specific in terms of numbers or percentages and the specific years being referred to. For instance, it is not very informative to state only that "The number of college students who cheat probably has increased" or that "There will be an increase in job growth." The authors of Examples 9.5.1 and 9.5.2 avoided this problem by being specific in citing percentages and the time frame (italics and bold are added for emphasis).

Example 9.5.1[5]

Names a specific time frame:

Over the years, research in this area has documented a steady increase in cheating and unethical behavior among college students (Brown & Emmett, 2001). ***Going as far back as 1941, Baird (1980) reported that college cheating had increased from 23% in 1941 to 55% in 1970 to 75% in 1980. Moving forward, McCabe and Bowers (1994) reported that college cheating had increased from 63% in 1962 to 70% in 1993.***

More recently, Burke, Polimeni, and Slavin (2007) stated that "various studies suggest that we may be at the precipice of a culture of academic malfeasance, where large numbers of students engage in various forms of cheating." The Center for Academic Integrity at Oklahoma State University (2009), conducted a

---

[4] Buehler, C., O'Brien, M., & Walls, J. K. (2011). Mothers' part-time employment: Child, parent, and family outcomes. *Journal of Family Theory & Review, 3*, 256–272.

[5] Burton, J. H., Talpade, S., & Haynes, J. (2011). Religiosity and test-taking ethics among business school students. *Journal of Academic and Business Ethics, 4*, 1–8.

large-scale survey of 1,901 students and 431 faculty members and found some very disturbing results, showing that 60% of college students engaged in at least one behavior that violated academic integrity and that 72% of undergraduate business majors reported doing this, versus 56% from other disciplines. ***Brown, Weible, and Olmosk (2010) also reported that the percentage of cheating in undergraduate management classes in 2008 was close to 100%, which was an increase from the recorded 49% in 1988.***

Example 9.5.2[6]
Names a specific time frame:

With the current economy showing signs of a sluggish recovery, employers are cautiously optimistic about what the future holds. Mixed indicators in the unemployment rate, depending on location, may mean an increase in job growth for certain industries. ***A recent economic report released by* USA Today *shows the strongest 12-month national job growth*** in Construction (3.9%), Leisure and Hospitality (3.4%), Education and Health Services (2.9%), and Professional and Business Services (2.9%) while traditionally strong and stable sectors such as Government (–0.3%) and Utilities (0.3%) are showing slower growth rates (Job Growth Forecast, 2011).

✔ Guideline 6: If citing a classic or landmark study, identify it as such.

Make sure that you identify the classic or landmark studies in your review. Such studies are often pivotal points in the historical development of the published literature. In addition, they are often responsible for framing a particular question or a research tradition, and they also may be the original source of key concepts or terminology used in the subsequent literature. Whatever their contribution, you should identify their status as classics or landmarks in the literature. Consider Example 9.6.1, in which a landmark study (one of the earliest investigations on the topic) is cited.

Example 9.6.1[7]
Identifies a landmark study:

A few studies have examined the direct and indirect links between victimization and achievement in elementary school over time. **In one of the earliest investigations on this topic** [emphasis added], Kochenderfer and Ladd (1996) showed that peer victimization experiences served as a precursor of school adjustment problems (e.g., academic achievement, school avoidance, loneliness) across the kindergarten year.

---

[6] Butler, T. H., & Berret, B. A. (2012). A generation lost: The reality of age discrimination in today's hiring practices. *Journal of Management and Marketing Research, 9*, 1–11.

[7] Juvonen, J., Wang, Y., & Espinoza, G. (2011). Bullying experiences and compromised academic performance across middle school grades. *Journal of Early Adolescence, 31*, 152–173.

✓ Guideline 7: If a landmark study was replicated, mention that and indicate the results of the replication.

As noted in the previous guideline, landmark studies typically stimulate additional research. In fact, many are replicated a number of times, using different groups of participants or by adjusting other research design variables. If you are citing a landmark study and it has been replicated, you should mention that fact and indicate whether the replications were successful. This is illustrated in Example 9.7.1.

Example 9.7.1[8]
Points at replications:

Since the time of this study, a number of *other content analyses have replicated these results* (emphasis added) (Belkaoui & Belkaoui, 1976; Busby & Leichty, 1993; Culley & Bennett, 1976; England, Kuhn, & Gardner, 1983; Lysonski, 1983; Sexton & Haberman, 1974; Venkatesan & Losco, 1975; Wagner & Banos, 1973). During the past 40 years, only one of the stereotypes found by Courtney and Lockeretz (1971) has shown evidence of amelioration: the image of women as homebound. As women have entered the workforce in growing numbers, advertisements have increasingly shown them in work settings outside the home (Busby & Leichty, 1993; Sullivan & O'Connor, 1988).

✓ Guideline 8: Discuss other literature reviews on your topic.

If you find an earlier published review on your topic, it is important to discuss it in your review. Before doing so, consider the following questions:

How is the other review different from yours?
Is yours substantially more current?
Did you delimit the topic in a different way?
Did you conduct a more comprehensive review?
Did the earlier reviewer reach the same major conclusions that you reached?
Did you reach the same major conclusions as the earlier reviewer?

How worthy is the other review of your readers' attention?
What will they gain, if anything, by reading it?
Will they encounter a different and potentially helpful perspective on the problem area?
What are its major strengths and weaknesses?

✓ Guideline 9: Refer the reader to other reviews on issues that you will not be discussing in detail.

If you find it necessary to refer to a *related issue* that cannot be covered in depth in your review, it is appropriate to refer the reader to other reviews, as in Example 9.9.1.

---

[8] Neptune, D., & Plous, S. (1997). Racial and gender biases in magazine advertising. *Psychology of Women Quarterly*, *21*, 627–644.

Needless to say, your review should completely cover the specific topic you have chosen. It is not acceptable to describe just a portion of the literature on your topic (as you defined it) and then refer the reader to another source for the remainder. However, the technique illustrated in Example 9.9.1 can be useful for pointing out literature that may be of interest to the reader but will not be reviewed in detail in the review you are writing (italics and bold are added for emphasis).

Example 9.9.1[9]

Refers readers to other sources for details:

A wealth of research has documented teachers' assessment practices and beliefs (...*for a review, see Brookhart, 2004*), but few of these studies consider these practices from an SRL perspective. In the present study....

✓ Guideline 10: Justify comments such as "no studies were found."

If you find a gap in the literature that deserves mention in your literature review, explain how you arrived at the conclusion that there is a gap. At the very least, explain how you conducted the literature search, which databases you searched, and the dates and other parameters you used. You do not need to be overly specific, but the reader will expect you to justify your statement about the gap.

To avoid misleading your reader, it is a good idea early in your review to make statements such as the one shown in Example 9.10.1. This will protect you from criticism if you point out a gap when one does not actually exist. In other words, you are telling your reader that there is a gap as determined by the use of *a particular search strategy*.

Example 9.10.1[10]

Describes the strategy for searching literature:

We systematically searched for relevant studies until February 2011. We started with an initial set of reports on children with incarcerated parents collected in our previous research on this topic. Four methods were used to search for additional studies. First, keywords were entered into 23 electronic databases and Internet search engines. The keywords entered were (*prison** or *jail** or *penitentiary* or *imprison** or *incarcerat** or *detention*) and (*child** or *son** or *daughter** or *parent** or *mother** or *father**) and (*antisocial** or *delinquen** or *crim** or *offend** or *violen** or *aggressi** or *mental health* or *mental illness* or *internaliz** or *depress** or *anxiety* or *anxious* or *psychological** or *drug** or *alcohol** or *drink** or *tobacco* or *smok** or *substance* or *education** or *school* or *grade** or *achievement*).

Second, bibliographies of prior reviews were examined (Dallaire, 2007; S. Gabel, 2003; Hagan & Dinovitzer, 1999; Johnston, 1995; Murray, 2005; Murray

---

[9] Davis, D. S., & Neitzel, C. (2011). A self-regulated learning perspective on middle grades classroom assessment. *The Journal of Educational Research, 104,* 202–215.

[10] Murray, J., Farrington, D. P., & Sekol, I. (2012). Children's antisocial behavior, mental health, drug use, and educational performance after parental incarceration: A systematic review and meta-analysis. *Psychological Bulletin, 138,* 175–210.

& Farrington, 2008a; Myers et al., 1999; Nijnatten, 1998) as well as edited books on children of incarcerated parents (Eddy & Poehlmann, 2010; K. Gabel & Johnston, 1995; Harris & Miller, 2002; Harris, Graham, & Carpenter, 2010; Shaw, 1992b; Travis & Waul, 2003). Third, experts in the field were contacted to request information about any other studies that we might not have located. The first group of experts contacted consisted of about 65 researchers and practitioners who we knew were professionals with an interest in children with incarcerated parents. The second group consisted of about 30 directors of major longitudinal studies in criminology....

✓ Guideline 11: Avoid long lists of nonspecific references.

In academic writing, references are used in the text of a written document for at least two purposes. First, they are used to give proper credit to an author of an idea or, in the case of a direct quotation, of a specific set of words. A failure to do so would constitute plagiarism. Second, references are used to demonstrate the breadth of coverage given in a manuscript. In an introductory paragraph, for instance, it may be desirable to include references to several key studies that will be discussed in more detail in the body of the review. However, it is inadvisable to use long lists of references that do not specifically relate to the point being expressed. For instance, in Example 9.11.1, the long list of nonspecific references in the first sentence is probably inappropriate. Are these all empirical studies? Do they report their authors' speculations on the issue? Are some of the references more important than others? It would have been better for the authors to refer the reader to a few key studies, which themselves would contain references to additional examples of research in that particular area, as illustrated in Example 9.11.2.

Example 9.11.1
First sentence in a literature review (too many nonspecific references):

Numerous writers have indicated that children in single-parent households are at greater risk for academic underachievement than children from two-parent households (Adams, 2012; Block, 2011; Doe, 2011; Edgar, 2012; Hampton, 2009; Jones, 2012; Klinger, 2008; Long, 2011; Livingston, 2010; Macy, 2011; Norton, 2012; Pearl, 2012; Smith, 2009; Travers, 2010; Vincent, 2011; West, 2008; Westerly, 2009; Yardley, 2011).

Example 9.11.2
An improved version of Example 9.11.1:

Numerous writers have suggested that children in single-parent households are at greater risk for academic underachievement than children from two-parent households (e.g., see Adams, 2012, and Block, 2011). Three recent studies have provided strong empirical support for this contention (Doe, 2011; Edgar, 2012; Jones, 2012). Of these, the study by Jones (2012) is the strongest, employing a national sample with rigorous controls for....

Notice the use of "e.g., see…," which indicates that only some of the possible references are cited for the point that the writers have suggested. You may also use the Latin abbreviation *cf.* (which means *compare*).

✔ Guideline 12: If the results of previous studies are inconsistent or widely varying, cite them separately.

It is not uncommon for studies on the same topic to produce inconsistent or widely varying results. If so, it is important to cite the studies separately in order for the reader to interpret your review correctly. The following two examples illustrate the potential problem. Example 9.12.1 is misleading because it fails to note that the previous studies are grouped according to the two extremes of the percentage range given. Example 9.12.2 illustrates a better way to cite inconsistent findings.

Example 9.12.1
Inconsistent results cited as a single finding (undesirable):

In previous studies (Doe, 2011; Jones, 2012), parental support for requiring students to wear school uniforms in public schools varied considerably, ranging from only 19% to 52%.

Example 9.12.2
Improved version of Example 9.12.1:

In previous studies, parental support for requiring students to wear school uniforms has varied considerably. Support from rural parents varied from only 19% to 28% (Doe, 2011), while support from suburban parents varied from 35% to 52% (Jones, 2012).

✔ Guideline 13: Speculate on the reasons for inconsistent findings in previous research.

The authors of Example 9.13.1 speculate on inconsistent findings regarding shame about in-group moral failure.

Example 9.13.1[11]
Speculation of inconsistent findings of previous research (desirable):

We think that the inconsistent findings regarding shame about in-group moral failure may result from the rather broad conceptualization of shame in past work. As Gausel and Leach (2011) recently pointed out, different studies of shame have conceptualized the emotion as involving quite different combinations of appraisal and feeling. Some previous work conceptualizes shame as a combination of the appraisal of *concern for condemnation* and an attendant *feeling of rejection*. Most

---

[11] Gausel, N., Leach, C. W., Vignoles, V. L., & Brown, R. (2012). Defend or repair? Explaining responses to in-group moral failure by disentangling feelings of shame, rejection, and inferiority. *Journal of Personality and Social Psychology, 102*, 941–960.

previous work conceptualizes shame as a combination of the appraisal that the self *suffers a defect* and an attendant *feeling of inferiority*.

✓ Guideline 14: Cite all relevant references in the review section of a thesis, dissertation, or journal article.

When writing a thesis, a dissertation, or an article for publication in which the literature review precedes a report of original research, you should usually first cite all the relevant references in the literature review of your document. Avoid introducing new references to literature in later sections, such as the results or discussion sections. Make sure you have checked your entire document to ensure that the literature review section or chapter is comprehensive. You may refer back to a previous discussion of a pertinent study when discussing your conclusions, but the study should have been referenced first in the literature review at the beginning of the thesis, dissertation, or article.

✓ Guideline 15: Emphasize the need for your study in the literature review section or chapter.

When writing a thesis, a dissertation, or an article for publication in which the literature review precedes a report of original research, you should use the review to help justify your study. You can do this in a variety of ways, such as pointing out that your study (a) closes a gap in the literature, (b) tests an important aspect of a current theory, (c) replicates an important study, (d) retests a hypothesis using new or improved methodological procedures, (e) is designed to resolve conflicts in the literature, and so on.

Example 9.15.1 was included in the literature review portion of a research report designed to examine the relation of ADHD to substance use among undergraduate college students. In their review, the authors point out gaps in the literature and indicate how their study fills them. This is a strong justification for the study.

Example 9.15.1[12]
Justifies a study:

This study addressed limitations of the previous literature by controlling for CD [conduct disorder] symptoms, examining different symptom dimensions of ADHD (e.g., hyperactivity/impulsivity, inattention) related to substance use, and exploring both continuous levels of ADHD symptoms and categorical ADHD based on clinically significant symptomatology. The importance of controlling for CD symptoms has been well-documented (e.g., Flory & Lynam, 2003), although to our knowledge, no previous studies on ADHD and college students have controlled for CD. Further, previous research has highlighted the importance of understanding symptom dimension differences among individuals with ADHD (e.g., Mikami, Huang-Pollock, Pfiffner, McBurnett, and Hangai, 2007), which may in turn help to inform specific prevention and intervention efforts. Finally, because ADHD has not been widely studied among college students, it is important to ex-

---

[12] Glass, K., & Flory, K. (2012). Are symptoms of ADHD related to substance use among college students? *Psychology of Addictive Behaviors, 26*, 124–132.

amine the full range of symptomatology, and so including both a continuous and categorical measurement of ADHD symptoms can help to clarify the relation between ADHD and substance use.

Activities for Chapter 9

Directions: For each of the model literature reviews that your instructor assigns, answer the following questions. The model literature reviews are presented near the end of this book.

1. Did the author begin by identifying the broad problem area while avoiding global statements? Explain.

2. Did the author indicate why the topic being reviewed is important? Explain.

3. Did the author distinguish between research findings and other sources of information by using appropriate wording? Explain.

4. Did the author indicate why certain studies are important? Explain.

5. If the author commented on the timeliness of the topic, was he or she specific in describing the time frame? Explain.

6. Was a landmark study cited? If yes, was it identified as a landmark? Was there any indication that it was replicated?

7. Are other literature reviews on the same topic discussed?

8. Are there references to other reviews on related issues that are not discussed in detail in the model literature review?

9. If the author said "no studies were found" on some aspect of the topic, was this statement justified (as indicated in this chapter)?

10. Did the author provide long lists of nonspecific references?

11. If results of previous studies are inconsistent or widely varying, were they cited separately?

Chapter 10

Guidelines for Developing a Coherent Essay

This chapter is designed to help you refine your first draft by guiding you in developing a coherent essay. Remember that a literature review should not be written as a series of connected summaries (or annotations) of the literature you have read. Instead, it should have a clearly stated argument, and it should be developed in such a way that all of its elements work together to communicate a well-reasoned account of that argument.

✔ **Guideline 1: If your review is long, provide an overview near the beginning of the review.**

When writing a long literature review, it is important to provide readers with an explicit road map of your argument. This is usually done in the introductory section of the review, which should include an overview of what will be covered in the rest of the document. Example 10.1.1 illustrates this.

Example 10.1.1[1]
An effective road map at the beginning of a review:

The major purpose of the present…review is to provide a comprehensive analysis of three broad questions. First, do incentives to cooperate promote and sustain cooperation in small group social dilemmas? Second, what variables might influence the effectiveness of incentives? Finally, do reward and punishment differ in their ability to promote and sustain cooperation? As we discuss shortly, we adopt an interdependence-theoretical analysis for understanding whether incentives might promote cooperation and when these incentives might be especially effective.

✔ **Guideline 2: Near the beginning of a review, state explicitly what will and will not be covered.**

Some topics are so broad that it will not be possible to cover the research completely in your review, especially if you are writing a term paper, which may have page-length restrictions imposed by your instructor, or an article for publication, in which reviews traditionally are relatively short. In such cases, you should state explicitly, near the beginning of your review, what will and will not be covered (i.e., the delimitations of your review). The excerpt in Example 10.2.1 illustrates application of this guideline. Note

---

[1] Balliet, D., Mulder, L. B., & Van Lange, P. A. M. (2011). Reward, punishment, and cooperation: A meta-analysis. *Psychological Bulletin*, *137*, 594–615.

that the reviewers first provide a definition and indicate that their review includes *deceiving* and *lying* (as being interchangeable). They then state that the review will be limited to two criteria.

Example 10.2.1[2]
A statement of the delimitations of a review:

We define deception as a deliberate attempt to mislead others. Falsehoods communicated by people who are mistaken or self-deceived are not lies, but literal truths designed to mislead are lies. Although some scholars draw a distinction between *deceiving* and *lying* (e.g., Bok, 1978), we use the terms interchangeably. As Zuckerman et al. (1981) did in their review, we limit our analysis to behaviors that can be discerned by human perceivers without the aid of any special equipment. We also limit our review to studies of adults, as the dynamics of deceiving may be markedly different in children (e.g., Feldman, Devin-Sheehan, & Allen, 1978; Lewis, Stanger, & Sullivan, 1989; Shennum & Bugental, 1982).

✓ Guideline 3: Specify your point of view early in the review.

As has been emphasized previously, your literature review should be written in the form of an essay that has a particular point of view after looking at the research. This point of view serves as the thesis statement of your essay (the assertion or proposition that is supported in the remainder of the essay).

The expression of your point of view does not need to be elaborate or detailed (although it can be). In Example 10.3.1, the reviewers briefly indicate their point of view (that SES, cognitive-emotional factors, and health may be dynamically linked). This informs readers very early in the review that this overarching point of view guides the interpretation and synthesis of the literature.

Of course, you should settle on a point of view only *after* you have read and considered the body of literature as a whole. In other words, this guideline indicates when you should *express* your point of view (early in the review), not when you should develop a point of view.

Example 10.3.1[3]
Early summary of the path of an argument:

The associations between SES and cognitive-emotional factors have not been presented in any recent, enumerative reviews (but see the review of SES and psychiatric disorders by Kohn, Dohrenwend, & Mirotznik, 1998), and we therefore analyze this research in more detail. Following our review and critical analysis, we present a framework for understanding the pathways that may dynamically link SES, cognitive-emotional factors, and health. Finally, we conclude with recommendations for future research to better address the proposed mediation hypothesis.

---

[2] DePaulo, B. M., Lindsay, J. J., Malone, B. E., Muhlenbruck, L., Charlton, K., & Cooper, H. (2003). Cues to deception. *Psychological Bulletin, 129,* 74–118.
[3] Gallo, L. C., & Matthews, K. A. (2003). Understanding the association between socioeconomic status and physical health: Do negative emotions play a role? *Psychological Bulletin, 129,* 10–51.

✓ Guideline 4: Aim for a clear and cohesive essay. Avoid annotations.

It has been emphasized several times thus far that an effective literature review should be written in the form of an essay. Perhaps the single most reported problem for novice academic writers is their difficulty in abandoning the use of annotations in the body of a literature review.

Annotations are brief summaries of the contents of articles. Stringing together several annotations in the body of a review may describe what research is available on a topic, but it fails to organize the material for the reader. An effective review of literature is organized to make a point. The writer needs to describe how the individual studies relate to one another. What are the relative strengths and weaknesses? Where are the gaps, and why do they exist? All these details and more need to support the author's main purpose for writing the review. The detailed outline developed in Chapter 8 describes the path of the argument, but it is up to the writer to translate this into a prose account that integrates the important details of the research literature into an essay that communicates a point of view.

Example 10.4.1 shows how a number of studies can be cited together as part of a single paragraph. Clearly, then, the organization of the paragraph is topical—not around the reports of individual authors.

Example 10.4.1[4]
A single paragraph with multiple sources:

College has long been a key pathway to financial, physical, and social-psychological well-being (Brand & Xie, 2010; House, 2002; Hout, 1988), and its role in differentiating family patterns has grown (McLanahan, 2004). College graduates are, on average, more likely to get married and stay married than others, and they are more likely to have and raise their children in marriage (Ellwood & Jencks, 2004; Goldstein & Kenney, 2001; Martin, 2006; Raley & Bumpass, 2003)....

✓ Guideline 5: Use subheadings, especially in long reviews.

Because long reviews, especially those written for theses and dissertations, often deal with articles from more than one discipline area, it is advisable to use subheadings. If you decide to use subheadings, place them strategically to help advance your argument and allow the reader to follow your discussion more easily. The topic outline you prepared in Chapter 8 can help you to determine where they should be placed, though you may need to recast some of the topic headings as labels rather than statements.

✓ Guideline 6: Use transitions to help trace your argument.

Strategic transitional phrases can help readers to follow your argument. For instance, you can use transitions to provide readers with textual clues that mark the progression of a discussion, such as when you begin paragraphs with *First*, *Second*, and

---

[4] Musick, K., Brand, J. E., & Davis, D. (2012). Variation in the relationship between education and marriage: Marriage market mismatch? *Journal of Marriage and Family*, *74*, 53–69.

Third to mark the development of three related points. Of course, any standard writing manual will contain lists of transitional expressions commonly used in formal writing.

These transitions should not be overused, however. Especially in a short review, it may not be necessary to use such phrases to label the development of three related points when each is described in three adjacent paragraphs. Another problem often found in short reviews is the overuse of what Bem (1995) calls "meta-comments," which are comments about the review *itself* (as opposed to comments about the literature being reviewed).[5] For instance, in Example 10.6.1, the writers restate the organization of the review (i.e., this is an example of a meta-comment) partway through the document. While there is nothing inherently wrong with making meta-comments, you should avoid frequent restatements that rehash what you have already stated.

Example 10.6.1
Example of overuse of meta-comments:

Recall that this paper deals with how question-asking in children has been used to explain a variety of learning styles. Also recall that we have reviewed the research on the use of question-asking in the classroom and have reached some tentative conclusions regarding its conclusions. Now, we will consider two basic types of questions that young children frequently ask, noting that….

✓ Guideline 7: If your topic reaches across disciplines, consider reviewing studies from each discipline separately.

Some topics naturally transcend discipline boundaries. For instance, if you were writing about diabetes management among teenage girls, you would find relevant sources in several discipline areas, including health care, nutrition, and psychology. The health care literature, for instance, might deal with variations in insulin therapies (such as variations in types of insulin used or the use of pumps versus syringes to deliver the insulin). The nutrition journals, on the other hand, might include studies on alternative methods for managing food intake in the search for more effective methods to control episodes of insulin shock. Finally, the psychological literature might offer insights into the nature of the stressors common to adolescent girls, especially with respect to how these stressors may interfere with the girls' decision-making processes concerning self-monitoring, nutrition choices, and value orientations. While these examples are hypothetical, it is easy to see how such a review might benefit from being divided into three sections, with the findings from each discipline area reviewed separately.

✓ Guideline 8: Write a conclusion for the end of the review.

The end of your literature review should provide closure for the reader. That is, the path of the argument should end with a conclusion of some kind. How you end a literature review, however, will depend on your reasons for writing it. If the review was written to stand alone, as in the case of a term paper or a review article for publication,

---

[5] Bem, D. J. (1995). Writing a review article for *Psychological Bulletin. Psychological Bulletin, 118,* 172–177.

the conclusion needs to make clear how the material in the body of the review has supported the assertion or proposition presented in the introduction. On the other hand, a review in a thesis, dissertation, or journal article presenting original research usually leads to the research questions that will be addressed.

If your review is long and complex, you should briefly summarize the main threads of your argument, then present your conclusion. Otherwise, you may cause your reader to pause in order to try to reconstruct the case you have made. Shorter reviews usually do not require a summary, but this judgment will depend on the complexity of the argument you have presented. You may need feedback from your faculty adviser or a friend to help you determine how much you will need to restate at the end. Example 10.8.1 presents a brief summary and conclusion section that appeared at the end of a long literature review. In most cases, for very long reviews, a more detailed summary would be desirable.

Example 10.8.1[6]

A summary and conclusion section at the end of a long review:

There is a general belief in society that frequent exposure to print has a long-lasting impact on academic success, as if practicing reading is the miracle drug for the prevention and treatment of reading problems (for reviews, see Dickinson & McCabe, 2001; Phillips, Norris, & Anderson, 2008). This comprehensive meta-analysis of print exposure provides some scientific support for this belief. Our findings are consistent with the theory that reading development starts before formal instruction, with book sharing as one of the facets of a stimulating home literacy environment. Books provide a meaningful context for learning to read, not only as a way of stimulating reading comprehension but also as a means of developing technical reading skills even in early childhood. In preconventional readers, we found that print exposure was associated moderately with oral language and basic knowledge about reading. Reading books remained important for children in school who were conventional readers....

✔ Guideline 9: Check the flow of your argument for coherence.

One of the most difficult skills to learn in academic writing is how to evaluate one's own writing for coherence. Coherence refers to how well a manuscript holds together as a unified document. It is important to ask yourself how well the various elements of your review connect with one another. This requires that you carefully evaluate the effectiveness of the rhetorical elements of your document that tell the reader about its structure and about the relationships among its elements. Subheadings often go a long way in identifying a manuscript's structure. Transitional expressions and other kinds of rhetorical markers also help to identify relationships among sections, as in "the next example," "in a related study," "a counter-example," and "the most recent (or relevant) study." Obviously, there are many more such examples. Remember, these kinds of rhetorical devices are useful navigational tools for your reader, especially if the details of the review are complex.

---

[6] Mol, S. E., & Bus, A. G. (2011). To read or not to read: A meta-analysis of print exposure from infancy to early adulthood. *Psychological Bulletin, 137*, 267–296.

Activities for Chapter 10

Directions: For each of the model literature reviews that your instructor assigns, answer the following questions. The model literature reviews are presented near the end of this book.

1. If the review is long, did the author provide an overview of the review near its beginning? Explain.

2. Did the author explicitly state what would and would not be covered in the review? Explain.

3. Is the review a clear and cohesive essay? Explain.

4. Did the author avoid annotations? Explain.

5. If the review is long, did the author use subheadings? Explain.

6. Did the author use transitions to help trace his or her argument? Explain.

7. If the topic reaches across disciplines, did the author review studies from each discipline separately?

8. Did the author write a conclusion for the end of the review?

9. Is the flow of the argument coherent?

Chapter 11

Guidelines on Style, Mechanics, and Language Usage

The previous two chapters dealt with general issues involved in writing a literature review. This chapter presents guidelines that focus on more specific issues related to style, mechanics, and language usage. These issues are important in producing a draft that is free of mechanical errors.

✓ Guideline 1: Compare your draft with your topic outline.

The topic outline you prepared after reading Chapter 8 traced the path of the argument for the literature review. Now that your first draft is completed, compare what you have written with the topic outline to make sure you have properly fleshed out the path of the argument.

✓ Guideline 2: Check the structure of your review for parallelism.

The reader of a literature review, especially a long, complex review, needs to be able to follow the structure of the manuscript while internalizing the details of the analysis and synthesis. A topic outline will typically involve parallel structural elements. For instance, a discussion of weaknesses will be balanced by a discussion of strengths, arguments for a position will be balanced by arguments against, and so on. These expectations on the part of the reader stem from long-standing rhetorical traditions in academic writing. Therefore, you need to check your manuscript to make sure that your descriptions are balanced properly. This may require that you explain a particular lack of parallelism, perhaps by stating explicitly that no studies were found that contradict a specific point (see Guideline 10 in Chapter 9 if this applies to your review).

✓ Guideline 3: Avoid overusing direct quotations, especially long ones.

One of the most stubborn problems for novice academic writers in the social and behavioral sciences is the overuse of quotations. This is understandable, given the heavy emphasis placed in college writing classes on the correct use of the conventions for citing others' words. In fact, there is nothing inherently wrong with using direct quotations. However, problems arise when they are used inappropriately or indiscriminately.

A direct quotation presented out of context may not convey the full meaning of the author's intent. When a reader struggles to understand the function of a quotation in a review, the communication of the message of the review is interrupted. Explaining the full context of a quotation can further confuse the reader with details that are not essential for the purpose of the review at hand. By contrast, paraphrasing the main ideas of an author is usually more efficient and makes it easier to avoid extraneous details. In addition, paraphrasing eliminates the potential for disruptions in the flow of a review due to the different writing styles of various authors.

Finally, it is seldom acceptable to begin a literature review with a quotation. Some students find it hard to resist doing this. Remember that it is usually very difficult for the reader to experience the intended impact of the quotation when it is presented before the author of the literature review has established the proper context.

✓ Guideline 4: Check your style manual for correct use of citations.

Make sure you check the style manual used in your field for the appropriate conventions for citing references in the text. For instance, the *Publication Manual of the American Psychological Association* (2010) specifies the following guidelines for citations.

a. You may formally cite a reference in your narrative in one of several ways. At the conclusion of a statement that represents someone else's thoughts, you cite the author's last name and the year of publication, separated by a comma, set off in parentheses, as in this example: (Doe, 2012). If you use the author's name in the narrative, simply give the year of publication in parentheses immediately following the name, as in "Doe (2012) noted that…."

b. When you cite multiple authors' names in parentheses, use the ampersand (&) instead of the word *and*. If the citation is in the narrative, use the word *and*.

c. Use semicolons to separate multiple citations in parentheses, as in this example: (Black, 2011; Brown, 2012; Green, 2011).

d. When you cite a secondary source, be sure you have made it clear, as in this example: (Doe, as cited in Smith, 2012). Note that only Smith (2011) would be placed in the reference list.

✓ Guideline 5: Avoid using synonyms for recurring words.

The focus of a review of empirical research should be on presenting, interpreting, and synthesizing other writers' ideas and research findings as clearly and precisely as possible. This may require you to repeat words that describe routine aspects of several studies. Students who are new to academic writing sometimes approach the task as though it were a creative writing exercise. *It is not!* Literature reviews should include information about many studies (and other types of literature), all of which readers should be able to internalize quickly. Therefore, it is important to adhere to the use of conventional terms, even if they should recur. Clarity is best achieved when the writer consistently uses conventional terms throughout, especially when referring to details about a study's methodology or some other technical aspect of the research.

In general, it is best not to vary the use of labels. For instance, if a study deals with two groups of participants, and the researcher has labeled them Groups 1 and 2, you should usually avoid substituting more creative phrases (e.g., "the Phoenix cohort" or "the original group of youngsters"). On the other hand, if alternative labels help to clarify a study's design (e.g., when Group 1 is the control group and Group 2 the experimental group), use the substitute expressions instead, but remain consistent throughout your discussion. Example 11.5.1 illustrates how the use of synonyms and "creative" sentence construction can confuse readers. At various points, the first group is referred to as the "Phoenix cohort," as "Group I," and as the "experimental group," which is bound to cause confusion. Example 11.5.2 is an improved version in which the writer consistently uses the terms *experimental group* and *control group* to identify the two groups.

Example 11.5.1
Inconsistent use of identifying terms:

The Phoenix cohort, which was taught to correctly identify the various toy animals by name, was brought back to be studied by the researchers twice, once after 6 months and again at the end of the year. The other group of youngsters was asked to answer the set of questions only once, after 6 months, but they had been taught to label the animals by color rather than by name. The performance of Group I was superior to the performance of Group II. The superior performance of the experimental group was attributed to....

Example 11.5.2
Improved version of Example 11.5.1:

The experimental group was taught to identify toy animals by color and was retested twice at 6-month intervals. The control group, which was taught to identify the toys by name, was retested only once after 6 months. The performance of the experimental group was superior to the performance of the control group. The superior performance of the experimental group was attributed to....

✔ Guideline 6: Spell out all acronyms when you first use them, and avoid using too many.

So many acronyms have become part of our everyday lexicon that it is easy to overlook them during the editing process. Some examples are school acronyms, such as UCLA and USC; professional acronyms, such as APA and MLA; and acronyms from our everyday lives, such as FBI, FDA, and GPA. As obvious as this guideline may seem, it is quite common to find these and other examples of acronyms that are never spelled out. Make sure you check your document carefully for acronyms and spell them out the first time you use them.

Sometimes, it is useful to refer to something by its acronym, especially if its full title is long and you need to refer to it several times. For instance, the Graduate Writing Assessment Requirement for students in the California State University system is commonly referred to as the GWAR. In general, you should avoid using too many acronyms, especially ones that are not commonly recognized, like GWAR. In a complex literature review, using a few acronyms may be helpful, but using too many may be confusing.

✓ Guideline 7: Avoid the use of contractions. They are inappropriate in formal academic writing.

Contractions are a natural part of language use. They are one example of the natural process of linguistic simplification that accounts for how all languages change, slowly but surely, over time. Many instructors, even some English composition instructors, tolerate the use of contractions on the assumption that their use reflects the changing standards of acceptability in modern-day American English. In spite of such attitudes, however, it is almost always *inappropriate* to use contractions in formal academic writing.

✓ Guideline 8: When used, coined terms should be set off by quotations.

It is sometimes useful to coin a term to describe something in one or two words that would otherwise require a sentence or more. Coined terms frequently become part of common usage, as with the noun "lunch," which is now commonly used as a verb (e.g., Did you *lunch* with Jane yesterday?). However, coined terms should be used sparingly in formal academic writing. If you decide to coin a term, set it off with quotation marks the first time it is used to indicate that its meaning cannot be found in a standard dictionary.

✓ Guideline 9: Avoid slang expressions, colloquialisms, and idioms.

Remember that academic writing is *formal* writing. Therefore, slang, colloquialisms, and idioms are not appropriate in a literature review. While many slang terms such as *cool* (meaning "good") and *ain't* are becoming part of our conversational language repertoire, they should be avoided altogether in formal writing. Colloquialisms, such as *thing* and *stuff*, should be replaced with appropriate noncolloquial terms (e.g., *item*, *feature*, and *characteristic*). Similarly, idioms, such as "to rise to the pinnacle" and "to survive the test," should be replaced by more formal expressions, such as *to become prominent* or *to be successful*.

✓ Guideline 10: Use Latin abbreviations in parenthetic material. Elsewhere, use English translations.

The Latin abbreviations shown below with their English translations are commonly used in formal academic writing. With the exception of et al., these abbreviations are limited to parenthetic material. For instance, the Latin abbreviation in parentheses at the end of this sentence is proper: (i.e., this is a correct example). If the word or phrase is not in parentheses, you should use the English translation: That is, this is also a correct example. In addition, note the punctuation required for each of these abbreviations. Note especially that there is no period after *et* in et al.

cf.	compare	e.g.,	for example	et al.	and others
etc.	and so forth	i.e.,	that is	vs.	versus, against

✓ Guideline 11: Check your draft for common writing conventions.

There are a number of additional writing conventions that all academic disciplines require. Check your draft to ensure you have applied all the following items before you give it to your instructor to read.

a. Make sure you have used complete sentences.

b. It is sometimes acceptable to write a literature review in the first person. However, you should avoid excessive use of the first person.

c. It is inappropriate to use sexist language in academic writing. For instance, it is incorrect to always use masculine or feminine pronouns (he, him, his vs. she, her, hers) to refer to a person when you are not sure of the person's gender (as in, "the teacher left her classroom...," when the teacher's gender is not known). Often, sexist language can be avoided through use of the plural form ("the teachers left their classrooms..."). If you must use singular forms, alternate between masculine and feminine forms or use *he or she*.

d. You should strive for clarity in your writing. Thus, you should avoid indirect sentence constructions, such as, "In Smith's study, it was found...." An improved version would be, "Smith found that...."

e. In general, the numbers zero through nine are spelled out, but numbers 10 and above are written as numerals. Two exceptions to this rule are numbers assigned to a table or figure and measurements expressed in decimals or in metric units.

f. Always capitalize nouns followed by numerals or letters when they denote a specific place in a numbered series. For instance, this is Item f under Guideline 11 in Chapter 11. (Note that *I*, *G*, and *C* are capped.)

g. Always spell out a number when it is the first word or phrase in a sentence, as in, "Seventy-five participants were interviewed...." Sometimes a sentence can be rewritten so that the number is not at the beginning, as in "Researchers interviewed 75 participants...."

✓ Guideline 12: Write a concise and descriptive title for the review.

The title of a literature review should identify the field of study you have investigated as well as tell the reader your point of view. However, it should also be concise and describe what you have written. In general, the title should not draw attention to itself. Rather, it should help the reader to adopt a proper frame of reference with which to read your paper. The following suggestions will help you to avoid some common problems with titles.

a. **Identify the field but do not describe it fully.** Especially with long and complex reviews, it is not advisable that you try to describe every aspect of your argument. If you do, the result will be an excessively long and detailed title. Your title should provide your reader with an easy entry into your paper. It should not force the reader to pause in order to decipher it.

b. **Consider specifying your bias, orientation, or delimitations.** If your review is written with an identifiable bias, orientation, or delimitation, it may be desirable to specify it in the title. For instance, if you are critical of some aspect of the literature, consider using a phrase such as, *A Critique of...* or *A Critical Evaluation* *of...* as part of your title. Subtitles often can be used effectively for this purpose. For instance, "The Politics of Abortion: A Review of the Qualitative Research" has a subtitle indicating that the review is delimited to qualitative research.

c. **Avoid "cute" titles.** Avoid the use of puns, alliteration, or other literary devices that detract from the content of the title. While a title such as "Phonics vs. 'Hole' Language" may seem clever if your review is critical of the whole language approach to reading instruction, it will probably distract readers. A more descriptive title, such as "Reading as a Natural or Unnatural Outgrowth of Spoken Language," will give the reader of your review a better start in comprehending your paper.

d. **Keep it short.** Titles should be short and to the point. Professional conference organizers will often limit titles of submissions to about nine words in order to facilitate the printing of hundreds of titles in their program books. While such printing constraints are not at play with a term paper or a chapter heading, it is still advisable to try to keep your review title as simple and short as possible. A good rule of thumb is to aim for a title of about 10 words, plus or minus three.

✓ Guideline 13: Strive for a user-friendly draft.

You should view your first draft as a work in progress. As such, it should be formatted in a way that invites comments from your readers. Thus, it should be legible and laid out in a way that allows the reader to react easily to your ideas. The following list contains some suggestions for ensuring that your draft is user-friendly. Ask your faculty adviser to review this list and add additional items as appropriate.

a. **Spell-check, proofread, and edit your manuscript.** Word-processing programs have spell-check functions. Use the spell-check feature before asking anyone to read your paper. However, there is no substitute for editing your own manuscript carefully, especially because the spell-check function can overlook some of your mistakes (e.g., *see* and *sea* are both correctly spelled, but the spell-check function will not highlight them as errors if you type the wrong one). Remember that your goal should be an error-free document that communicates the content easily and does not distract the reader with careless mechanical errors.

b. **Number all pages.** Professors sometimes write general comments in the form of a memo in addition to their notes in the margins. Unnumbered pages make such comments more difficult to write because professors have no page numbers to refer to in their memos.

c. **Double-space the draft.** Single-spaced documents make it difficult for the reader to write specific comments or suggest alternate phrasing.

d. **Use wide margins.** Narrow margins may save paper, but they restrict the amount of space available for your instructor's comments.

e. **Use a stapler or a strong binder clip to secure the draft.** Your draft is one of many papers your instructor will read. Securing the document with a stapler or a strong clip will make it easier to keep your paper together. If you use a folder or a binder to hold your draft, make sure that it opens flat. Plastic folders that do not open flat make it difficult for your professor (or editor) to write comments in the margins.

f. **Identify yourself as the author, and include a telephone number or e-mail address.** Because your draft is one of many papers your instructor will read, it is important to identify yourself as the author. Always include a cover page with your name and a telephone number or e-mail address in case your professor wants to contact you. If you are writing the literature review as a term paper, be sure to indicate the course number and title as well as the date.

g. **Make sure the draft is printed clearly.** In general, you should avoid using printers with ribbons unless you make sure the print is dark enough to be read comfortably. Similarly, if you submit a photocopy of your draft, make sure the copy is dark enough. Always keep a hard copy for your records! Student papers sometimes get misplaced, and hard drives on computers sometimes crash.

h. **Avoid "cute" touches.** In general, you should avoid using color text for highlighted words (use italics instead), mixing different size fonts (use a uniform font size throughout except for the title), or using clip art or any other special touches that may distract the reader by calling attention to the physical appearance of your paper instead of its content.

✓ Guideline 14: Use great care to avoid plagiarism.

If you are uncertain about what constitutes plagiarism, consult your university's student code of conduct. It is usually part of your university's main catalog and is reprinted in several other sources that are readily available to students. For instance, the University of Washington's Psychology Writing Center provides a writing guide titled *Academic Responsibility* (http://web.psych.washington.edu/writingcenter/). On the main page, click the "Writing Guides" link, which will take you to a list of handouts in PDF format. Under the "Avoiding Plagiarism" heading, you will find a statement on academic responsibility prepared by the university's Committee on Academic Conduct (1994),[1] which discusses six types of plagiarism.

(1) Using another writer's words without proper citation;

(2) using another writer's ideas without proper citation;

(3) citing a source but reproducing the exact words of a printed source without quotation marks;

(4) borrowing the structure of another author's phrases or sentences without crediting the author from whom it came;

(5) borrowing all or part of another student's paper or using someone else's outline to write your own paper; and

(6) using a paper-writing service or having a friend write the paper for you.

It is easy to quarrel about whether borrowing even one or two words would constitute plagiarism or whether an idea is really owned by an author. However, plagiarism is easily avoided simply by making sure that you cite your sources properly. If you have any doubt about this issue with respect to your own writing, ask your instructor. Plagiarism is a very serious matter.

---

[1] Committee on Academic Conduct. (1994). *Bachelor's degree handbook*. University of Washington.

✓ Guideline 15: Get help if you need it.

It should be obvious from the content of this chapter that the expectations of correctness and accuracy in academic writing are high. If you feel that you are unable to meet these demands at your current level of writing proficiency, you may need to get help. International students are often advised to hire proofreaders to help them meet their instructors' expectations. Most universities offer writing classes, either through the English department or in other disciplines. Some offer workshops for students struggling with the demands of thesis or dissertation requirements, and many universities have writing centers that provide a variety of services for students. If you feel you need help, talk with your instructor about the services available at your university. You should not expect your instructor to edit your work for style and mechanics.

Activities for Chapter 11

1. Examine the titles of the model literature reviews near the end of this book.

- How well does each title serve to identify the field of the review?

- Do the titles of the articles specify the authors' points of view in the review?

2. Now consider the first draft of your own literature review.

- Compare your first draft with the topic outline you prepared. Do they match? If not, where does your draft differ from the outline? Does this variation affect the path of the argument of your review?

- Find two or three places in your review where your discussion jumps to the next major category of your topic outline. How will the reader know that you have changed to a new category (i.e., did you use subheadings or transitions to signal the switch)?

Chapter 12

Incorporating Feedback
and Refining the First Draft

At this point in the writing process, you have completed the major portion of your critical review of the literature. However, your work is not yet done. You should now undertake the important final steps in the writing process—redrafting your review.

New writers often experience frustration at this stage because they are now expected to take an impartial view of a piece of writing in which they have had a very personal role. In the earlier stages, as the writer, you were the one analyzing, evaluating, and synthesizing other writers' work. Now, your draft is the subject of your own and your readers' analysis and evaluation. This is not an easy task, but it is a critical *and* necessary next step in writing an *effective* literature review.

The first step in accomplishing this role reversal is to put the manuscript aside for a period of time, thereby creating some distance from the manuscript and from your role as the writer. Second, remind yourself that the writing process is an ongoing negotiation between a writer and the intended audience. This is why the role reversal is so important. You should now approach your draft from the perspective of someone who is trying to read and understand the argument being communicated.

The redrafting process typically involves evaluating and incorporating feedback. That feedback may come from an instructor and your peers, or it may come from your own attempts to refine and revise your own draft. If you are writing a literature review as a term paper, solicit feedback from your professor at key points during the writing process, either by discussing your ideas during an office visit or, if your professor is willing, by submitting a first draft for comments. If it is for a thesis or dissertation, your earliest feedback will be from your faculty adviser, although you should also consider asking fellow students and colleagues for comments. If the review is for an article intended for publication, you should seek feedback from instructors, fellow students, and colleagues.

As the writer, you should determine which comments you will incorporate and which you will discard, but the feedback you receive from these various sources will give you valuable information on how to improve the communication of your ideas to your audience. The following guidelines are designed to help you through this process.

✔ Guideline 1: The reader is always right.

This guideline is deliberately overstated to draw your attention to it because it is the most important one in the redrafting process. If an educated reader does not understand one of your points, the communication process has not worked. Therefore, you should almost always seriously consider changing the draft to make it clearer for the reader. It will usually be counterproductive to defend the draft manuscript. Instead, you should try to determine why the reader did not understand it. Did you err in your analysis? Did you provide insufficient background information? Would the addition of more explicit transitions between sections make it clearer? These questions, and others like these, should guide your discussions with readers of your manuscript whom you chose to provide you with feedback.

✓ Guideline 2: Expect your instructor to comment on the content.

It is important for you to obtain your instructor's feedback on the *content* of your manuscript early in the redrafting process. If your first draft contained many stylistic and mechanical errors, such as misspellings or misplaced headings, your instructor may feel compelled to focus on these matters and defer the comments on the content until the manuscript is easier to read.

✓ Guideline 3: Concentrate first on comments about your ideas.

As the previous two guidelines suggest, your first priority at this stage should be to make sure that your ideas have come across as you intended. Of course, you should note comments about stylistic matters and eventually attend to them, but your first order of business should be to ensure that you have communicated the argument you have developed. Thus, you need to carefully evaluate the feedback you receive from all your sources—your fellow students as well as your instructor—because at this stage you need to concentrate your efforts on making sure that your paper communicates your ideas effectively and correctly. (Some important matters concerning style, language use, and grammar are covered in Chapter 13.)

✓ Guideline 4: Reconcile contradictory feedback by seeking clarification.

You may encounter differences of opinion among those who review your draft document. For instance, it is not unusual for members of a thesis or dissertation committee to give you contradictory feedback. One member may ask that you provide additional details about a study, while another member may want you to de-emphasize it. If you encounter such differences of opinion, it is your responsibility to seek further clarification from both sources and negotiate a resolution of the controversy. First, make sure that the different opinions were not due to one person's failure to comprehend your argument. Second, discuss the matter with both individuals and arrive at a compromise.

✓ Guideline 5: Reconcile comments about style with your style manual.

Make sure that you have carefully reviewed the particular style manual that is required for your writing task. If your earliest experience with academic writing was in an English department course, you may have been trained to use the Modern Language Association's *MLA Handbook for Writers of Research Papers*.[1] Many university libraries

---

[1] Gibaldi, J. (2008). *MLA style manual and guide to scholarly publishing* (3rd ed.). New York, NY: Modern Language Association of America.

advise that theses and dissertations follow *The Chicago Manual of Style*.[2] However, the most widely used manual in the social and behavioral sciences is the *Publication Manual of the American Psychological Association*.[3] If you are preparing a paper for publication, check the specific periodical or publisher for guidelines on style before submitting the paper. Finally, many academic departments and schools will have their own policies with respect to style. Regardless of which style manual pertains to your writing task, remember that you are expected to adhere to it meticulously. As you consider incorporating any feedback you receive, make sure that it conforms to the required style manual.

✓ Guideline 6: Allow sufficient time for the feedback and redrafting process.

Students often experience frustration when they are faced with major structural or content revisions and have an imminent deadline. You can expect to have to prepare at least one major redraft of your literature review, so you should allow yourself plenty of time for it. Professional writers often go through three or more drafts before they consider a document to be a final draft. While you may not have quite so many drafts, you should allow enough time to comfortably go through at least several revisions of your document.

Activities for Chapter 12

1. Ask two friends to read the draft of your literature review and comment on the content. Compare their comments.

   - On which points did your friends agree?

   - On which points did they disagree? Which of the two opinions will you follow? Why?

   - Consider the places in your review that your friends found hard to follow. Rewrite these passages, keeping in mind that you want your friends to understand your points.

2. Write five questions designed to guide your instructor or your friends in giving you feedback on the content of your review.

   - Reread your review draft, and respond to your own questions by pretending you are your instructor.

   - Revise your draft according to your own feedback.

   - Reconsider the five questions you wrote for your instructor or your friends. Which questions would you leave on your list? What questions would you add?

---

[2] University of Chicago Press. (2010). *The Chicago manual of style* (16th ed.). Chicago: University of Chicago Press.

[3] American Psychological Association. (2010). *Publication manual of the American Psychological Association* (6th ed.). Washington, DC: Author.

Notes

Chapter 13

Preparing a Reference List[1]

The guidelines in this chapter for preparing reference lists are consistent with the principles in the *Publication Manual of the American Psychological Association* (APA), which is the most frequently used style manual in the social and behavioral sciences. The APA Manual can be purchased at most college and university bookstores and is available for purchase online at www.apa.org.

✔ Guideline 1: Place the reference list at the end of the review under the main heading "References."

The main heading "References" should be centered. It is the last element in a review except for author contact information or appendices, if any.

✔ Guideline 2: A reference list should refer only to sources cited in the literature review.

Writers often have some sources that, for one reason or another, were not cited in their reviews. References for these uncited materials should *not* be included in the reference list at the end of a literature review.

✔ Guideline 3: List references alphabetically by author's surname.

For sources with multiple authors, use the surname of the first author (i.e., the first author mentioned at the beginning of the source).

✔ Guideline 4: Use hanging indents for the second and subsequent lines of references.

A hanging indent is created when the first line is *not* indented but the subsequent ones are indented, as in Example 13.4.1, where the surnames of the authors stand out in the left margin of the list.

Example 13.4.1
Three references in alphabetical order with hanging indents:

Apple, D. W. (2012). Experimental evidence of the XYZ phenomenon. *The Journal of New Developments, 55*, 99–104.

---

[1] This chapter was adapted from Pan, M. L. (2008). *Preparing literature reviews: Qualitative and quantitative aproaches* (3rd ed.). Glendale, CA: Pyrczak Publishing. All rights reserved. Reprinted with permission.

Boy, C. C. (2010). New evidence on the validity of the XYZ phenomenon. *Journal of Psychological Renderings, 44*, 454–499.

Catty, F. B., & Jones, C. M. (2012). The XYZ phenomenon reexamined. *Journal of Social and Economic Justice, 167*, 19–26.

✓ Guideline 5: Learn how to create hanging indents using a word processor.

Word-processing programs make it easy to create hanging indents. For instance, to create a hanging indent using Microsoft Word

1. Type a reference as a paragraph without any indents.

2. Click on the reference with the right mouse button, and then click on "Paragraph." A dialog box will appear.

3. Within the dialog box, click on the down-arrowhead below "Special," then click on the word "Hanging." (Note that at this point, Word will suggest a size for the indent under the word "By.")

4. Click OK.[2]

✓ Guideline 6: Italicize the titles of journals and their volume numbers.

As most students know from basic composition classes, the titles of books should be italicized. Likewise, the titles of journals should be italicized.

Typically, all issues of a journal for a given year constitute a volume. Volume 1 consists of all issues the first year a journal was published, Volume 2 consists of all issues the second year, and so on. Within each volume, all page numbers are sequential. In other words, the first page of the first issue of a year is page 1. For the next issue of the same year, the page numbers pick up where the previous issue left off. For instance, if the first issue of the year ends on page 98, the second issue of the year begins with page 99.

In light of the above, it is clear that all a reader needs in order to locate an article is the title of the journal as well as the volume number and page numbers. Issue numbers are not essential for this purpose.

Volume numbers should be italicized. (Issue numbers do not need to be included in a reference.)

Example 13.6.1 has both the title of the journal (*Journal of Marriage and Family*) and its volume number (*74*) italicized.

Example 13.6.1
A reference with the journal title and volume number italicized:

Petts, R. J. (2012). Single mothers' religious participation and early childhood behavior. *Journal of Marriage and Family, 74*, 251–268.

---

[2] If the default size suggested by Word is too large or small, right-click again on the reference, click on "Paragraph" again, and change the number of inches under "By."

✓ Guideline 7: Pay particular attention to capitalization.

Style manuals specify when to capitalize in reference lists. For instance, in APA style, only the first letter of the first word in the main title (and subtitle, if any) of an article title is capitalized. This is true even though all important words in the titles of articles *in the journals themselves* are capitalized. This illustrates that some matters of style cannot be logically deduced. Attention to details in a style manual is required.

✓ Guideline 8: Pay particular attention to punctuation.

Failure to use proper punctuation in a reference list could lead to corrections on a student's review. In APA style for print journals, for instance, there should always be a period after the close of the parentheses around the year of publication and at the end of the reference.

✓ Guideline 9: Do not add extraneous material such as abbreviations for page numbers.

Page numbers in APA style for journals are the last two numbers in a reference. APA style does not use abbreviations such as "pp." for page numbers.

✓ Guideline 10: Provide the date and URL in references for material published on the Internet.

Because material published on the Web may be modified from time to time, it is important to indicate the date on which material from the Internet was retrieved. Also, be sure to provide the full URL (such as www.example.com/retrieve) as well as any other identifying information, such as the name of the author, if known. This guideline is illustrated in Example 13.10.1.

Example 13.10.1
A reference to material retrieved from the Internet:

Jones, A. A. (2011). *Some new thoughts on material evidence in the XYZ matter*. Retrieved from www.newexample.org/specimen

✓ Guideline 11: Format references to books in accordance with a style manual.

Example 13.11.1 shows a reference to a book formatted in APA style.

Example 13.11.1
A reference to a book in APA style:

Doe, B. D., & Smith, V. A. (2012). *The big book of little thoughts* (2nd ed.). New York, NY: New Template Press.

✓ **Guideline 12: Double-check the reference list against the citations in the body of the review.**

In addition to checking that all cited material is referenced in the reference list, check that the spelling of the authors' names is the same in both places. Also, check to see that the years of publication in the citations and in the reference list are consistent.

Concluding Comment

To cite a type of source not covered in this chapter, consult a comprehensive style manual, such as the APA Manual, which specifies how to cite many types of specialized sources, such as a newsletter article, an unpublished paper presented at a professional meeting, a published technical report, a book, and so on.

Activities for Chapter 13

1. Examine the reference lists in the journal articles you collected for your literature review. What percentage of the reference lists are in APA style?

2. Will you be following APA style when preparing a reference list? If not, which style manual will you use?

3. Will you be citing any types of sources not covered in this chapter (e.g., a newsletter)? If yes, have you consulted a style manual to determine how to prepare the reference for it? Was the style manual useful? Explain.

Chapter 14

Comprehensive Self-Editing Checklist for Refining the Final Draft

The final draft should be as accurate and error-free as possible in terms of both its content and its mechanics and style. After you have carefully considered the feedback you received from your peers and academic advisers, and after you have revised the manuscript in light of their input, you should carefully edit your manuscript a final time. The purpose for this final review is accuracy.

The items in the following checklist are grouped according to some of the major criteria instructors use in evaluating student writing. Most of these criteria are absolutely critical when one is writing a thesis or dissertation. However, your instructor may relax some of them in the case of term papers written during a single semester.

You will find that most of the items on the checklist were presented in the earlier chapters as guidelines, but many additional ones have been added in an attempt to cover common problems that are sometimes overlooked by student writers. You should show this checklist to your instructors and ask that they add or eliminate items according to their own preferences.

Keep in mind that the checklist is designed to help you to refine the manuscript. Ultimately, the extent of perfection you achieve will depend on how meticulously you edit your own work.

Adherence to the Writing Process for Editing and Redrafting

_____ 1. Have you asked your instructors to review this checklist and to add or delete items according to their preferences?

_____ 2. After finishing your last draft, did you set your manuscript aside for several days before you began to revise it (i.e., did you create an appropriate distance from your manuscript before changing roles from "writer" to "reader")?

_____ 3. Did you ask one or more persons to review your manuscript?

_____ 4. Have you addressed all the questions raised by your reviewers?

_____ 5. Did you reconcile all differences of opinion among your reviewers?

Importance or Significance of the Topic

_____ 6. Is your topic important, from either a theoretical or a practical perspective?

_____ 7. Does it present a fresh perspective or identify a gap in the literature (i.e., does it address a question not previously addressed)?

_____ 8. Is your topic's significance or importance demonstrated and justified?

_____ 9. Is this an appropriate topic for your field of study?

_____ 10. Is the topic timely in terms of what is being reported in the research literature?

_____ 11. Does the title of your manuscript adequately describe the subject of your review?

Organization and Other Global Considerations

_____ 12. Does your review include an introduction along with a discussion and conclusions section?

_____ 13. Did you include a reference list?

_____ 14. Does the length and organization of your review follow the criteria set forth by (a) your instructor, if you are writing a term paper; (b) your committee chair, if you are writing a thesis or dissertation; or (c) the publication guidelines of the journal you have targeted, if you are writing for publication?

Effectiveness of the Introduction

_____ 15. Does your introduction describe the scope of the literature you have reviewed and why the topic is important?

_____ 16. Did you describe in your introduction the general structure of your paper?

_____ 17. Does your introduction identify the line of argumentation you have followed in your manuscript?

_____ 18. Does the introduction state what will and will not be covered, if this is appropriate?

_____ 19. Does the introduction specify your thesis statement or point of view, if this is relevant?

Currency and Relevance of the Literature Cited

_____ 20. Did you review the most current articles on the topic?

_____ 21. Are the studies you reviewed current?

_____ 22. If you have included older articles, did you have a good reason for including them?

_____ 23. Have you explained why you have described some findings as being strong?

_____ 24. Have you explained why you have described other findings as being weak?

_____ 25. Did you identify the major patterns or trends in the literature?

_____ 26. Have you identified in your manuscript the classic or landmark studies you cited?

_____ 27. Did you specify the relationship of these classic studies to subsequent studies they may have influenced?

Thoroughness and Accuracy of the Literature Reviewed

_____ 28. Is the coverage of your review adequate?

_____ 29. Have you noted and explained the gaps in the literature?

_____ 30. Have you described any pertinent controversies in the field?

_____ 31. If you answered "yes" to Item 30, did you make clear which studies fall on either side of the controversy?

_____   32.   Have you checked the draft for parallelism?

_____   33.   Have you noted and explained the relationships among studies, such as which ones came first? Which ones share similarities? Which ones have differences?

_____   34.   Did you indicate the source of key terms or concepts?

_____   35.   Are there gaps in the body of your manuscript?

Coherence and Flow of the Path of the Argument

_____   36.   Does each study you reviewed correspond with a specific part of your topic outline?

_____   37.   Have you deleted citations to studies you decided not to include in your review because they do not relate to the path of your argument?

_____   38.   Is the path of your argument made clear throughout the manuscript?

_____   39.   Does each part of your review flow logically from the preceding part?

_____   40.   If you have used "meta-comments" (see Chapter 10, Guideline 6), are they essential?

_____   41.   If you have used subheadings, do they help to advance your argument?

_____   42.   If you have not used subheadings, would adding them help to advance your argument?

_____   43.   Is your manuscript coherent, or would additional transitional devices help to clarify how it holds together?

Effectiveness of the Conclusion

_____   44.   Does your conclusion provide closure for the reader?

_____   45.   Does your conclusion make reference to the line of argumentation you specified in the introduction?

Accuracy of Citations and the Reference List

_____   46.   Have you checked your style manual's guidelines for citing references in the narrative (e.g., when to use parentheses, how to cite multiple authors, and how to cite a secondary source)?

_____   47.   Have you checked each citation in the manuscript to make sure that it appears on your reference list?

_____   48.   Have you checked all entries on the reference list to make sure that each one is cited in your manuscript?

_____   49.   Have you eliminated all entries from your reference list that are not cited in the manuscript?

_____   50.   Are most of the dates of the studies included in the reference list within the recent past?

_____   51.   Have you checked for accuracy and consistency between the dates in your manuscript and the dates in your reference list?

_____   52.   Have you checked the accuracy of the spelling of the authors' names in your manuscript and in your reference list?

Mechanics and Overall Accuracy of the Manuscript

_____ 53. Did you read and edit your manuscript carefully?

_____ 54. Did you perform a final spell-check of the entire manuscript?

_____ 55. Are your margins set appropriately?

_____ 56. Did you number all the pages?

_____ 57. Is your manuscript double-spaced?

_____ 58. Did you include your full name (and, for theses and dissertations, your telephone number or e-mail address)?

Appropriateness of Style and Language Usage

_____ 59. Have you carefully reviewed the appropriate style manual for your field?

_____ 60. Have you checked your manuscript for consistency with your style manual?

_____ 61. Are your headings formatted in accordance with the guidelines specified in the appropriate style manual?

_____ 62. If you used Latin abbreviations (such as i.e., e.g., etc.), are they in parentheses, and have you checked for the required punctuation?

_____ 63. If you have used long quotations, are they absolutely necessary?

_____ 64. Does each quotation contribute significantly to the review?

_____ 65. Can any of these quotations be paraphrased?

_____ 66. Did you avoid the use of synonyms for important key terms and concepts?

_____ 67. If you have coined a new term, is it set off in quotations the first time it is used?

_____ 68. Have you avoided slang terms, colloquialisms, and idioms?

_____ 69. Have you avoided contractions?

_____ 70. Have you included any annotations that are not linked to the path of the argument of your review?

_____ 71. Have you avoided using a series of annotations?

_____ 72. Have you spelled all acronyms in full on first mention?

_____ 73. If you have used the first person, is it appropriate?

_____ 74. Have you avoided using sexist language?

_____ 75. If you used numbers in the narrative of your review, did you ensure that you spelled the numbers zero through nine in full?

_____ 76. If you used a noun followed by a number to denote a specific place in a sequence, did you capitalize the noun (as in "Item 76" of this checklist)?

_____ 77. If you used a number to begin a sentence, did you spell it in full?

Grammatical Accuracy

_____ 78. Did you check your manuscript for grammatical correctness?

_____ 79. Is every sentence of your manuscript a complete sentence?

_____ 80. Have you avoided using indirect sentence constructions (as in, "In Galvan's study, it was found....")?

_____ 81. Have you been consistent in your use of tenses (e.g., if you use the present tense in describing one study's findings, do you use this tense throughout, unless you are commenting on the historical relationship among studies)?

_____ 82. Have you checked for the proper use of commas and other punctuation marks?

_____ 83. Have you attempted to avoid complicated sentence structures?

_____ 84. If you have any long sentences (e.g., several lines), have you attempted to break them down into two or more sentences?

_____ 85. If you have any long paragraphs (e.g., a page or longer), have you attempted to break them down into two or more paragraphs?

Additional Editing Steps for Non-Native English Speakers and Students With Serious Writing Difficulties

_____ 86. If your proficiency in English is not at a high level, have you asked a proof-reader for assistance?

_____ 87. Have you checked the entire manuscript for the proper article usage (e.g., a, an, the)?

_____ 88. Have you checked the manuscript for proper use of prepositions?

_____ 89. Have you checked each sentence for proper subject-verb agreement?

_____ 90. Have you checked the manuscript for proper use of idiomatic expressions?

Additional Guidelines Suggested by Your Instructor

_____ 91. _____

_____ 92. _____

_____ 93. _____

_____ 94. _____

_____ 95. _____

Notes

Model Literature Reviews for Discussion and Evaluation

Notes

Cyberbullying Among College Students[1]

On January 14, 2010, 15-year-old Phoebe Prince took her life after being cyberbullied. After her death, classmates revealed that she had been relentlessly cyberbullied by text messages and posts on social net-
5 working sites (Johnson, 2010). On September 22, 2010, 18-year-old Tyler Clementi jumped to his death from the George Washington Bridge after his roommate streamed video of him and another male over the Internet (Friedman, 2010). Traditional bullying is
10 moving into the technological realm, and cyberbullying is becoming a growing problem. As a result, 34 states have adopted or are in the process of adopting laws against cyberbullying (National Conference of State Legislatures, 2011).

Defining Traditional Bullying and Cyberbullying

15 Olweus (1993) defined traditional bullying as repeated exposure to negative actions by one or more other people. Bullying can be direct, such as physically beating someone up, or indirect, which includes non-face-to-face methods like spreading rumors. This
20 definition contains components that overlap with the current definition of cyberbullying (Figure 1). Cyberbullying is a repeated, intentional act done with the purpose of harming another person through technologies such as e-mail, cell phone messaging, social net-
25 working websites, chat rooms, and instant messaging (Beran & Li, 2005; Bhat, 2008; Campbell, 2005; Patchin & Hinduja, 2006), which can be perpetrated by a single individual or a group of people (Smith et al., 2008). Unlike traditional bullying, cyberbullying does
30 not require a face-to-face confrontation or a physical location to convene and can be completely anonymous (Dehue, Bolman, & Völlink, 2008; Mason, 2008).

Most studies have defined cyberbullying in similar ways with only slight variations. For example, Ma-
35 son (2008) categorized cyberbullying as a "form of psychological cruelty" that included a new form of bullying that is simply a more "covert form of verbal and written [traditional] bullying" (p. 323). Also, some researchers do not include the repetition component
40 when defining cyberbullying (e.g., Privitera & Campbell, 2009; Raskauskas & Stoltz, 2007; Slonje & Smith, 2008). However, to leave this aspect out overgeneralizes cyberbullying by including incidents that happened only once or by chance. Other researchers

45 also include the component of a power differential between the victim and the perpetrator of cyberbullying (Hinduja & Patchin, 2007; Mason, 2008; Privitera & Campbell, 2009). A power imbalance could be based on actual power criteria, such as physical
50 strength, body build, age, or on technological ability (Vandebosch & Van Cleemput, 2008). However, we do not believe the power differential is a necessary element to the definition of cyberbullying due to the anonymity and security offered by cyberbullying. The
55 anonymity provided by technology can actually help create a power advantage, where cyberbullying can be a way for smaller victims of traditional bullying to get revenge on their more powerful aggressor(s) (Campbell, 2005; Dehue et al., 2008; Li, 2007a; Ybarra &
60 Mitchell, 2004).

Li (2007a) outlined seven different forms of cyberbullying that constitute this new phenomenon. The seven categories of cyberbullying are: flaming, online harassment, cyberstalking, denigration, masquerading,
65 outing, and exclusion. *Flaming* involves the electronic transmission of angry, rude, and vulgar messages, whereas *online harassment* is the repeated sending of messages. *Cyberstalking* entails threats of harm or intimidation. *Denigration* (put-downs) involves send-
70 ing cruel, and possibly untrue, information about a person to others. Pretending to be someone else and sharing information to damage a person's reputation or relationships is classified as *masquerading*. *Outing* is the sharing of sensitive or private information about a
75 person to others. Finally, *exclusion* involves maliciously leaving someone out of a group online.

Prevalence Rates of Cyberbullying

Since studies define cyberbullying in slightly different ways and with different age groups, diverse prevalence rates have been reported. Overall, preva-
80 lence rates of cyberbully victimization ranged from 4.8% (Sourander et al., 2010) to 55.3% (Dilmac, 2009) across all age groups. The Second Youth Internet Safety survey, a national survey collected in 2004 ($N = 1,500$), reported the overall prevalence rate for cyber-
85 bullying between the ages of 10 and 17 to be 9% (Ybarra, Mitchell, Wolak, & Finkelhor, 2006). This was a 50% increase in prevalence from a similar survey taken in 2000 (Ybarra & Mitchell, 2004). Within

---

[1] Literature review excerpt from Schenk, A. M., & Fremouw, W. J. (2012). Prevalence, psychological impact, and coping of cyberbully victims among college students. *Journal of School Violence, 11,* 21–37. Copyright © 2012 by Taylor & Francis Group, LLC. All rights reserved. Reprinted with permission.

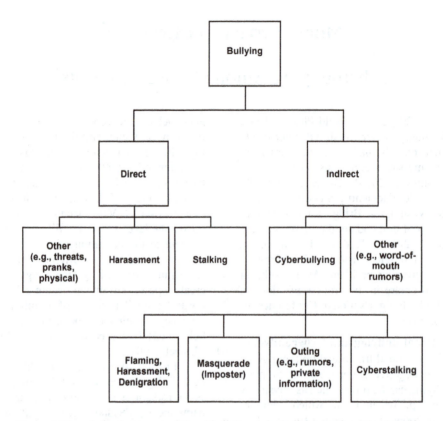

Figure 1. The relation between traditional bullying, cyberbullying, and stalking behaviors

smaller and more specific studies, the rates vary. The
90 following summarizes the prevalence rates of cyberbullying from middle school, high school, college, and
workplace samples.

At the middle school level, Canadian students
completed a self-report questionnaire regarding their
95 experiences with cyberbullying (Li, 2007a). Results
showed that 24.9% of the sample ($n = 177$) were victims of cyberbullying. A sample of seventh-grade students ($n = 461$) in both Canada and China completed
the same questionnaire and found one in three students
100 had been a victim of cyberbullying (Li, 2007b). Of
those victims, over 40% had been cyberbullied more
than three times. In addition, Beran and Li (2005)
sampled 432 Canadian middle school students and
reported that 21% of students had been frequently cy-
105 berharassed (i.e., cyberbullied).

Studies have included both middle school and
high school children to examine prevalence rates of
cyberbullying across adolescence. Using a sample of
92 children from the United States, ages 11 to 16,
110 Smith and colleagues (2008) found that 6.6% of students had been bullied "often" (two or three times a
month) and 15.6% had experienced cyberbullying at
least once or twice. Among 2,215 Finland youth, ages
13 to 16, 4.8% had been cyberbullied within the last 6
115 months (Sourander et al., 2010). Hinduja and Patchin
(2008) reported the prevalence of cyberbullying

among 384 Americans, up to age 17, as 30%. Additionally, Slonje and Smith (2008) assessed experiences
with cyberbullying of 360 Swedish students, ages 12
120 to 20. The overall cyberbullying victimization rate for
that sample was 11.7%.

To date, there is little research examining cyberbullying with a college population. However, Kraft
and Wang (2010) conducted one such study that inves-
125 tigated both cyberbullying and cyberstalking among
college students in the United States (New Jersey).
They reported prevalence rates of 10% for cyberbully
victims and 9% for cyberstalking victims among a
sample of 471 participants. Only one other study has
130 been found that examines cyberbullying among college students. This study was conducted at a university
in Turkey and found much higher prevalence rates of
cyberbully victimization at 55.3% of the 666 students
in the sample (Dilmac, 2009). This prevalence rate can
135 be explained by the fact the researchers counted being
a victim of cyberbullying at least once in their lifetime.
More research utilizing a college-age sample is necessary to better understand the prevalence rate among
this population.

In the workplace, Privitera and Campbell (2009)
140 reported that 10.7% of male Australian Manufacturing
Workers' Union employees ($n = 103$) had been cyberbullied. These results support the idea that traditional

bullying is changing with technological advancements,
145 not only in schools, but beyond.

Impact of Cyberbully Victimization

Victims of cyberbullying experience a variety of emotional impacts, with most showing an increase in emotional distress (Ybarra & Mitchell, 2004). Typical responses to cyberbully victimization included frustra-
150 tion, anger, and sadness. Additionally, the more cyberbullying that was experienced, the more offline problems victims exhibited (Hinduja & Patchin, 2007). Beran and Li (2005) identified feeling angry and crying as the most frequent reactions with feeling
155 sad, hurt, anxious, embarrassed, afraid, and blaming one's self as other common emotional responses. An American-based study found victims of cyberbullying had significantly lower self-esteem than other middle school students who had no experience with cyberbul-
160 lying (Patchin & Hinduja, 2010). Finkelhor, Mitchell, and Wolak (2000) found that approximately one third (32%) of cyberbully victims experienced at least one symptom of stress: 31% were upset, 19% were afraid, and 18% felt embarrassed as a result of being cyber-
165 bullied.

Specific behavioral impacts reported from Canadian cyberbully victims in Grades 7–9 were poor concentration, low school achievement, and absenteeism (Beran & Li, 2005). Consciously avoiding the Internet,
170 dwelling on the harassment, feeling jumpy or irritable, and losing interest in things were also found to be common experiences among cyberbullying victims. Adolescent victims were more likely to have behavior problems, consume alcohol, smoke, and have low
175 school commitment than adolescent nonvictims (Mason, 2008). A population-based study of cyberbullying in adolescents from Finland found victims experienced emotional and peer problems, headaches, recurrent abdominal pain, problems sleeping, and not feeling
180 safe at school compared to nonvictims (Sourander et al., 2010). Cyberbullying experienced in the workplace was typically associated with negative physical health, negative emotional well-being, impacted social and family relationships, as well as a reduction in staff
185 morale, commitment, job satisfaction, and a breakdown of work relationships (Privitera & Campbell, 2009).

Cyberbully victimization was also associated with clinical symptomology. Ybarra (2004) found that
190 victims of cyberbullying, ages 10 through 17, endorsed more depressive symptoms than nonvictims. Furthermore, Fauman (2008) identified common psychological consequences related to cyberbully victimizas as depression, anxiety, suicidal ideation, and poor con-
195 centration, as well as a sense of helplessness and low self-esteem. Thomas (2006) also found anxiety, school phobia, depression, lowered self-esteem, emotional

distress, and suicide were acknowledged as potential results of being a victim of cyberbullying among ado-
200 lescents, ages 13 through 18. Raskauskas and Stoltz (2007) recognized that extreme cases of cyberbully victimization have been linked to adolescent suicide.

Empirically, Hinduja and Patchin (2010) investigated the relation between suicidal behaviors (ideation,
205 attempts/experiences) among traditional and cyberbully victims and perpetrators. Their research revealed a link between youth who experienced traditional or cyberbullying, as either perpetrator or victim, and more suicidal thoughts and an increased likelihood of
210 attempting suicide compared to a control group. This relation was stronger for victims, rather than perpetrators, of both forms of bullying.

Research has shown that the impact on cyberbully victims is substantial and negative. Some factors
215 that can escalate the severity of the impact are the increased difficulty to escape the cyberbullying, as well as the countless bystanders that can view this private information due to the ease of electronic transmission (Bhat, 2008; Campbell, 2005; Slonje & Smith, 2008).

Methods for Coping With Cyberbully Victimization

Coping strategies to deal with cyberbullying var-
220 ied across empirical studies. For example, some victims in the United States removed themselves from the particular website, stayed offline for a period of time, talked about their experience with a friend, and a few
225 informed a teacher or an adult about what they experienced (Hinduja & Patchin, 2007). Telling someone and blocking or avoiding the technological device were viewed as the best methods, although doing nothing/ignoring, blocking one's identity, keeping a record of offensive e-mails and texts, reporting the occurrence to police/authorities, contacting the service provider, asking the perpetrator to stop, and fighting back were also identified as methods for dealing with cyberbully victimization in 11 through 16 year olds in England
235 (Smith et al., 2008). In addition, pretending to ignore it, really ignoring it, deleting all the bully's messages, and bullying the bully were other strategies identified by a sample ($n = 1,211$) of primary school children and first-year pupils of secondary schools in the Nether-
240 lands (Dehue et al., 2008).

It is evident that victims of cyberbullying negatively react to the experience and cope in a variety of ways. To date, the majority of research has been done using school-age children and adolescents. Research is
245 necessary to identify the prevalence of cyberbullying in a college sample, how this age group is impacted by their victimization, and what coping strategies are utilized. Cyberbullying is especially relevant for this age group since they are typically just out of high school
250 where cyberbullying is still prevalent, and they are

more independent from parental influences. There also needs to be more research focusing on cyberbullying in the United States, as much of the current research has been conducted internationally.

255   To date, the two studies that examined cyberbullying among college students have laid important groundwork on this new phenomenon. This study builds upon those by obtaining another prevalence rate for cyberbullying among college students in the United

260 States, as well as utilized standardized measures (e.g., SCL-90-R, Suicidal Behaviors Questionnaire-Revised [SBQ-R]) to better understand the psychological impact cyberbullying can have on victims. Additionally, this study expands others by assessing coping strate-

265 gies victims employ.

Purpose

The purpose of this study was to examine the prevalence rate of cyberbullying, the psychological impact, and the coping strategies utilized by college-student victims. Differences in suicidal behaviors be-

270 tween victims of cyberbullying and control participants were explored. Gender differences in the results were also examined.

References

Beran, T., & Li, Q. (2005). Cyber-harassment: A study of a new method for an old behavior. *Journal of Educational Computing Research, 32*, 265–277.

Bhat, C. S. (2008). Cyber bullying: Overview and strategies for school counselors, guidance officers, and all school personnel. *Australian Journal of Guidance and Counselling, 18*, 53–66.

Campbell, M. A. (2005). Cyber bullying: An old problem in a new guise? *Australian Journal of Guidance and Counselling, 15*, 68–76.

Dehue, F., Bolman, C., & Völlink, T. (2008). Cyberbullying: Youngsters' experiences and parental perceptions. *CyberPsychology & Behavior, 11*, 217–223.

Dilmac, B. (2009). Psychological needs as a predictor of cyber bullying: A preliminary report on college students. *Educational Sciences: Theory and Practice, 9*, 1307–1325.

Fauman, M. A. (2008). Review of "Cyber bullying: Bullying in the digital age." *The American Journal of Psychiatry, 165*, 780–781.

Finkelhor, D., Mitchell, K. J., & Wolak, J. (2000). *Online victimization: A report on the nation's youth.* Alexandria, VA: National Center for Missing and Exploited Children.

Friedman, E. (2010). Victim of secret dorm sex tape posts Facebook goodbye, jumps to his death. *ABC News.* Retrieved from http://abcnews.go.com/US/victim-secret-dorm-sex-tape-commits-suicide/story?id=11758716

Hinduja, S., & Patchin, J. W. (2007). Offline consequences of online victimization: School violence and delinquency. *Journal of School Violence, 6*, 89–112.

Hinduja, S., & Patchin, J. W. (2008). Cyberbullying: An exploratory analysis of factors related to offending and victimization. *Deviant Behavior, 29*, 129–156.

Hinduja, S., & Patchin, J. W. (2010). Bullying, cyberbullying, and suicide. *Archives of Suicide Research, 14*, 206–221.

Johnson, O. (2010). Bullying eyed in girl's death. *Boston Herald.* Retrieved from http://news.bostonherald.com/news/regional/view/20100123bullying-_eyed_in_girls_death/srvc=home&position-also

Kraft, E., & Wang, J. (2010). An exploratory study of the cyberbullying and cyberstalking experiences and factors related to victimization of students at a public liberal arts college. *International Journal of Technologies, 1*, 74–91.

Li, Q. (2007a). Bullying in the new playground: Research into cyberbullying and cyber victimization. *Australian Journal of Educational Technology, 23*, 435–454.

Li, Q. (2007b). New bottle but old wine: A research of cyberbullying in schools. *Computers in Human Behavior, 23*, 1777–1791.

Mason, K. L. (2008). Cyberbullying: A preliminary assessment for school personnel. *Psychology in the Schools, 45*, 323–348.

National Conference of State Legislatures. (2011). *State cyberstalking, cyberharassment, and cyberbullying laws.* Retrieved from http://www.ncsl.org/default.aspx?tabid=13495

Olweus, D. (1993). *Bullying at school: What we know and what we can do.* Oxford, England: Blackwell.

Patchin, J. W., & Hinduja, S. (2006). Bullies move beyond the schoolyard: A preliminary look at cyberbullying. *Youth Violence and Juvenile Justice, 4*, 148–169.

Patchin, J. W., & Hinduja, S. (2010). Cyberbullying and self-esteem. *Journal of School Health, 80*, 614–621.

Privitera, C., & Campbell, M. (2009). Cyberbullying: The new face of workplace bullying? *CyberPsychology & Behavior, 12*, 395–400.

Raskauskas, J., & Stoltz, A. D. (2007). Involvement in traditional and electronic bullying among adolescents. *Developmental Psychology, 43*, 564–575.

Slonje, R., & Smith, P. K. (2008). Cyberbullying: Another main type of bullying? *Scandinavian Journal of Psychology, 49*, 147–154.

Smith, P. K., Mahdavi, J., Carvalho, M., Fisher, S., Russell, S., & Tippett, N. (2008). Cyberbullying: Its nature and impact in secondary school pupils. *Journal of Clinical Psychology and Psychiatry, 49*, 376–385.

Sourander, A., Brunstein-Klomek, A., Ikonen, A., Lindroos, J., Luntamo, T., Koskelainen, M., & Helenius, H. (2010). Psychological risk factors associated with cyberbullying among adolescents: A population-based study. *Archive of General Psychiatry, 67*, 720–728.

Thomas, S. P. (2006). From the editor: The phenomenon of cyberbullying. *Issues in Mental Health Nursing, 27*, 1015–1016.

Vandebosch, H., & Van Cleemput, K. (2008). Defining cyberbullying: A qualitative research into the perceptions of youngsters. *CyberPsychology & Behavior, 11*, 499–503.

Ybarra, M. L., & Mitchell, K. J. (2004). Youth engaging in online harassment: Associations with caregiver-child relationships, Internet use, and personal characteristics. *Journal of Adolescence, 27*, 319–336.

Ybarra, M. L., Mitchell, K. J., Wolak, J., & Finkelhor, D. (2006). Examining characteristics and associated distress related to Internet harassment: Findings from the second youth Internet safety survey. *Pediatrics, 118*, 1169–1177.

Ybarra, M. L. (2004). Linkages between depressive symptomatology and Internet harassment among young regular Internet users. *CyberPsychology & Behavior, 7*, 247–257.

Address correspondence to: Allison M. Schenk, Department of Psychology, West Virginia University, Morgantown, WV 26505. E-mail: Allison.schenk@mail.wvu.edu

Waterpipe Smoking Among College Students in the United States[1]

ABSTRACT. **Objective**: To review the literature on college student waterpipe use with a focus on undergraduates in the United States. **Participants**: Undergraduate students. **Methods**: Studies were accessed using the databases PubMed, MEDLINE, PsycINFO, and Academic Search Premier. Searches included combinations of the following keywords: "waterpipe," "hookah," "shisha," "nargila," "argileh," "hubble bubble," "college," "university," and "student." **Results**: Results demonstrate that approximately 1 in 5 American college students report past-year waterpipe use. Results also suggest that there are a number of established correlates of waterpipe smoking, including male gender, Arab ethnicity, cigarette smoking, and the belief that waterpipe smoking is less harmful than cigarette smoking. **Conclusions**: Despite its harmful health effects, waterpipe smoking is quite common among college students. Future research with better methodologies and theoretical frameworks are needed to advance the field.

Waterpipe use (alternatively called hookah, shisha, nargila, argileh, or hubble bubble) is a 400-year-old form of smoking in which tobacco is heated with charcoal and its smoke is passed through water prior to inhalation. The typical waterpipe contains a "head" filled with tobacco, a glass bowl filled with water, and a hose for inhaling or "puffing." The waterpipe has traditionally been associated with Middle Eastern cultures; however, in recent years, its use has spread to North America and Europe.

Like all forms of tobacco use, waterpipe smoking increases the risk for a variety of adverse health outcomes. More specifically, its use has been associated with esophageal cancer,[1,2] chromosomal aberrations,[3] decreased pulmonary and cardiovascular function,[4,5] low birth weight,[6] infertility,[7] dental problems,[8,9] and infectious diseases.[10,11] Waterpipe smokers have also been known to report symptoms of tobacco dependence, including craving[12,13] and repeated quit attempts.[14] However, despite these harmful health outcomes, there has been a distinct increase in the popularity of waterpipe use, particularly in the Middle East, where, in some cultures, lifetime prevalence rates are as high as 70%.[12,15]

Waterpipe smoking is particularly prevalent among university students and other young adults.[16,17] There are several factors that could account for this. First, waterpipe tobacco is relatively inexpensive, a fact touted by many waterpipe forums and websites. Second, unlike other tobacco products, waterpipe tobacco can be purchased online, making it particularly accessible to university students, who are likely to have easy Internet access. Moreover, many waterpipe websites do not verify age, a fact that may attract underage smokers. Third, waterpipe smoking has become integrated into the "social scene" on many university campuses. There has been a notable rise in the number of "hookah bars" and "waterpipe cafes" near college campuses,[18] and many students cite socialization as a primary motivation for their waterpipe use.[19] Fourth, in the 1990s, a new form of sweetened waterpipe tobacco called Maassel was introduced. Maassel is produced in a variety of flavors (fruit, toffee, coffee, etc.) and tends to be more appealing to young adults than the unflavored tobacco traditionally used in the waterpipe.[12] Finally, many young adults mistakenly believe that waterpipes are safer than cigarettes (i.e., that waterpipes contain less nicotine, are not addictive, etc.) and that their use does not constitute "smoking."[20]

Although a number of individual studies have documented the prevalence and correlates of waterpipe use among university students, there have been no systematic reviews of this literature. The present article aims to fill this gap by examining (1) the prevalence of waterpipe smoking among college students, (2) demographic correlates of waterpipe smoking, (3) beliefs about waterpipe smoking, and (4) relationships between waterpipe smoking and cigarette smoking. We will also review methodological limitations of existing waterpipe studies and suggest directions for future research.

Methods

Identification of Studies

We conducted a literature search using the databases PubMed, MEDLINE, PsycINFO, and Academic Search Premier. Searches included combinations of the following keywords: "waterpipe," "hookah," "shisha," "nargila," "argileh," "hubble bubble," "college," "university," and "student." Studies that combined data from college students and noncollege students in analyses (e.g., Maziak et al.)[21] were excluded from this review. Studies that focused on graduate or professional students, rather than undergraduates, were also excluded. This review primarily focuses on college

[1] Literature review from Grekin, E. R., & Ayna, D. (2012). Waterpipe smoking among college students in the United States: A review of the literature. *Journal of American College Health, 60*, 244–249. Copyright © 2012 by Taylor & Francis Group, LLC. All rights reserved. Reprinted with permission.

students in the United States; however, data from Middle Eastern students are also presented throughout 80 the article for comparison purposes.

We identified 16 studies of college student waterpipe smoking that used 14 different samples. All 16 studies had been published since 2001. Seven of the 16 studies examined waterpipe smoking among college students in the United States or Europe.[16,17,22–26] (Table 1). The remaining 9 studies examined waterpipe smoking among college students in the Middle East[27–35] (Table 2).

Table 1
Studies Examining Waterpipe Use Among College Students in the United States or Europe

Authors	Sample	Study design	% Reporting lifetime smoking	% Reporting past-year smoking	% Reporting past-month smoking
Primack et al.[22]	8,745 students at 8 universities	Online survey	29.5	—	7.2
Eissenberg et al.[23]	744 freshmen in introductory psychology courses	Online survey	—	—	20.0
Grekin and Ayna[16]	602 students in psychology courses	Online survey	15.1	12.4	—
Jackson and Aveyard[17]	937 students in randomly selected courses	Paper-and-pencil survey	37.9	—	21.1
Primack et al.[24]	3,600 randomly selected students	Online survey	41.0	30.6	9.5
Smith-Simone et al.[25*]	411 freshmen at a private university	Online survey	28.0	—	15.3
Smith et al.[26*]	411 freshmen at a private university	Online survey	28.0	—	15.3

Note. Studies marked with an asterisk (*) use the same sample.

Table 2
Studies Examining Waterpipe Use Among College Students in the Middle East

Authors	Sample	Study design	% Reporting lifetime smoking	% Reporting past-year smoking	% Reporting past-month smoking
Azab et al.[28]	548 students at 4 universities in Jordan	Interviewer-administered questionnaire	61.1	—	42.7
Roohafza et al.[35]	233 university students in Iran	Interviewer-administered questionnaire	—	—	19.2
Mandil et al.[34]	1,057 university students in United Arab Emirates	Paper-and-pencil survey	—	—	5.6
Chaaya et al.[33]	416 students at American University in Beirut	Interviewer-administered questionnaire	43.0	—	28.3
Maziak et al.[19*]	587 university students in Syria	Interviewer-administered questionnaire	45.3	—	14.7
Maziak et al.[21*]	587 university students in Syria	Interviewer-administered questionnaire	45.3	—	14.7
Tamim et al.[29*]	1,964 students attending 5 universities in Lebanon	Paper-and-pencil survey	—	—	32.4
Tamim et al.[27]	533 students attending 4 universities in Lebanon	Paper-and-pencil survey	—	—	43.3

Note. Studies marked with an asterisk (*) use the same sample. One study cited in the review (Labib et al.[32]) did not include a comparison group of nonsmokers and, therefore, prevalence rates from this sample could not be included in the table.

Results

Prevalence of Waterpipe Use

Among studies conducted in the United States or Europe, *lifetime* waterpipe smoking rates ranged from 15.1% to 41.0% (*M* = 30.3%, *SD* = 10.1%), *past-year* smoking rates ranged from 12.4% to 30.6% (*M* = 21.5%, *SD* = 12.9%), and *past-month* smoking rates ranged from 7.2% to 21.1% (*M* = 14.6%, *SD* = 6.2%; Table 1). Of the 9 studies examining waterpipe use among Middle Eastern college students, *lifetime* smoking rates ranged from 43.0% to 61.1% (*M* = 49.8%, *SD* = 9.9%). None of the Middle Eastern studies reported *past-year* smoking rates. *Past-month* or *current* smoking rates ranged from 5.6% to 43.3% (*M* = 26.6%, *SD* = 14.2%; Table 2).

Several conclusions can be drawn from these prevalence data. First, rates of waterpipe use in the United States and Europe are quite high, with approximately 1 in 5 college students reporting past-year waterpipe smoking. In comparison, approximately 30% of college students report past-year cigarette smoking,[36] suggesting that although cigarette smoking remains the most popular form of tobacco use among American college students, waterpipe smoking is a close second. Second, the limited data that are available suggest that rates of waterpipe smoking among Middle Eastern college students are substantially higher than rates among Western samples, with approximately 1 in 4 Middle Eastern college students reporting waterpipe use during the past month.

Gender Differences in Waterpipe Use

With the exception of Primack et al.,[24] all of the studies in this review found that males were more likely than females to report waterpipe use.[16,17,22,23, 25–35] These gender differences were particularly pronounced when examining current, as opposed to lifetime, use. For example, Smith-Simone et al.[25] conducted a cross-sectional Internet survey of 411 college freshmen and found that, among females, 77.4% were never smokers, 13.6% were ever smokers, and 9.0% were current smokers. In contrast, among males, 67% were never smokers, 11.8% were ever smokers, and 21.2% were current smokers. Similarly, Maziak et al.[30] conducted interviews with 587 randomly selected university students in Syria and found that 62.6% of men and 29.8% of women reported lifetime waterpipe use, whereas 25.5% of men and 4.9% of women reported past-month waterpipe use. It should be noted that in the United States, there are few reported gender differences in cigarette smoking among college samples.[37] Thus, the factors that make waterpipe use more popular among males than females cannot be generalized to all tobacco products.

Ethnic/Racial Differences in Waterpipe Use

Two of the studies in this review found that students of Arab descent, attending college in the United States or Europe, were significantly more likely than their non-Arab peers to report waterpipe use. Specifically, Grekin and Ayna[16] found that 62% of Arab students, as opposed to 11% of non-Arab students, had used a waterpipe in their lifetime. Similarly, Jackson and Aveyard[17] found that 81.3% of Arab students had tried a waterpipe, as compared with 38.1% of White students, 26.1% of Black students, and 40.9% of Asian students. No other studies have compared waterpipe use among Arab versus non-Arab students outside of the Middle East.

All of the remaining American studies found that Black students were less likely than students of other races to use a waterprpe.[22–26] For example, Primack et al.[22] found that 13.3% of Black students had smoked a waterpipe as compared with 31.4% of White students, 23.2% of Asian students, and 33.2% of students who identified as "other" or "mixed." Similarly, Eissenberg et al.[23] found that 35.5% of White students, 9.1% of Black students, and 33.7% of students identifying as "other" reported past-30-day waterpipe use. These data are consistent with the broader literature on race and substance use, which suggests that Black college students are less likely than their White counterparts to smoke cigarettes or to use alcohol.[37,38]

Beliefs About Waterpipe Smoking

Five studies have examined beliefs about waterpipe smoking among American and European college students.[17,23–26] Overall, these studies suggest that college students perceive waterpipe use to be less harmful and more socially acceptable than cigarette use. For example, Smith-Simone et al.[25] conducted a cross-sectional Internet survey of 411 freshmen at a private university and found that students believed waterpipe smoking to be less addicting and more socially acceptable than cigarette smoking. Students also believed that they were more likely to be influenced by friends to use a waterpipe as opposed to cigarettes in the next year and that friends looked "cooler" when using waterpipes versus cigarettes. Using the same sample, Smith et al.[26] found that 37% of participants perceived waterpipe use to be less harmful than cigarette use. In addition, current (odds ratio [OR] = 6.77) and lifetime (OR = 3.19) waterpipe smokers were more likely than never smokers to perceive waterpipe use as less harmful than cigarette use, suggesting that beliefs about waterpipe harmfulness may play a role in the initiation and/or maintenance of smoking.

Primack et al.[24] sent an online survey to 3,600 randomly selected university students as part of the National College Health Assessment (the researchers paid to have waterpipe questions added to their university's version of the survey). Data from the 647 students who responded indicated that more than half of the sample (52%) believed waterpipe smoking to be less addictive than cigarette smoking. In addition, multivariate models revealed associations between past-year waterpipe use (yes/no) and (1) low perceived harm (believing waterpipe smoking is less harmful than cigarette smoking; OR = 2.54), (2) low perceived addictiveness (believing waterpipe smoking is less addictive than cigarette smoking; OR = 4.64), (3) perception of high social acceptability (believing that waterpipe smoking is socially acceptable among peers; OR = 20.00), and (4) high perception of popularity (believing that a large percentage of college students have smoked a waterpipe; OR = 4.72).

Eissenberg et al.[23] conducted an online survey of waterpipe use among 744 college freshmen enrolled in introductory psychology courses. Compared with never smokers, those who had smoked in the past month were more likely to believe that (1) waterpipe smoking is socially acceptable among peers (OR = 3.71), (2) waterpipe smoking makes peers look "cool" (OR = 2.47), (3) waterpipes are less harmful than cigarettes (OR = .31), and (4) waterpipes are less addicting than cigarettes (OR = .65).

Finally, Jackson and Aveyard[17] administered a cross-sectional paper-and-pencil questionnaire to 937 students in randomly selected courses at Birmingham University in the United Kingdom. They then sent a follow-up survey to the 75 students who reported at least monthly waterpipe use. Twenty-one of the 75 heavy users responded to the follow-up survey. All but 1 of these heavy users considered waterpipe smoking to be socially acceptable, and 68.4% thought that waterpipe smoking was less harmful than cigarette smoking.

Associations Between Waterpipe Smoking and Cigarette Smoking

Four studies have examined relationships between waterpipe smoking and cigarette smoking among American and European college students, and all four have found significant associations between the two forms of tobacco use.[16,17,23,24] For example, Eissenberg et al.[23] found that past-month waterpipe use was associated with a greater likelihood of having smoked cigarettes (OR = 10.44) and cigars/cigarillos (OR = 6.31). Similarly, Grekin and Ayna[16] found that cigarette users were twice as likely as noncigarette users to report lifetime waterpipe use. Strong cigarette/waterpipe associations have also been found in studies of Middle Eastern college students.[29–31]

To date, however, no studies have longitudinally assessed cigarette versus waterpipe trajectories. Thus, it is unclear whether cigarette use typically precedes or follows waterpipe use or whether waterpipe use is more frequent or intense among students who simultaneously use cigarettes.

It is also important to note that, although cigarette smoking is a robust correlate of waterpipe use, a substantial proportion of waterpipe users do not smoke cigarettes. For example, Primack et al.[24] found that 35.4% of students who had smoked a waterpipe in the past year had never smoked a cigarette. Similarly, Jackson and Aveyard[17] found that 65% of regular (at least monthly) waterpipe smokers had never smoked cigarettes. It is not clear what factors are associated with the exclusive use of waterpipes (i.e., waterpipe use in the absence of cigarette smoking). However, preliminary data suggest that the two forms of tobacco have different correlates. For example, male gender seems to be predictive of a waterpipe, but not cigarette use.[37] Similarly, club and intramural athletic participation appears to protect against cigarette smoking, but not waterpipe smoking.[22] These data suggest that waterpipes and cigarettes are viewed differently by different groups of people; however, more data are needed to delineate common and unique risk factors for the two types of tobacco products.

Comment

Future Directions/Limitations

The literature on waterpipe smoking among college students has grown rapidly over the past 10 years. However, there are still relatively few studies in this area, and many potential waterpipe smoking predictors have not been examined (e.g., peer smoking, smoking expectancies, smoking motives, alcohol/drug use comorbidity, anxiety/depression/stress, etc.). In addition, there are several methodological limitations that limit our ability to draw conclusions about college student waterpipe use. First, most existing waterpipe studies use data from convenience (e.g., introductory psychology students), rather than representative samples. In addition, the few studies that attempt to recruit representative samples suffer from low response rates. For example, Primack et al.[24] sent an online survey to 3,600 randomly selected university students as part of the National College Health Assessment; however, only 18.6% of recruited students completed the survey. Notably, there are often important differences between survey responders and nonresponders, and it is, therefore, difficult to generalize from existing data to the broader population of college student waterpipe smokers. Nationally representative studies and representative single campus studies are needed to accurately examine the prevalence and correlates of waterpipe smoking.

Second, all existing student waterpipe studies are cross-sectional, rather than longitudinal or prospective. As a result, it is unclear which variables precede and predict the development of waterpipe use. In addition, it is impossible to draw conclusions about typical trajectories of waterpipe use (e.g., does waterpipe use

295 tend to peak during adolescence and decline throughout the third decade of life, like alcohol and drug use?).

Third, most student waterpipe smoking data are based on online surveys, rather than interviews or 300 laboratory tasks. Although online surveys are ideal for assessing certain, standardized correlates of waterpipe use (e.g., personality, beliefs, attitudes, demographic information), there are many substance use correlates that cannot be adequately measured with surveys, such 305 as neuropsychological functioning, laboratory-based impulsivity, and *Diagnostic and Statistical Manual of Mental Disorder* diagnoses.

Fourth, no college student waterpipe studies have examined waterpipe dependence, as opposed to simple 310 quantity and frequency of use. Waterpipe dependence is a fuzzy concept that is difficult to define due to the social/intermittent nature of waterpipe smoking and its high comorbidity with cigarette use. However, several researchers have proposed methods of characterizing 315 waterpipe dependence,[39] and at least one factor-analyzed scale has been published.[40] Thus, it would be useful for future studies to explore characteristics of waterpipe dependence among student populations.

Fifth, very few college student studies have examined interactions between potential predictors of 320 examined interactions between potential predictors of waterpipe use. It would be useful to know whether relationships between independent variables and waterpipe use differ depending on gender, ethnicity, age, personality, and a variety of other variables.

325 Sixth, no studies have explored the role of culture in the initiation and maintenance of waterpipe use. More specifically, although one set of studies has examined waterpipe smoking among Middle Eastern students and another set of studies has examined 330 smoking among Western students, no studies have explored differential predictors and correlates of waterpipe smoking among students in Middle Eastern versus Western cultures. This type of international data would provide information about the unique cultural 335 contexts that support or inhibit waterpipe use.

Finally, the literature on college student waterpipe smoking is decidedly atheoretical. Theoretical frameworks that explain current empirical findings and suggest directions for future research would add 340 greatly to the field.

Despite these limitations, the existing literature points to a variety of potential waterpipe smoking interventions for college students. For example, it is clear that college students as a whole, and waterpipe 345 smokers in particular, believe that waterpipe use is less harmful than cigarette use. Providing information about the harmful health effects of waterpipe tobacco (e.g., through college counseling centers, peer mentors, student orientation sessions, etc.) may help to 350 decrease its use. It may also be useful to develop tar-

355 geted prevention/intervention programs for those most likely to smoke waterpipes (i.e., males, cigarette smokers, Arab students in the United States, etc.). Finally, at the societal level, efforts are needed to decrease the accessibility of waterpipe tobacco to underage smokers by monitoring online waterpipe tobacco availability and waterpipe sales to underage smokers.

Conclusions

Despite its associated health risks, the prevalence of waterpipe smoking among college students is quite high, with approximately 1 in 5 students reporting past-year use. There are also a number of established correlates of waterpipe smoking, including male gender, Arab ethnicity, cigarette smoking, and the belief that waterpipe smoking is less harmful than cigarette 365 smoking. Though intriguing, the existing literature on college student waterpipe smoking is small and future studies using different methodologies and better theoretical frameworks are needed to advance our knowledge in this area.

References

1. Gunaid AA, Sumairi AA, Shidrawi RG, et al. Oesophageal and gastric carcinoma in the Republic of Yemen. *Br J Cancer*. 1995;71:409–410.
2. Nasrollahzadeh D, Kamangar F, Aghcheli K, et al. Opium, tobacco, and alcohol use in relation to oesophageal squamous cell carcinoma in a high-risk area of Iran. *Br J Cancer*. 2008;98:1857–1963.
3. Yadav JS, Thakur S. Genetic risk assessment in hookah smokers. *Cytobios*. 2000;101:101–113.
4. Kiter G, Ucan ES, Ceylan E, Kilinc O. Water-pipe smoking and pulmonary functions. *Respir Med*. 2000;94:891–894.
5. Mutairi SS, Shihab-Eldeen AA, Mojiminiyi OA, Anwar AA. Comparative analysis of the effects of hubble-bubble (sheesha) and cigarette smoking on respiratory and metabolic parameters in hubble-bubble and cigarette smokers. *Respirology*. 2006;11:449–455.
6. Nuwayhid IA, Yamout B, Azar G, Al Kouatly Kambris M. Narghile (hubble-bubble) smoking, low birth weight, and other pregnancy outcomes. *Am J Epidemiol*. 1998;148:375–383.
7. Inhorn MC, Buss KA. Ethnography, epidemiology, and infertility in Egypt. *Soc Sci Med*. 1994;3:671–686.
8. Dar-Odeh NS, Abu-Hammad OA. Narghile smoking and its adverse health consequences: a literature review. *Br Dent J*. 2009;206:511–573.
9. Natto S, Baljoon M, Bergstrom J. Tobacco smoking and periodontal health in a Saudi Arabian population. *J Periodontol*. 2005;76:1919–1926.
10. Munckhof WJ, Konstantinos A, Wamsley M, Mortlock M, Gilpin CA. A cluster of tuberculosis associated with use of marijuana water pipe. *Int J Tuberc Lung Dis*.2003;7:860–865.
11. Steentoft J, Wittendorf J, Andersen JR. Tuberculosis and water pipes as source of infection. *Ugeskr Laeger*. 2006;198:904–907.
12. Maziak W, Eissenberg T, Ward KD. Patterns of waterpipe use and dependence: Implications for intervention development. *Pharmacol Biochem Behav*. 2005;80:173–179.
13. Maziak W, Rastam S, Ibrahim I, Ward K, Shihadeh A, Eissenberg T. CO exposure, puff topography, and subjective effects in waterpipe tobacco smokers. *Nicotine Tob Res*. 2009;11:806–811.
14. Ward K, Hammal F, VanderWeg M, et al. Are waterpipe users interested in quitting? *Nicotine Tob Res*. 2005;7:149–156.
15. Knishkowy B, Amitai Y. Water-pipe (waterpipe) smoking: An emerging health risk behavior. *Pediatrics*. 2005;116:e113–e119.
16. Grekin ER, Ayna D. Argileh use among college students in the United States: An emerging trend. *J Stud Alcohol Drugs*. 2008;69:412–415.
17. Jackson DJ, Aveyard P. Waterpipe smoking in students: Prevalence, risk factors, symptoms of addiction, and smoke intake. Evidence from one British university. *BMC Public Health*. 2008;8:174.
18. Cobb C, Ward K, Maziak W, Shihadeh A, Eissenberg T. Waterpipe tobacco smoking: An emerging health crisis in the United States. *Am J Health Behav*. 2010;34:275–285.
19. Maziak W, Eissenberg T, Rastam S, et al. Beliefs and attitudes related to waterpipe smoking among university students in Syria. *Ann Epidemiol*. 2004;14:646–654.

20. Ward KD, Eissenberg T, Gray JN, Srinivas V, Wilson N, Maziak W. Characteristics of U.S. waterpipe users: A preliminary report. *Nicotine Tob Res.* 2007;9:1339–1346.

21. Maziak W, Rastam S, Eissenberg T, et al. Gender and smoking status based analyses of views regarding waterpipe and cigarette smoking in Aleppo, Syria. *Prev Med.* 2004;38:479–484.

22. Primack BA, Fertman CI, Rice KR, Adachi-Mejia AM, Fine MJ. Waterpipe and cigarette smoking among college athletes in the United States. *J Adolesc Health.* 2010;46:45–51.

23. Eissenberg T, Ward KD, Smith-Simone S, Maziak W. Waterpipe tobacco smoking on a U.S. college campus: Prevalence and correlates. *J Adolesc Health.* 2008;42:526–529.

24. Primack BA, Sidani J, Agarwal AA, Shadel WG, Donny EF, Eissenberg T. Prevalence and associations with waterpipe tobacco smoking among U.S. university students. *Ann Behav Med.* 2008;36:81–86.

25. Smith-Simone SY, Curbow BA, Stillman FA. Differing psychosocial risk profiles of college freshmen waterpipe, cigar and cigarette smokers. *Addict Behav.* 2008;33:1619–1624.

26. Smith SY, Curbow B, Stillman FA. Harm perception of nicotine products in college freshmen. *Nicotine Tob Res.* 2001;9:977–982.

27. Tamim H, Musharrafieh U, Almawi WY. Smoking among adolescents in a developing country. *Aust N Z J Public Health.* 2001;25:185–186.

28. Azab M, Khabour OF, Alkaraki AK, Eissenberg T, Alzoubi KH, Primack BA. Waterpipe tobacco smoking among university students in Jordan. *Nicotine Tob Res.* 2010;12:606–612.

29. Tamim H, Terro A, Kassem H, et al. Tobacco use by university students in Lebanon, 2001. *Addiction.* 2003;98:933–939.

30. Maziak W, Fouad MF, Asfar T, et al. Prevalence and characteristics of narghile smoking among university students in Syria. *Int J Tuberc Lung Dis.* 2004;8:882–889.

31. Maziak W, Hammal F, Rastam S, et al. Characteristics of cigarette smoking and quitting among university students in Syria. *Prev Med.* 2004;39:330–336.

32. Labib N, Radwan G, Makhail N, et al. Comparison of cigarette and waterpipe smoking among female university students in Egypt. *Nicotine Tob Res.* 2006;9:591–596.

33. Chaaya M, El-Roueiheb Z, Chemaitelly H, Azar G, Nasr J, Al-Sahab B. Argileh smoking among university students: A new tobacco epidemic. *Nicotine Tob Res.* 2004;6:457–463.

34. Mandil A, Hussein A, Omer H, Turki G, Gaber I. Characteristics and risk factors of tobacco consumption among University of Sharjah students, 2005. *East Mediterr Health J.* 2007;13:1449–1458.

35. Roohafza H, Sadeghi M, Shahnam M, Bahonar A, Sarafzadegan N. Perceived factors related to cigarette and waterpipe (ghelyan) initiation and maintenance in university students of Iran. *Int J Public Health.* 2011;56:175–180.

36. Johnston LD, O'Malley PM, Bachman JG, Schulenberg JE. *Monitoring the Future: National Survey Results on Drug Use, 1975–2007. Volume II: College Students and Adults Ages 19–45.* Bethesda, MD: National Institute on Drug Abuse; 2008. NIH publication 08-6418B.

37. Johnston LD, O'Malley PM, Bachman JG, Schulenberg JE. *Monitoring the Future: National Survey Results on Drug Use, 1975–2009. Volume II: College Students and Adults Ages 19–50.* Bethesda, MD: National Institute on Drug Abuse, 2010. NIH publication 10-7585.

38. Grant BF, Dawson DA, Stinson FS, Chou SP, Dufour MC, Pickering RP. The 12-month prevalence and trends in DSM-IV alcohol abuse and dependence. *Alcohol Res Health.* 2006;29:79–91.

39. Asfar T, Ward KD, Eissenberg T, Maziak W. Comparison of patterns of use, beliefs, and attitudes related to waterpipe between beginning and established smokers. *BMC Public Health.* 2005;5:19.

40. Salameh P, Waked M, Aoun Z. Waterpipe smoking: Construction and validation of the Lebanon Waterpipe Dependence Scale (LWDS-11). *Nicotine Tob Res.* 2008;10:149–158.

About the authors: *Dr. Grekin* and *Ms. Ayna* are with the Department of Psychology at Wayne State University in Detroit, Michigan.

Address correspondence to: Emily R. Grekin, PhD, Department of Psychology, Wayne State University, 5057 Woodward Avenue, 7th floor, Detroit, MI 48202. E-mail: grekine@wayne.edu

The Effect of Student Discussion Frequency on Mathematics Achievement[1]

Mathematical discourse in the form of classroom discussion is considered an effective strategy for increasing student mathematics achievement. Sharing ideas through discussion allows students to organize their reasoning and encourages them to justify their solution strategies (D'Ambrosio, Johnson, & Hobbs, 1995; Silver, Kilpatrick, & Schlesinger, 1990). The act of putting thought into words helps students to structure and clarify their reasoning. Talking about mathematics communicates the concept(s) to others but also helps communicate the concept(s) to the individual speaking (Pimm, 1987; Silver et al., 1990). This act of reflection allows individuals to further clarify their own thinking and restructure it when appropriate.

It seems acceptable that an understanding of mathematical concepts should translate into higher achievement in mathematics itself. A deepened understanding of mathematical concepts is an advocated benefit of peer discussion. Therefore, having students discuss mathematics with one another should increase mathematical achievement. Yet, this seemingly obvious logical consequence does not appear to be fully supported in the empirical literature. That is, although some studies show higher achievement for students who discuss mathematics more frequently (e.g., Hiebert & Wearne, 1993; Mercer & Sams, 2006), literature exists that shows frequent student discussion of mathematics has a negative effect on achievement (i.e., Shouse, 2001). Such a discrepancy in the literature pressed us to question what the true effect of student discussion was, whether such an effect was positive or negative, and why the results in the various studies differed. Finding answers to such questions is the goal of the present study. To achieve this goal, we used a large-scale dataset collected in the United States (Early Childhood Longitudinal Study) to investigate the general effect of discussion on mathematics achievement as well as differences of such effect between different classrooms/schools.

Benefits of Mathematical Discussion

Mathematics education literature has strongly supported the academic benefits of mathematical classroom discussion (hereafter referred to as *mathematical discussion*). Describing results from Stigler and Hiebert (1997), Grouws (2004) cited the Trends in International Mathematics and Science Study (TIMSS) as evidence that having students share solution methods and solve problems together increases mathematics achievement. Stigler and Hiebert (1997) evaluated video collected from 231 classrooms, including 100 in Germany, 50 in Japan, and 81 in the United States, with one lesson videotaped in each eighth-grade classroom. Qualitative findings suggested that students in the U.S. classrooms engaged in mathematics at a lower average grade level, which concur with the quantitative findings from. However, teachers in the United States were observed to be much less likely to have students develop mathematical concepts (about 22% in the United States compared with 78% in Germany and 82% in Japan) and much more likely to simply state mathematical concepts (78% in the United States compared with 22% in Germany and 18% in Japan). It is notable that engaging students in discussing math concepts was considered a part of developing mathematical concepts. However, Grouws (2004) identified a separate finding in the study that focused on a particular distinction made in Japanese mathematics classrooms. Japanese students were identified as being more likely than their American counterparts to discuss mathematical solution strategies with one another. In concordance with Grouws (2004), D'Ambrosio et al. (1995) suggested that mathematical discussion is a means of increasing mathematics achievement. By observing more frequent math discussion in classrooms where more advanced mathematics were done by students, the results provided by Stigler and Hiebert (1997), and described by Grouws (2004), suggest that more frequent discussion may be related to higher achievement.

Observing six different second-grade U.S. classrooms, Hiebert and Wearne (1993) found that two of six teachers observed asked students to explain and justify their mathematics significantly more than the other teachers in the study. In addition, students of these two teachers had higher gains in content knowledge than the students of the other four teachers. In comparing one of the classrooms to three of similar beginning achievement, Hiebert and Wearne (1993) noted:

[1] Literature review excerpt from Kosko, K. W., & Miyazaki, Y. (2012). The effect of student discussion frequency on fifth-grade students' mathematics achievement in U.S. schools. *The Journal of Experimental Education*, *80*(2), 173–195. Copyright © 2012 by Taylor & Francis Group, LLC. All rights reserved. Reprinted with permission.

90 Compared to A, B, and C, Classroom D students worked fewer place-value and computation problems, spent more time on each problem, engaged in more whole-class discussion, and shared more of the discourse by describing their solution strategies and explaining their responses (p. 419).

95 A similar distinction was noted between classrooms E and F, in which students were recognized as higher achieving, but students in class E engaged in more frequent discussion and saw higher achievement gains.

A more recent study, conducted by Mercer and 100 Sams (2006) in Britain, compared achievement for fifth-grade students of teachers who received training in conducting math discussion and teachers who did not receive such training. Mercer and Sams (2006) found that the prior set of students discussed math 105 more frequently than did the latter group and also had statistically significant higher gains in mathematics achievement. Although Mercer and Sams (2006) and Hiebert and Wearne (1993) focused on the quality of discussion and frequency, in both studies more fre-110 quent math discussion resulted in higher gains in math achievement.

Koichu, Berman, and Moore (2007) found evidence that incorporating language related to heuristic literacy, the use of heuristics in problem solving, and 115 appropriate heuristic language in mathematical discourse into classroom dialogue increased achievement scores. In their experiment Koichu et al. (2007) engaged eighth-grade students in two Israeli classrooms in problem solving. Students solved problems in 120 groups before discussing them as a class, similar to what Grouws (2004) described of successful peer discussions in Japanese mathematics classrooms. Koichu et al. (2007) found that incorporating heuristics into student dialogue significantly increased mathematics 125 achievement scores.

Evaluating data from the 1988 National Education Longitudinal Study (NELS), Shouse (2001) used a regression analysis and found that more frequent 10th-grade student discussion in mathematics had a slightly 130 negative effect on mathematics achievement. Although small in magnitude, the findings were statistically significant. Tenth-grade students were asked how often they participated in student discussions about mathematics. As stated, results showed that more frequent 135 student discussion had a small negative effect on mathematics achievement. This result contradicts much of what reform-oriented mathematics advocates in relation to student discussion as well as the aforementioned studies.

Implementation of Mathematical Discussion

140 The previous section aimed to describe the background of literature linking the frequency of mathematical discussion to higher mathematics achievement. However, the studies supporting a positive relation

between frequent math discussion and math achieve-145 ment (e.g., Mercer & Sams, 2006; Stigler & Hiebert, 1997) also articulate the quality of the more frequently occurring discussions of mathematics. There are also several other qualitative studies that describe teacher practices in implementing effective mathematical dis-150 course (e.g., Truxaw & DeFranco, 2007; Wood, 1999; Yackel & Cobb, 1996). Contrasting these studies are other qualitative investigations that observed teachers engaging students in more frequent discussion, but discussion that was not deemed effective in engaging 155 students in deep mathematical thinking.

One such study was conducted by Manouchehri and St. John (2006), who, in describing some of their findings, compared two episodes of classroom talk where there was a large degree of student participa-160 tion. The teachers in each classroom actively engaged students in the discussion, and on the surface, the two classrooms appeared similar. However, in one classroom the teacher explained and justified mathematical positions where in the other classroom the students did 165 so. More specifically, although students in both classrooms engaged in the discussions frequently, students in one classroom took more ownership of the discussion than students in the other classroom.

Kazemi and Stipek (2001) observed students in 170 fourth- and fifth-grade classrooms and found that while all observed teachers had similar levels of mathematical discussion, some teachers were more likely to require students to explain and justify their mathematics than other teachers. All teachers asked 175 their students to describe how they solved problems, but one group of teachers asked students to discuss such descriptions and other teachers asked students whether they agreed with the descriptions or not.

The two studies presented in the preceding para-180 graphs highlight the fact that more frequent mathematical discussion does not necessarily equate with more effective or higher quality mathematical discussion. Yet, what is not clear is the degree to which the two do not equate. As stated earlier in the literature 185 review, it is logical that more effective mathematical discussion should occur in accord with higher frequencies of mathematical discussion. Many of the studies describing the link between higher math achievement and mathematical discussion suggest this is the case. 190 Yet, the studies presented in this section suggest that it is not always the case. The slightly negative effect of frequent math discussion found by Shouse (2001) may be evidence of this or it may simply be evidence of an incomplete analysis of the problem.

Overview

195 What seems apparent from the review of literature is that there are two issues that need to be addressed in analysis. The first is whether there is a posi-

tive relation between more frequent math discussion and math achievement on average. The second is whether this effect varies between classrooms, which would be evidence of the different quality of frequent math discussions observed by qualitative studies (i.e., Kazemi & Stipek, 2001; Manouchehri & St. John, 2006).

Therefore, the primary research question in this study is whether frequency of student discussion about mathematics has a significant positive effect on mathematics achievement on average across classrooms and schools. In addition to this primary research question, it is prudent to investigate whether there are differences in the effectiveness of discussion in some classrooms as compared with others, because this may help explain conflicting results in the literature. Thus, a secondary research question is to determine whether there is significant variability of the effect of discussion on mathematics achievement across teachers, classrooms, or schools, and if it is found, to identify the characteristics of these constituents that can explain such variability.

References

D'Ambrosio, B., Johnson, H., & Hobbs, L. (1995). Strategies for increasing achievement in mathematics. In R. W. Cole (Ed), *Educating everybody's children: Diverse teaching strategies for diverse learners* (pp. 121–137). Alexandria, VA: Association for Supervision and Curriculum Development.

Grouws, D. A. (2004). Mathematics. In G. Cawelti (Ed.), *Handbook of research on improving student achievement* (3rd ed., pp. 160–178). Arlington, VA: Education Research Service.

Hiebert, J., & Wearne, D. (1993). Instructional tasks, classroom discourse, and students' learning in second-grade arithmetic. *American Educational Research Journal, 30*, 393–425.

Kazemi, E., & Stipek, D. (2001). Promoting conceptual thinking in four upper-elementary mathematics classrooms. *The Elementary School Journal, 102*(1), 59–80.

Koichu, B., Berman, A., & Moore, M. (2007). The effect of promoting heuristic literacy on the mathematical aptitude of middle-school students. *International Journal of Mathematical Education in Science and Technology, 38*(1), 1–17.

Manouchehri, A., & St. John, D. (2006). From classroom discussions to group discourse. *Mathematics Teacher, 99*, 544–551.

Mercer, N., & Sams, C. (2006). Teaching children how to use language to solve math problems. *Language and Education, 20*, 507–528.

Pimm, D. (1987). *Speaking mathematically: Communication in mathematics classrooms*. New York, NY: Routledge & Kegan Paul.

Shouse, R. (2001). The impact of traditional and reform-style practices on students' mathematical achievement. In T. Loveless (Ed.), *The great curriculum debate: How should we teach reading and math?* Washington, DC: Brookings Institution Press.

Silver, E. A., Kilpatrick, J., & Schlesinger, B. (1990). *Thinking through mathematics: Fostering inquiry and communication in mathematics classrooms*. New York, NY: College Entrance Examination Board.

Stigler, J. W., & Hiebert, J. (1997). Understanding and improving classroom mathematics instruction. *Phi Delta Kappa, 79*(1), 14–21.

Truxaw, M. P., & DeFranco, T. C. (2007). Lessons from Mr. Larson: An inductive model of teaching for orchestrating discourse. *Mathematics Teacher, 101*, 268–272.

Wood, T. (1999). Creating a context for argument in mathematics class. *Journal for Research in Mathematics Education, 30*, 171–191.

Yackel, E., & Cobb, P. (1996). Sociomathematical norms, argumentation, and autonomy in mathematics. *Journal Research in Mathematics Education, 27*, 458–477.

Authors' notes: The authors share joint first authorship of this article. The sequence of names was agreed on by the authors.

About the authors: *Karl W. Kosko* is a postdoctoral fellow at the University of Michigan. His research interests center around mathematical communication, with a special interest in the self-regulation of mathematical communication. *Yasuo Miyazaki* is an associate professor in the School of Education at Virginia Tech. His research interests include methodological and application issues on hierarchical linear/nonlinear modeling, longitudinal data analysis, and latent variable modeling, with particular recent interest in multilevel factor analysis and multilevel measurement models.

Address correspondence to: Karl W. Kosko, School of Education, University of Michigan, 610 East University Avenue, Room 2404, Ann Arbor, MI 48109. E-mail: kwkosko@umich.edu

Notes

MODEL LITERATURE REVIEW D

Behaviors in Couples With a History of Infidelity[1]

Although most Americans (up to 97%) believe that engaging in extramarital sex is wrong (Johnson et al., 2002), prevalence rates of infidelity remain high with approximately 22%–25% of men and 11%–15% of women admitting to engaging in extramarital sex (for a review of rates and correlates of extradyadic involvement [EDI], see Allen et al., 2005). EDI—that is, sexual involvement with a person outside the primary dyad—typically is associated with problems for partners and their relationship. Many negative emotional and behavioral correlates of EDI have been documented including partner violence, acute anxiety, depression, suicidal ideation, and symptoms similar to those of posttraumatic stress disorder (Cano & O'Leary, 2000; Gordon, Baucom, & Snyder, 2004). Relationship distress and dissolution are also commonly associated with EDI, with infidelity being the most frequently cited cause of divorce (Amato & Previti, 2003).

While prior literature has examined a broad range of correlates of infidelity, studies examining specific characteristics of communication related to EDI are rare. In a recent observational longitudinal study (Allen et al., 2008), women's infidelity was predicted by lower levels of their own premarital positive communication and by higher levels of negative communication and invalidation by both partners. Men's infidelity was predicted by their own lower levels of premarital positive communication and by higher invalidation communication by their partner. Thus, findings suggest that problems in communication are a significant risk factor for engaging in infidelity (as well as for general marital distress; Fincham & Beach, 1999; Markman, Rhoades, Stanley, Ragan, & Whitton, 2010). Indeed, existing infidelity interventions incorporate communication skill building as a core treatment component (Baucom, Snyder, & Gordon, 2009).

Conflict communication serves as an important indicator of both current and future relationship functioning (Markman et al., 2010). Dissatisfied couples are more likely to engage in negative conflict communication behaviors including criticism, defensiveness, contempt, and withdrawal (Gottman, 1993). One of the most widely studied and well-documented negative communication patterns is the demand/withdraw pattern in conflict communication. During conflict interactions, distressed couples often display a dyadic conflict pattern in which one spouse blames, nags, criticizes, or pressures the other for change, while the other spouse withdraws or avoids conflict (Christensen & Heavey, 1990). This demand/withdraw pattern correlates strongly with relationship dissatisfaction (Eldridge, Sevier, Jones, Atkins, & Christensen, 2007; Ridley, Wilhelm, & Surra, 2001), and is seen more often during problem discussions among couples seeking marital therapy and divorcing couples compared with nondistressed couples (Christensen & Shenk, 1991).

Gender differences in demand and withdraw conflict behaviors have been demonstrated in multiple studies. As a group, dissatisfied wives tend to demand change from their husbands, whereas dissatisfied husbands tend to withdraw from conflict with their wives (Caughlin & Vangelisti, 2000; Christensen & Heavey, 1990; Christensen & Shenk, 1991; Eldridge et al., 2007). Several theoretical perspectives have been proposed to account for this gender difference in conflict behavior including power differences, intimacy regulation, and gender roles (Caughlin & Vangelisti, 2000; Christensen & Heavey, 1990; Nichols & Rohrbaugh, 1997). However, recent empirical evidence suggests that demand and withdraw behavior is often dependent on the context in which it occurs (Holley, Sturm & Levenson, 2010; Vogel, Murphy, Werner-Wilson, Cutrona, & Seeman, 2007) and that one omnibus theoretical model may not adequately explain variations in demand and withdraw behavior. With this in mind, it is important to evaluate not only gender differences but contextual factors that might influence individual demand and withdraw behavior in couple conflict discussions.

The present study examined demand and withdraw behaviors in conflict discussions among couples with and without a history of sexual EDI. Based on the existing literature on EDI and relationship distress, it could generally be predicted that couples with a history of EDI would have higher demand and withdraw behaviors compared with those couples without such history of EDI in their relationship.

References

Allen, E. S., Atkins, D., Baucom, D. H., Snyder, D. K., Gordon, K. C., & Glass, S. P. (2005). Intrapersonal, interpersonal, and contextual factors in engaging in and responding to extramarital involvement. *Clinical Psychology: Science and Practice, 12*, 101–130.

---

[1] Literature review excerpt from Balderrama-Durbin, C. M., Allen, E. S., & Rhoades, G. K. (2012). Demand and withdraw behaviors in couples with a history of infidelity. *Journal of Family Psychology, 26*, 11–17. Copyright © 2011 by the American Psychological Association. All rights reserved. Reprinted with permission.

Allen, E. S., Rhoades, G. K., Stanley, S. M., Markman, H. J., Williams, T., Melton, J., & Clements, M. L. (2008). Premarital precursors of marital infidelity. *Family Process, 47*, 243–259.

Amato, P. R., & Previti, D. (2003). People's reasons for divorcing: Gender, social class, the life course, and adjustment. *Journal of Family Issues, 24*, 602–626.

Baucom, D. H., Snyder, D. K., & Gordon, K. C. (2009). *Helping couples get past the affair: A clinician's guide*. New York, NY: Guilford Press.

Cano, A., & O'Leary, K. D. (2000). Infidelity and separations precipitate major depressive episodes and symptoms of nonspecific depression and anxiety. *Journal of Consulting and Clinical Psychology, 68*, 774–781.

Caughlin, J. P., & Vangelisti, A. L. (2000). An individual difference explanation of why married couples engage in the demand/withdraw pattern of conflict. *Journal of Social and Personal Relationships, 17*, 523–551.

Christensen, A., & Heavey, C. L. (1990). Gender and social structure in the demand/withdraw pattern of marital conflict. *Journal of Personality and Social Psychology, 59*, 73–81.

Christensen, A., & Shenk, J. L. (1991). Communication, conflict, and psychological distance in nondistressed, clinic, and divorcing couples. *Journal of Consulting and Clinical Psychology, 59*, 459–463.

Eldridge, K. A., Sevier, M., Jones, J., Atkins, D. C., & Christensen, A. (2007). Demand-withdraw communication in severely distressed, moderately distressed, and nondistressed couples: Rigidity and polarity during relationship and personal problem discussions. *Journal of Family Psychology, 21*, 218–226.

Fincham, F. D., & Beach, S. R. H. (1999). Conflict in marriage: Implication for working with couples. *Annual Review of Psychology, 50*, 47–77.

Gordon, K. C., Baucom, D. H., & Snyder, D. K. (2004). An integrative intervention for promoting recovery from extramarital affairs. *Journal of Marital and Family Therapy, 30*, 1–12.

Gottman, J. M. (1993). The roles of conflict engagement, escalation, and avoidance in marital interaction: A longitudinal view of five types of couples. *Journal of Consulting and Clinical Psychology, 61*, 6–15.

Holley, S. R., Sturm, V. E., & Levenson, R. W. (2010). Exploring the basis of gender differences in the demand-withdraw pattern. *Journal of Homosexuality, 57*, 666–684.

Johnson, C. A., Stanley, S. M., Glenn, N. D., Amato, P. A., Nock, S. L., Markman, H. J., & Dion, M. R. (2002). *Marriage in Oklahoma: 2001 baseline statewide survey on marriage and divorce*. Oklahoma City, OK: Oklahoma Department of Human Services.

Markman, H. J., Rhoades, G. K., Stanley, S. M., Ragan, E. P., & Whitton, S. W. (2010). The premarital communication roots of marital distress and divorce: The first five years of marriage. *Journal of Family Psychology, 24*, 289–298.

Nichols, M. P., & Rohrbaugh, M. J. (1997). Why do women demand and men withdraw? The role outside the career and family involvements. *The Family Journal: Counseling and Therapy for Couples and Families, 5*, 111–119.

Ridley, C. A., Wilhelm, M. S., & Surra, C. A. (2001). Married couples' conflict responses and marital quality. *Journal of Social and Personal Relationships, 18*, 517–534.

Vogel, D. L., Murphy, M. J., Werner-Wilson, R. J., Cutrona, C. E., & Seeman, J. (2007). Sex differences in the use of demand and withdraw behavior in marriage: Examining the social structure hypothesis. *Journal of Counseling Psychology, 54*, 165–177.

Address correspondence to: Christina M. Balderrama-Durbin, Department of Psychology–Mailstop 4235, College Station, TX 77843-4235. Email: balderrama-durbin@tamu.edu

The Prevalence of Stalking Among College Students[1]

Stalking Vignette

Heather's class ended, and she left the classroom. She noticed Tom hanging around outside the door again. She wished there was another way out. He approached, said hello, and began walking with her. Heather was uncom-
5   fortable with Tom's unwanted attention because this was not the first time he had waited for her. He gave her a small gift and asked her out again. Heather told him she did not want the gift and did not want to go on a date. She once more explained to him that she already had a
10   boyfriend, and she did not want Tom to pursue her anymore. Tom replied that she was just playing hard to get and that she would eventually come around. Heather told him that he was acting like a stalker and should just leave her alone. As he turned to leave, Heather felt re-
15   lieved, but worried and anxious about the next encounter. She wondered if she should skip her class next time just to avoid him.

The aforementioned vignette is representative of early stalking encounters that students experience on
20   college campuses. Researchers have found that approximately 21% of college students have been stalked.[1-6] Further, data from a national sample indicate that 74% of stalking victims were between 18 and 39 years of age.[7] College students of both genders re-
25   port being stalked, ranging from 13% to 52.4% of female students[1-6] and 11% to 23.2% of males.[4,5,8] Those who report being stalked note that the episodes last two years on average,[9] constituting approximately half of the time it takes to earn an undergraduate degree.
30   Collectively, these prevalence rates demonstrate that stalking victimization poses a threat to many college students and their academic success.

Stalking victims can be negatively affected psychologically and physically when the frequency and
35   severity of the stalking episodes escalate, which can interfere with their normal routine.[1,7,8,10-13] More specifically, stalking victimization often leads to adverse problems, such as mild to extreme fearfulness, drug abuse, depression, anxiety, sleep disorders, headaches,
40   and stomach problems.[1,8,10-13] As a result, students may turn to college health and counseling centers for assistance. In fact, university counseling centers report that at least 33% of their student clientele desire psychological intervention for crimes of interpersonal
45   violence, including being stalked.[14] Victims are likely to make drastic changes to their lifestyle. For example, they may change their school, job, or city in which

they live.[1,7,8] Importantly, those who are stalked may not go on to graduate on time as approximately 20%
50   relocate; of those, 11% move out of town.[7] Lifestyle changes in conjunction with the psychological and physical repercussions of being stalked may result in students dropping out of college altogether. For these reasons, stalking should be addressed by colleges and
55   universities that are focused on student safety which, in turn, impacts retention, progression, and graduation.

Although previous research demonstrates that stalking is a significant social concern, prevalence rates vary widely.[1,2,5,8,9] According to a meta-analysis,
60   there are several methodological reasons for these inconsistent prevalence rates. One reason for this variability is a lack of consistency in how stalking was measured.[9] For example, some researchers asked if the respondent had been stalked within the last 12 months,
65   and others asked about lifetime prevalence rates.[5] Further, how researchers determine whether stalking has taken place varies considerably among studies; this would include asking respondents if they had been stalked by anyone during their lifetime based on the
70   respondent's personal definition[8] or based on a definition provided by the researchers.[2] Others have asked respondents if they had been stalked by an intimate person within the past year based on the respondent's personal definition.[1] To our knowledge, only one study
75   addressed the prevalence of stalking during college enrollment. However, participants were labeled as stalking victims by the researchers, not by self-identification.[3]

Another reason for differences in reported preva-
80   lence rates is based on the characteristics of the sample. For example, general population samples have lower prevalence rates than college student samples.[7] Even reported rates within college student samples vary based on the demographics of the university's
85   population.[3] For example, previous research suggests that prevalence rates would be higher for an all-women's college compared to an all-men's college.[9]

Additionally, most state laws include in their definition of stalking unwanted, repeated, implicit, or
90   explicit threatening behavior or intrusions resulting in psychological distress and reasonable fear.[7,15] However, legal definitions can vary by state, and interpretations of the reasonable person standard can vary by individual. Thus, it is difficult to assess how wide-

---

[1] Literature review excerpt from McNamara, C. L., & Marsil, D. F. (2012). The prevalence of stalking among college students: The disparity between researcher and self-identified victimization. *Journal of American College Health*, 60, 168–174. Copyright © 2012 by Taylor & Francis Group, LLC. All rights reserved. Reprinted with permission.

95 spread stalking is on campuses due to these measurement, sampling, and legal issues.

In order to effectively determine whether a culture of violence exists, it is important for college campuses to focus on obtaining accurate data about the

100 prevalence of stalking that is part of a larger cycle of interpersonal violence. Although some college campuses have begun to recognize this problem, the manner in which crime statistics are reported and the way the issue is addressed vary by university. Federal law

105 mandates annual reporting of some crimes that occur on all campuses; however, this does not include instances of stalking.[16] As a result of these factors and because victims of violence often underreport, we do not have an accurate assessment of the prevalence

110 rates of interpersonal violence, particularly with college students. Therefore, it is not sufficient for universities to rely on police reports for accurate prevalence rates of stalking victimization.

Prevalence rates suggest that stalking behavior

115 may be perceived as normative in our society. According to the social norms theory, social norms are accepted explicit and implicit rules of behavior that govern how individuals interact with others. Unfortunately, sometimes perceived social norms are incor-

120 rect. In fact, many people may not endorse a particular social norm, yet because they believe others approve of that norm, they continue to tolerate it. Previous research demonstrates that using a social norms approach can be an effective framework for addressing

125 interpersonal violence, such as stalking.[17,18] To use the stalking vignette as an example, an individual may think that his/her peers believe it is acceptable for Tom to repeatedly pursue Heather despite being told that his behavior is unwanted. Although the individual may

130 not personally engage in that behavior, a social norm that is accepting of interpersonal violence would likely prevent the individual from intervening in that situation. By systematically changing these inaccurate social norms, tolerance for interpersonal violence will be

135 reduced, thus fostering more appropriate behaviors.

The Present Study

A first step in implementing a social norms framework is to determine rates of stalking, thus establishing a need to reform a culture of violence if one exists.[17] The purpose of this study was threefold. First,

140 we updated prevalence rates using self-identification (respondents' own definition) and behavioral measures (researcher definition) of stalking victimization. Second, we assessed whether students who affirm they have experienced stalking behaviors then label such

145 behaviors as stalking. Finally, we analyzed the demographic and behavioral factors that might predict stalking victimization. The findings from this research allow us to demonstrate the extent stalking is a problem for college students, to compare this sample to

150 national prevalence rates, and to educate personnel in higher education on how to recognize and prioritize stalking prevention and education issues for the campus community.

References

1. Amar, AF. Behaviors that college women label as stalking or harassment. *J Am Psychiatr Nurs Assoc.* 2007; 13: 210–220.
2. Fremouw, WJ and Westrup, MA. Pennypacker BA. Stalking on campus: The prevalence and strategies for coping with stalking. *J Forensic Sci.* 1997; 42: 666–669.
3. Buhi, ER, Clayton, H and Surrency, HH. Stalking victimization among college women and subsequent help-seeking behaviors. *J Am Coll Health.* 2008; 57: 419–425.
4. Fisher, BS, Cullen, FT and Turner, MG. *The Sexual Victimization of College Women,* Washington, DC: National Criminal Justice Reference Service, US Department of Justice; 2000. NCJRS Publication No. 182369.
5. Björklund, K, Häkkänen-Nyholm, H, Sheridan, L and Roberts, K. The prevalence of stalking among Finnish university students. *J Interpers Violence.* 2010; 25: 684–698.
6. Jordan, CE, Wilcox, P and Pritchard, AJ. Stalking acknowledgement and reporting among college women experiencing intrusive behaviors: Implications for the emergence of a "classic stalking case." *J Crim Just.* 2007; 35: 556–569.
7. Tjaden, P and Thoennes, N. *Stalking in America: Findings from the National Violence Against Women Survey,* Washington, DC: National Institute of Justice and Centers for Disease Control; 1998. Available at: http://www.ncjrs.gov/pdffiles/169592.pdf. Accessed June 30, 2010.
8. Bjerregaard, B. An empirical study of stalking victimization. *Violence Vict.* 2000; 15: 389–406.
9. Spitzburg, BH and Cupach, WR. The state of the art stalking: Taking stock of the emerging literature. *Aggress Violent Behav.* 2007; 12: 64–86.
10. Davis, KE, Coker, AL and Sanderson, M. Physical and mental health effects of being stalked for men and women. *Violence Vict.* 2002; 17: 429–443.
11. Pathe, M and Mullen, PE. The impact of stalkers on their victims. *Br J Psychiatry.* 1997; 170: 12–17.
12. Slashinski, MJ, Coker, AL and Davis, KE. Physical aggression, forced sex, and stalking victimization by a dating partner: An analysis of the National Violence Against Women Survey. *Violence Vict.* 2003; 18: 595–617.
13. Thomas, SDM, Purcell, R, Pathé, M and Mullen, PE. Harm associated with stalking victimization. *Aust N Z J Psychiatry.* 2008; 42: 800–806.
14. Gallagher, R, Gill, A and Sysko, H. *National Survey of Counseling Center Directors,* Alexandria, VA: International Association of Counseling Services; 2000.
15. Meloy, JR. *The Psychology of Stalking: Clinical and Forensic Perspectives.* New York, NY: Academic Press; 1998.
16. Office of Postsecondary Education, US Department of Education. *The Handbook for Campus Crime Reporting,* Washington, DC: US Department of Education; 2005. Available at: http://www2.ed.gov/admins/lead/safety/handbook.pdf. Accessed June 30, 2010.
17. Berkowitz, AD. Applications of social norms theory to other health and social justice issues. In *The Social Norms Approach to Preventing School and College Age Substance Abuse,* Edited by: Perkins, H W. 259–279. San Francisco, CA: Jossey-Bass; 2003.
18. Fabiano, PM, Perkins, HW, Berkowitz, A, Linkenbach, J and Stark, C. Engaging men as social justice allies in ending violence against women: Evidence for a social norms approach. *J Am Coll Health.* 2003; 52: 105–112.

About the authors: *Dr. McNamara* and *Dr. Marsil* are with the Department of Psychology at Kennesaw State University, Georgia.

School Social Workers' Experiences With Youth Suicidal Behavior[1]

Child and adolescent suicidal behavior, including ideation, attempt, and dying, is a national and preventable public health problem (Center for Substance Abuse Treatment, 2008) and a significant concern for school staff and administrators. In 2006 (the most recent year for which statistics are available), the third leading cause of death among U.S. youths ages 5 to 19 years was suicide, with 1,774 deaths. Rates (per hundred thousand) of youth suicide increase significantly with age: 0.18 for youths ages 5 to 12 years, 2.78 for youths 13 to 15, and 8.06 for youths 16 to 19 (Centers for Disease Control and Prevention [CDC], 2010a). The death by suicide of an individual student, or multiple students in cluster suicides, can be devastating to the members of the school community; challenges the emotional, legal, and administrative resources of the school; and requires an informed and coordinated response by school staff (including school social workers [SSWs], counselors, and teachers) and administrators (Callahan, 2002; Newgass & Schonfeld, 2005). However, the relative infrequency of suicide means that many school staff will never work with a youth who dies by suicide, so a more frequent concern for school staff is the much larger number of youths who present with suicidal ideation and attempt.

Unlike death by suicide, which is reported across all age groups by the CDC, there is no single source for information on youth suicide ideation and attempt. For example, the Youth Risk Behavior Survey (YRBS), which provides the baseline for rates of suicidal behavior among middle school (MS) and high school (HS) students, is not administered to elementary school (ES) students. The prevalence of suicidal ideation among children ages 6 to 12 years has been reported to be as low as 8.9% in a U.S. sample (Pfeffer, Zuckerman, Plutchik, & Mizruchi, 1984) and as high as 32.2% in a Brazilian sample (Bandim, Fonseca, & De Lima, 1997). Reisch, Jacobson, Sawdey, Anderson, and Henriques (2008) found that among a sample of youths ages 9 to 12, 8.9% reported attempting suicide. According to the YRBS, MS students reported that over their lifetime approximately 20% seriously thought about killing themselves, 13% made a plan, and 8% tried to kill themselves (Shanklin, Brener, McManus, Kinchen, & Kann, 2007). HS students reported that within the 12 months prior to the study, 14.5% seriously thought about killing them-

selves, 11.3% made a plan, 6.9% tried to kill themselves, and 2.0% received medical attention for their suicide attempt (Eaton et al., 2008). Recent research has suggested that although older adolescents might report more frequency and duration of suicidal ideation, even transient suicidal ideation among ES- and MS-age children is predictive of poorer outcomes in adulthood (Vander Stoep, McCauley, Flynn, & Stone, 2009). Despite the difficulties in comparing suicide risk across age groups, these data indicate that youths in ES, MS, and HS think about and attempt suicide. Consequently, the prevention of and intervention in youth suicidal ideation and attempt should be a primary focus of child and adolescent professionals, with school being perhaps the most important venue for these activities (Joe & Bryant, 2007).

Youths receive more mental health services in schools than in any other service sector, including specialty mental health service settings such as psychiatric hospitals, outpatient clinics, and residential treatment facilities (Rones & Hoagwood, 2000). Schools are a particularly important venue for mental health services delivery because school staff members have unparalleled access to at-risk youths. For example, a recent study reported that youths who receive special education services had significantly higher rates of suicidal ideation (previous 12 months = 31.5%) and suicide attempts (lifetime = 30%) than youths in juvenile justice, substance abuse treatment, county mental health, and child welfare (Chavira, Accurso, Garland, & Hough, 2010). According to a U.S. Department of Health and Human Services (2001) study, almost all schools have at least one staff member whose responsibilities include providing mental health services to students (Foster et al., 2005). Although these staff members are more likely to be school counselors (77%) nurses (69%), and school psychologists (68%) than social workers (44%), social workers have reported spending the largest percentage of time providing mental health services (57%), followed by school counselors (52%), school psychologists (48%), and nurses (32%). SSWs also reported spending more time providing crisis intervention services (7.4%) than school counselors (4.7%) or school psychologists (3.1%) (Agresta, 2004). Examples of crisis intervention services that SSWs are expected to provide include suicide prevention programming, risk assessment,

[1] Literature review excerpt from Singer, J. B., & Slovak, K. (2011). School social workers' experiences with youth suicidal behavior: An exploratory study. *Children & Schools*, *33*, 215–228. Copyright © 2011 by the National Association of Social Workers, Inc. All rights reserved. Reprinted with permission.

95 counseling, referral, and facilitation of hospitalization (Constable, 2008). In addition, SSWs are expected to provide suicide education and prevention programming to faculty and staff and families and the community (Gibbons & Struder, 2008).

100   Although the data suggest that SSWs play an integral role in providing mental health and crisis intervention services in schools, their experiences with suicidal youths, preparation to work with suicidal students, and role in the school regarding this issue is

105 currently undocumented. The limited scholarship on youth suicide and SSWs is most likely a natural extension of the fact that suicide has long been neglected as a focus of social work research (Joe & Neidermeyer, 2008); there is limited scholarship on school social

110 work (Franklin, Kim, & Tripodi, 2009); researchers have traditionally focused on consumers of services and program development rather than provider characteristics in treatment outcomes (Wampold, 2001); and across all of the helping professions, there is a limited

115 scholarship on the experiences of providers of services to suicidal youths. Therefore, to provide a context for the current study, we have summarized extant research on youth suicide and social workers, and relevant knowledge from research in allied and school profes-

120 sions.

Social Workers and Youth Suicide

     A review of the literature suggests that social workers have contributed empirical literature that pri-

175 marily describes risk factors and characteristics of suicidal youths and conceptual literature that addresses

125 practice, education, and policy related to social work with suicidal youths. For example, empirical studies by social workers on youth suicide since 1980 have

180 reported on the rise in suicide rates among African American male adolescents due to firearms; increased

130 risk for suicide due to sexual and physical abuse, depression, substance abuse, race and sexual orientation, and school exclusion; use of firearms in male adoles-

185 cent suicide and medication overdose in female adolescents; and the use of, and need for, youth suicide

135 prevention and intervention internationally (see Joe & Niedermeier, 2008, for a review; Walls, Freedenthal, & Wisneski, 2008). A recent study in Great Britain

190 reported that social work services were a significant factor in reducing suicide risk among socially disad-

140 vantaged youths (Pritchard & Williams, 2009). Other scholarship has addressed pedagogical and practice implications of suicide (Sanders, Jacobson, & Ting,

195 2008), development of evidence-based approaches to working with suicidal youths (Singer, 2006), and the

145 role of school-based social workers in the prevention of suicide (Peebles-Wilkins, 2006; Ward, 1995). Missing from the social work literature is information on

200 the experiences and perceptions of SSWs who work with suicidal youths.

School Staff and Youth Suicide

150   Although most research on suicide and schools has looked at staff training, curriculum-based programs, or screening programs (Eckert, Miller, DuPaul, & Riley-Tillman, 2003), a few studies have reported on the experiences, perceptions, attitudes, or beliefs of

155 school counselors, school psychologists, nurses, and teachers. Whereas the majority of school counselors reported experience working with youth suicidal ideation and attempt (King, Price, Telljohann, & Wahl, 1999; King & Smith, 2000), the majority of school

160 counselors and school psychologists reported no experience with youth suicide; those with experience reported between zero and six deaths by suicide during their employment (Debski, Spadafore, Jacob, Poole, & Hixson, 2007; King et al., 1999). Experience with sui-

165 cidal youths appears to be important. King et al. (1999) found that the more experience school counselors had with suicidal youths, the more confident they were in engaging in suicide prevention and intervention services.

170   A number of studies reported on school staff members' knowledge, attitudes, and graduate and professional training. Knowledge of risk factors varied by study and discipline, with rates as low as 9% for school health teachers, 34% for school counselors

175 (King & Smith, 2000), and 43% for school psychologists (Debski et al., 2007) and as high as 63% for school counselors in an earlier study (Peach & Reddick, 1991). School staff members reported increased knowledge and skills following gatekeeper trainings

180 like QPR (question, persuade, and refer) and ASIST (applied suicide intervention training skills) (Joe & Bryant, 2007).When school staff were part of crisis intervention teams or received specific training on suicide assessment and intervention, they reported

185 higher levels of self-confidence in identifying and intervening in a suicidal crisis (King & Smith, 2000). However, staff members from all disciplines reported insufficient professional training in suicide prevention, intervention, and postvention (Christian-son & Everall,

190 2008; Feldman & Freedenthal, 2006; King et al., 1999, 2000; King & Smith, 2000; Ries & Cornell, 2008). Adequate and appropriate training not only affects a school staff's ability to address youth suicide in the schools, but also may increase the likelihood of pro-

195 viding suicide awareness training for nonmental-health school staff. One limitation of extant literature is that there are no studies that looked at school staff at the ES level, possibly because there is

200 no training program that covers the developmental issues that staff at the ES level face. It is unclear whether a training program developed for secondary

education would improve services rendered by staff at an ES level.

Although education and training on youth suicide
205 is crucial to preparedness in this area, research suggests it is not a standard component of the educational programming for school mental health professionals. Debski et al. (2007) found that although 99% of school psychologists had received some form of suicide train-
210 ing, only 40% had received any of this training while completing their graduate programs. Feldman and Freedenthal (2006) found that 79% of MSW-level social work graduates did not receive any formal training in their graduate curriculums, and of the 21 percent
215 who received training in their graduate program, over three-fourths (76%) received four hours or fewer of suicide-related training. School staff who graduated more recently reported increased knowledge and training regarding adolescent suicide (Debski et al., 2007;
220 Feldman & Freedenthal, 2006; King & Smith, 2000). Although this suggests a positive trend, it appears that most school staff members are likely to obtain training on suicide from sources such as professional journals, workshops, on-the-job training, and college courses
225 (King et al., 2000). This may apply to SSWs as well.

In summary, a small body of research suggests that the level of training, experiences, and perceptions of working with suicidal youths varies by school staff discipline and that these factors influence the likeli-
230 hood of school staff intervening in a suicidal crisis. Because SSWs work at all grade levels, and because they assume a variety of roles in the school system (Whitted & Dupper, 2005), extant research on nonsocial workers cannot be generalized to social workers.
235 Undertaking a preliminary examination of SSWs' experiences with and perceptions of working with suicidal youths will address calls from researchers and policymakers for more research on youth suicide, particularly from social workers (Joe & Bryant, 2007;
240 Satcher, 1999; U.S. Department of Health and Human Services, 2001); respond to a recent call for more documentation of SSWs' activities (Franklin et al., 2009); and serve as a baseline and foundation for future research on SSWs' knowledge, skills, and per-
245 ceived effectiveness in suicide prevention and intervention activities.

Purpose of the Current Study

The purpose of the current study was to gather basic information on social workers' experience with and perceptions of suicidal youths across three school
250 levels (ES, MS, and HS) that could inform practice, policy, and future research. As an exploratory study, it neither tests hypotheses nor evaluates SSWs' knowledge, skills, or effectiveness in suicide intervention.

References

Agresta, J. (2004). Professional role perceptions of school social workers, psychologists, and counselors. *Children & Schools, 26*, 151–163.

Bandim, J. M., Fonseca, L., & De Lima, J. M. (1997). Prevalência da ideaçâo suicida numa populaçâo de escolares do nordeste Brasileiro. *Jornal Brasileiro de Psiquiatria, 46*, 477–481.

Callahan, J. (2002). School-based crisis intervention for traumatic events. In R. Constable, S. McDonald, & J. Flynn (eds.), *School social work: Practice, policy, and research perspective* (5th ed., pp. 481–500). Chicago: Lyceum Books.

Center for Substance Abuse Treatment. (2008). *Substance abuse and suicide prevention: Evidence and implications—A white paper* (DHHS Pub. No. SMA-08-4352). Rockville, MD: Substance Abuse and Mental Health Services Administration.

Centers for Disease Control and Prevention. (2010a). Web-based injury statistics query and reporting system. Retrieved from http://webappa.cdc.gov/sasweb/ncipc/mortrate10_sy.html

Centers for Disease Control and Prevention. (2010b, June 4). Youth risk behavior surveillance—United States, 2009. Surveillance summaries. *Morbidity and Mortality Weekly Report, 59*(SS-5), 1–142.

Centers for Disease Control and Prevention. (n.d.). Youth risk behavior surveillance survey: Comparisons between state or district and national results fact sheet. Retrieved from http://www.cdc.gov/HealthyYouth/yrbs/state_district_comparisons.htm

Chavira, D. A., Accurso, E. C., Garland, A. F., & Hough, R. (2010). Suicidal behavior among youth in five public sectors of care. *Child and Adolescent Mental Health, 15*(1), 44–51.

Christianson, C. L., & Everall, R. D. (2008). Constructing bridges of support: School counsellors' experiences of student suicide. *Canadian Journal of Counselling, 42*, 209–221.

Constable, R. (2008). The role of the school social worker. In C. R. Massat, R. T. Constable, S. McDonald, & J. P. Flynn (eds.), *School social work: Practice, policy and research perspectives* (7th ed., pp. 3–29). Chicago: Lyceum Books.

Debski, J., Spadafore, C. D., Jacob, S., Poole, D. A., & Hixson, M. D. (2007). Suicide intervention: Training, roles, and knowledge of school psychologists. *Psychology in the Schools, 44*, 157–170.

Eaton, D. K., Kann, L., Kinchen, S., Shanklin, S., Ross, J., Hawkins, J., et al. (2008, June 6). Youth risk behavior surveillance—United States, 2007. *Morbidity and Mortality Weekly Report, 57*(SS04), 1–131. Retrieved from http://www.cdc.gov/mmwr/PdF/ss/ss5704.pdf

Eckert, T. L., Miller, D. N., DuPaul, G. J., & Riley-Tillman, T. C. (2003). Adolescent suicide prevention: School psychologists' acceptability of school-based programs. *School Psychology Review, 32*(1), 57–76.

Feldman, B. N., & Freedenthal, S. (2006). Social work education in suicide intervention and prevention: An unmet need? *Suicide and Life-Threatening Behavior, 36*, 467–480.

Foster, S., Rollefson, M., Doksum, T., Noonan, D., Robinson, G., & Teich, J. (2005). *School mental health services in the United States, 2002–2003* (DHHS Publication No. [SMA] 05-4068). Rockville, MD: Center for Mental Health Services, Substance Abuse and Mental Health Services Administration.

Franklin, C., Kim, J. S., & Tripodi, S. J. (2009). A meta-analysis of published school social work outcome studies: 1980–2007. *Research on Social Work Practice, 19*, 667–677.

Gibbons, M., & Struder, J. (2008). Suicide awareness training for faculty and staff: A training model for school counselors. *Professional School Counseling, 11*, 272–276.

Joe, S., & Bryant, H. (2007). Evidence-based suicide prevention screening in schools. *Children & Schools, 29*, 219–227.

Joe, S., & Niedermeier, D. (2008). Preventing suicide: A neglected social work research agenda. *British Journal of Social Work, 38*, 507–530.

King, K. A., Price, J. H., Telljohann, S. K., & Wahl, J. (1999). How confident do high school counselors feel in recognizing students at risk for suicide? *American Journal of Health Behavior, 23*, 457–467.

King, K. A., Price, J. H., Telljohann, S. K., & Wahl, J. (2000). Preventing adolescent suicide: Do high school counselors know the risk factors? *Professional School Counseling, 3*, 255–263.

King, K. A., & Smith, J. (2000). Project SOAR: A training program to increase school counselors' knowledge and confidence regarding suicide prevention and intervention. *Journal of School Health, 70*, 402–407.

Newgass, S., & Schonfield, D. (2005). School crisis intervention, crisis prevention, and crisis response. In A. R. Roberts (Ed.), *Crisis intervention handbook: Assessment, treatment and research* (3rd ed., pp. 499–518). New York: Oxford University Press.

Peach, L., & Reddick, T. L. (1991). Counselors can make a difference in preventing adolescent suicide. *School Counselor, 39*(2), 107–116.

Peebles-Wilkins, W. (2006). Evidence-based suicide prevention. *Children & Schools, 28*, 195–196.

Pfeffer, C. R., Zuckerman, S., Plutchik, R., & Mizruchi, M. S. (1984). Suicidal behavior in normal school children: A comparison with child psychiatric inpatients. *Journal of the American Academy of Child Psychiatry, 23,* 416–423.

Pritchard, C., & Williams, R. (2009). Does social work make a difference? A controlled study of former "looked-after-children" and "excluded-from-school" adolescents now men aged 16–24 subsequent offences, being victims of crime and suicide. *Journal of Social Work, 9,* 285–307.

Reisch, S. K., Jacobson, G., Sawdey, L., Anderson, J., & Henriques, J. (2008). Suicide ideation among later elementary school-aged youth. *Journal of Psychiatric and Mental Health Nursing, 15,* 263–277.

Ries, C., & Cornell, D. (2008). An evaluation of suicide gatekeeper training for school counselors and teachers. *Professional School Counseling, 11,* 386–394.

Rones, M., & Hoagwood, K. (2000). School-based mental health services: A research review. *Clinical Child and Family Psychology Review, 3,* 223–241.

Sanders, S., Jacobson, J. M., & Ting, L. (2008). Preparing for the inevitable: Training social workers to cope with client suicide. *Journal of Teaching in Social Work, 28,* 1–18.

Shanklin, S. L., Brener, N., McManus, T., Kinchen, S., & Kann, L. (2007). *Youth risk behavior survey: 2005 middle school.* Retrieved from http://www.cdc.gov/HealthyYouth/yrbs/middleschool2005/index.htm

Singer, J. B. (2006). Making stone soup: Evidence-based practice for a suicidal youth with comorbid attention-deficit/hyperactivity disorder and major depressive disorder. *Brief Treatment and Crisis Intervention, 6,* 234–247.

U.S. Department of Health and Human Services. (2001). *National strategy for suicide prevention: Goals and objectives for action.* Washington, DC: U.S. Government Printing office.

Vander Stoep, A., McCauley, E., Flynn, C., & Stone, A. (2009). Thoughts of death and suicide in early adolescence. *Suicide and Life-Threatening Behaviors, 39,* 599–613.

Walls, N. E., Freedenthal, S., & Wisneski, H. (2008). Suicidal ideation and attempts among sexual minority youths receiving social services. *Social Work, 53,* 21–29.

Wampold, B. E. (2001). *The great psychotherapy debate: Models, methods, and findings.* Mahwah, NJ: Laurence Erlbaum Associates.

Ward, B. R. (1995). The school's role in the prevention of youth suicide. *Social Work in Education, 17,* 92–100.

Whitted, K. S., & Dupper, D. R. (2005). Best practices for preventing or reducing bullying in schools. *Children & Schools, 27,* 167–175.

About the authors: *Jonathan B. Singer*, Ph.D., LCSW, is assistant professor, School of Social Work, Temple University, 1301 Cecil B. More Avenue, Philadelphia, PA 19122 (e-mail: jbsinger@temple.edu). *Karen Slovak*, Ph.D., is associate professor, Social Work, Ohio University Zanesville.

Demographic and Academic Trends in Drinking Patterns and Alcohol-Related Problems[1]

Researchers and college administrators alike have engaged in a continuing effort to better understand the nature of college drinking and best practices for prevention and intervention. Alcohol abuse and [5] alcohol-related problems are considered among the most serious public health threats on American college campuses (e.g., Wechsler, Davenport, Dowdall, Moeykens, & Castillo, 1994). Some national surveys suggest 44% of college students engage in heavy episodic [10] drinking at least occasionally (Wechsler, Molnar, Davenport, & Baer, 1999). Further, the misuse of alcohol by college students is associated with a wide variety of negative effects, such as date rape, violent behavior, poor academic performance, vandalism, injury, high-[15] risk sexual behavior (Eigen, 1991; Wechsler & Isaac, 1991; Presley, Meilman, & Lyerla, 1995), and even death.

The Effect of Demographic Characteristics on College Drinking

Gender

Male gender is often cited as a significant risk factor for heavy drinking in college. College men con-[20] sistently have been found to drink more than college females (Humara & Sherman, 2004; Perkins, 1992). Measures of national trends among college students show more than twice as many males than females report drinking 10 or more drinks per week (O'Malley [25] & Johnston, 2002). Further, men tend to binge drink and to report more alcohol-related problems than females as well (Wechsler, Dowdall, Davenport, & Castillo, 1995). Previous research has shown that men tend to perceive more permissive social and institu-[30] tional drinking norms relative to women and, consequently, present higher drinking rates than women. In addition to differences in perceptions, misperceptions, and behavior, there are significant differences in alcohol expectancies as well (Read, Wood, Lejuez, Palfai, [35] & Slack, 2004).

Ethnicity

Non-White ethnicity has been identified as a risk factor of alcoholism in the general population, but this association does not hold with the college population (Kahler, Read, Wood, & Palfai, 2003). In fact, across [40] four national surveys of college students, the data consistently show White students reporting the highest prevalence of heavy drinking, followed by Hispanic and Black students, respectively (O'Malley & Johnston, 2002). This pattern has been found in several na-[45] tional surveys of high-school-aged youth, such as the YRBS (Centers for Disease Control and Prevention, 2000, 2004) and MTF (Johnston, O'Malley, Bachman, & Schulenberg, 2004). Research that equates ethnicity and nationality, however, may not accurately capture [50] the drinking behavior of ethnic groups. For example, research that combines people of Asian origin into a single ethnicity may improperly describe groups that present significantly different drinking patterns, such as the Chinese and Koreans (Luczak, Wall, Shea, [55] Byun, & Carr, 2001).

Age

Heavy drinking among college students tends to increase as they approach legal drinking age and levels off after they reach legal drinking age. This pattern tends to result in alcohol abuse and underage drinking [60] by students younger than age 21 (Wechsler, Lee, Nelson, & Kuo, 2002). It is important to note, however, that college students of legal age present alcohol abuse problems as well, albeit less severe relative to underage students.

The Effect of Social and Academic Characteristics on College Drinking

Academic Class Level

[65] Consistent with the pattern implied by age, college freshmen present the most significant drinking problems on college campuses (Del Boca, Darkes, Greenbaum, & Goldman, 2004). Data on this point, however, are inconsistent. Core Alcohol and Drug [70] Survey (Core Institute, 2005) data, for example, suggested that college freshmen binge-drank less than their upper-class peers in 2004. The survey further indicated that freshmen were the lowest percentage of binge drinkers (45.3%), lower than sophomores [75] (49.1%), juniors (51.6%), and seniors (52.8%), respectively. Reports of average number of drinks by class level followed the same pattern.

---

[1] Literature review excerpt from Taylor, D. M., Johnson, M. B., Voas, R. B., & Turrisi, R. (2006). Demographic and academic trends in drinking patterns and alcohol-related problems on dry college campuses. *Journal of Alcohol and Drug Education, 50,* 35–54. Copyright © 2006 by the American Alcohol & Drug Information Foundation. All rights reserved. Reprinted with permission.

Furthermore, during high school, noncollege-bound students engage in heavy drinking more than college-bound students; however, after high school, noncollege-bound students show only a moderate increase in the prevalence of heavy drinking. Conversely, college-bound students drink significantly more after high school years, such that the prevalence of heavy drinking surpasses noncollege-bound students (O'Malley & Johnston, 2002).

Greek Status

Fraternity and sorority status has long been known to be a significant risk factor for college drinking (Larimer, Turner, Mallett, & Geisner, 2004). Greeks tend to drink more and to present more alcohol-related problems. As with college freshmen, many universities have designed alcohol-related prevention programs targeting this unique risk group. Further, research shows that the social and normative factors that lead to excessive drinking among Greeks are quite different from factors affecting the campus at large (Baer, 1994; Sher, Bartholow, & Nanda, 2001).

Academic Performance

College drinking can severely interfere with academic performance (Higher Education Center, 1997). A national survey of nearly 37,000 students at 66 four-year institutions revealed a strong relationship between alcohol consumption and grades (Presley, Meilman, Cashin, & Lyerla, 1996); whereas students with an A average consumed a little more than three drinks per week, B students had almost five drinks, C students more than six drinks, and D or F students reported nine drinks. Further, a survey of college administrators indicated their belief that alcohol is involved in 38% of cases of lack of academic success and 29% of cases of student attrition (Anderson & Gadaleto, 1997).

Drinking Behavior of Students on Dry Campuses

Although alcohol consumption in general represents a significant administration and policy problem on college campuses, underage and binge drinking are particularly troublesome for college administrators. In fact, underage drinking and binge drinking on college campuses have been described as a national public health crisis in research, media coverage, and by many government agencies (Wechsler, Molnar, Davenport, & Baer, 1999). Administrators have responded with an increase in prevention efforts and with the introduction of new prevention technologies (Wechsler et al., 2002). Although decreasing in number, many college campuses are completely dry or only allow alcohol on campus under very limited conditions and on a few modest occasions. To what extent do these measures buffer students from the detrimental effects of college drinking that is commonly found on other campuses? In short, how effective are restricted campus alcohol policies in reducing alcohol abuse and alcohol-related problems relative to general patterns found on U.S. college campuses?

College students vary significantly in their drinking patterns and associated problems; many demographic, academic, and social characteristics account for the variance. Campus alcohol policies may do little to counter national trends in college drinking. This research will describe the combined results of two surveys presented on two dry campuses in the western United States. Based on five years and nine semesters of survey data (2000–2004)[2] from two western universities, this report describes how various demographic and academic characteristics are associated with college drinking. Comparisons will be made between trends found in these data and research describing national trends.

References

Anderson, D. S., & Gadaleto, A. F. (1997). *Results of the 1997 college alcohol survey: Comparison with 1994 results and baseline year*. Fairfax, VA: George Mason University.

Baer, J. S. (1994). Effects of college residence on perceived norms for alcohol consumption: An examination of the first year in college. *Psychology of Addictive Behaviors, 8*, 43–50.

Centers for Disease Control and Prevention. (2000). *Youth risk behavior surveillance—United States, 1999*. Morbidity and Mortality Weekly Report (CDC Surveillance Summaries), 49(SS-5).

Centers for Disease Control and Prevention. (2004). *Youth risk behavior surveillance—United States, 2003*. Morbidity and Mortality Weekly Report, 53(SS-2).

Core Institute. (2005). *Measuring change, delivering results* [Online]. Southern Illinois University Carbondale. Accessed June 2005, from http://www.siu.edu/departments/coreinst/public_html/

Del Boca, F. K., Darkes, J., Greenbaum, P. E., & Goldman, M. S. (2004). Up close and personal: Temporal variability in the drinking of individual college students during their first year. *Journal of Consulting and Clinical Psychology, 72*(2), 155–164.

Eigen, L. D. (1991). *Alcohol practices, policies, and potentials of American colleges and universities: An OSAP White Paper*.

Higher Education Center. (1997). *College academic performance and alcohol and other drug use*. Newton, MA: Infofacts Resources.

Humara, M. J., & Sherman, M. F. (2004). Situational determinants of alcohol abuse among Caucasian and African American college students. *Addictive Behaviors, 24*(1), 135–158.

Johnston, L. D., O'Malley, P. M., Bachman, J. G., & Schulenberg, J. E. (2004). *Monitoring the future, national survey results on adolescent drug use: Overview of key findings, 2003*. Bethesda, MD: National Institute on Drug Abuse, U.S. Department of Health and Human Services, Public Health Service, National Institutes of Health.

Kahler, C. W., Read, J. P., Wood, M. D., & Palfai, T. P. (2003). Social environmental selection as a mediator of gender, ethnic, and personality effects on college student drinking. *Psychology of Addictive Behaviors, 17*(3), 226–234.

Larimer, M. E., Turner, A. P., Mallett, K. A., & Geisner, I. M. (2004). Predicting drinking behavior and alcohol-related problems among fraternity and sorority members: Examining the role of descriptive and injunctive norms. *Psychology of Addictive Behaviors, 18*(3), 203–212.

Luczak, S. E., Wall, T. L., Shea, S. H., Byun, S. M., & Carr, L. G. (2001). Binge drinking in Chinese, Korean, and White college students: Genetic and ethnic group differences. *Psychology of Addictive Behaviors, 15*(4), 306–309.

O'Malley, P. M., & Johnston, L. D. (2002). Epidemiology of alcohol and other drug use among American college students. *Journal of Studies on Alcohol* (Suppl. 14), 23–39.

Perkins, H. W. (1992). Gender patterns in consequences of collegiate alcohol abuse: A 10-year study of trends in an undergraduate population. *Journal of Studies on Alcohol, 53*(5), 458–462.

---

[2] Data, however, were not collected in the spring semester of 2001.

Presley, C. A., Meilman, P. W., Cashin, J. R., & Lyerla, R. (1996). *Alcohol and drugs on American college campuses: Use, consequences, and perceptions of the campus environment.* Volume III: 1991–1993. Carbondale, IL: Southern Illinois University at Carbondale, Core Institute.

Presley, C. A., Meilman, P. W., & Lyerla, R. (1995). *Alcohol on American college campuses: Use, consequences, and perceptions of the campus environment.* (Vol. 2). Carbondale, IL: The CORE Institute Student Health Programs, Southern Illinois University at Carbondale.

Read, J. P., Wood, M. D., Lejuez, C. W., Palfai, T. P., & Slack, M. (2004). Gender, alcohol consumption, and differing alcohol expectancy dimensions in college drinkers. *Experimental and Clinical Psychopharmacology, 12*(4), 298–308.

Sher, K. J., Bartholow, B. D., & Nanda, S. (2001). Short- and long-term effects of fraternity and sorority membership on heavy drinking: A social norms perspective. *Psychology of Addictive Behaviors, 15*(1), 42–51.

Wechsler, H., Davenport, A., Dowdall, G., Moeykens, B., & Castillo, S. (1994). Health and behavioral consequences of binge drinking in college: A national survey of students at 140 campuses. *Journal of the American Medical Association, 272*(21), 1672–1677.

Wechsler, H., Dowdall, G. W., Davenport, A., & Castillo, S. (1995). Correlates of college student binge drinking. *American Journal of Public Health, 85*(7), 921–926.

Wechsler, H., Isaac, N. (1991). *Alcohol and the college freshman: "Binge" drinking and associated problems*: A report to the AAA Foundation for Traffic Safety.

Wechsler, H., Lee, J. E., Nelson, T. F., & Kuo, M. (2002). Underage college students' drinking behavior, access to alcohol, and the influence of deterrence policies. Findings from the Harvard School of Public Health College Alcohol Study. *Journal of American College Health, 50*(5), 223–236.

Wechsler, H., Molnar, B. E., Davenport, A. E., & Baer, J. S. (1999). College alcohol use: A full or empty glass? *Journal of American College Health, 47,* 247–252.

About the authors: *Dexter M. Taylor*, Associate Research Scientist, Pacific Institute for Research and Evaluation, Calverton, Maryland. *Mark B. Johnson*, Research Scientist, Pacific Institute for Research and Evaluation, Calverton, Maryland. *Robert B. Voas*, Senior Research Scientist, Pacific Institute for Research and Evaluation, Calverton, Maryland. *Robert Turrisi*, Department of Biobehavioral Health & Prevention Research Center, The Pennsylvania State University, University Park, Pennsylvania.

Acknowledgment: The authors would like to thank the National Institute on Alcohol Abuse and Alcoholism (NIAAA) for their research support on grant numbers R37 AA12972, R37 AA12972-03S1, and K05 AA014260.

Address correspondence to: Dexter M. Taylor, Ph.D., Pacific Institute for Research and Evaluation, 11710 Beltsville Drive, Suite 125, Calverton, MD 20705-3102. E-mail: taylor@pire.org

Notes

Overnight Stays and Children's Relationships With Resident and Nonresident Parents After Divorce[1]

The assumption that the amount and frequency of children's contact with their nonresident parents (mostly fathers) is a significant factor in children's postseparation adjustment and well-being has been challenged by recent findings that it is not the frequency or quantity of contact that is important but the quality of the contact and what they do together (Amato & Gilbreth, 1999; Furstenberg & Cherlin, 1991; King & Sobolewski, 2006; Pryor & Rodgers, 2001; Stewart, 2003; Whiteside & Becker, 2000). Although the amount of time per se may not be the critical factor, it is likely that some contact arrangements and ways of distributing time may facilitate quality parenting and closer relationships between nonresident parents and their children. As one multidisciplinary group of 18 experts noted,

> Time distribution arrangements that ensure the involvement of both parents in important aspects of their children's everyday lives and routines—including bedtime and waking rituals, transitions to and from school, extracurricular and recreational activities—are likely to keep nonresident parents playing psychologically important and central roles in the lives of their children. (Lamb, Sternberg, & Thompson, 1997, p. 393)

For this reason, overnight stays and holiday stays may be an important means for nonresident parents maintaining "real" parenting relationships with potential benefits both for children and their nonresident parents. For children, overnight stays may facilitate involvement by their nonresident parents and foster closer and more enduring relationships; overnight stays may also help children feel that they have two homes rather than feel like visitors in one (Caruana & Smyth, 2004). Closer relationships and more authoritative parenting by nonresident parents have in turn been found to be associated with better medium- and long-term outcomes for children (Amato & Gilbreth, 1999; Aquilino, 2006; Dunn, 2004; King & Sobolewski, 2006; Manning & Lamb, 2003; White & Gilbreth, 2001).

For nonresident parents, involvement in their children's daily activities, including both routine and special moments, is likely to be more rewarding and sustaining than the more constrained and predominantly leisure activities of daytime-only contact (Hawthorne, 2005; Smyth, 2005; Stewart, 1999a). Two studies (one in Australia and one in the United States) indicate that contact involving overnight stays is more stable and more likely to endure over time than contact involving daytime-only visits (Gibson, 1992; Maccoby & Mnookin, 1992). In another Australian study, nonresident fathers with more overnight contact were more satisfied with the contact arrangements than those with day-only contact (Parkinson & Smyth, 2004; Smyth, 2005). Significantly, resident mothers whose children stayed overnight at least 18 nights per year were also more satisfied than those with little or no overnight contact, suggesting that they also may benefit from some respite from ongoing caregiving responsibilities (Caruana & Smyth, 2004; Funder, Harrison, & Weston, 1993).

There is, however, a paucity of evidence about the link between overnight stays and the quality of the relationship between nonresident parents and their children, the possible impact on the resident parent-child relationship, and any effect on the child's well-being. Little is also known about what factors may be associated with or predispose overnight stay arrangements. This is because few studies have specifically examined and separated out overnight stays or extended visits from daytime-only contact (Clarke-Stewart & Hayward, 1996; King, Harris, & Heard, 2004; Seltzer & Brandreth, 1994). As Smyth and Ferro (2002) point out, there is a lack of data "on some of the most rudimentary components of parent-child contact, such as the distinction between day-only contact versus sleepovers" (p. 54) and holiday versus term-time arrangements. Where information on overnight contact has been collected, it has often been part of a combined measure of contact that includes other forms of contact (in-person day-only contact and telephone contact; King, 2006; Menning, 2006), or the distribution of overnight stays over the year was very low.

The findings of the few studies that have analyzed the association between overnight stays and the quality of the nonresident parent-child relationship or outcomes for the children are mixed and, with the exception of Fabricius (2003) and Stewart (2003), have involved infants (Pruett, Ebling, & Insabella, 2004; Solomon & George, 1999). This study therefore fo-

---

[1] Literature review excerpt from Cashmore, J., Parkinson, P., & Taylor, A. (2008). Overnight stays and children's relationships with resident and nonresident parents after divorce. *Journal of Family Issues, 29,* 707–733. Copyright © 2008 by Sage Publications. All rights reserved. Reprinted with permission.

cused on three questions. First, what factors are asso- 145
ciated with an increased likelihood that children will
stay overnight with their nonresident parents? Second,
are overnight and extended stays, compared to
95 daytime-only contact, associated with greater perceived involvement and closer relationships between 150
children and their nonresident parents? If so, is this
association still significant after taking account of the
overall frequency of contact and factors such as con-
100 flict that may affect the likelihood of overnight contact? Third, is there any association between the 155
amount and type of contact (overnight stays or daytime-only contact) and the relationship between the
resident parent and the child? The data come from a
105 national study involving children's reports on the quality of their relationships with both their resident and 160
nonresident parents and the frequency and type of contact as well as the reports of their resident parents on
contact and their relationships with their children.

Factors Associated With Overnight Stays
165
110 Only a few studies have focused specifically on
overnight contact, but the findings in relation to various aspects of contact (mostly frequency or regularity)
indicate that a number of factors either have been or
are likely to be associated with overnight stays. Sev-
115 eral are characteristics of the child (age, gender, and 170
ethnicity), and others are characteristics of the interparental relationship (cooperative or conflictual parenting and trust) or the preseparation or postseparation
period and arrangements (involvement in parenting by
120 the nonresident parent before the separation, distance 175
between the parents' homes, and time since the separation).

The child's age is an obvious factor, with considerable debate on the effects on very young children of
125 overnight stays and being separated from their mothers 180
(Biringen et al., 2002; Gould & Stahl, 2001; Lamb &
Kelly, 2001; Solomon & Biringen, 2001; Warshak,
2002) but with little empirical evidence as yet (Pruett
et al., 2004; Solomon & George, 1999). In contrast to
130 the concern about overnight stays for infants and 185
young children, there has been little debate about the
merits or possible benefits of overnight stays for older
children and adolescents. Overnight stays may, for
example, provide the opportunity for nonresident par-
135 ents to engage with their adolescent children in more 190
routine activities and to have more unstructured time
to build the social capital necessary for positive outcomes and the successful transition to adulthood
(Coleman, 1988; Dubas & Gerris, 2002; King et al.,
140 2004). 195

The limited data on the frequency of overnight
stays indicate, however, that many adolescents do not
stay overnight, partly because of competing social
activities (Maccoby & Mnookin, 1992). In the United

States, just over 40% of 12- to 18-year-olds in the
1994–1996 National Longitudinal Study of Adolescent
Health reported that they had stayed overnight with
their nonresident fathers over the past 12 months,
58.5% of 12- to 18-year-olds reported that they never
stayed overnight with their nonresident fathers, and
23.5% did so only once or several times in the previous year; only 18% stayed overnight on a monthly
basis or more (Stewart, 2003).[2] Similarly, 45% of 12-
to 14-year-olds and 57% of 15- to 17-year-olds in a
nationally representative study in Australia never
stayed overnight (Australian Bureau of Statistics,
2006).

There do not appear to be any specific findings in
relation to child gender and overnight stays. Several
studies, however, have reported that nonresident fathers have more contact and more frequent and longer
visits with sons than with daughters (King et al., 2004;
Manning & Smock, 1999; Simpson, McCarthy, &
Walker, 1995) and that sons report being closer to their
nonresident fathers compared to what daughters report
(King et al., 2004; Sobolewski & King, 2005).

Several characteristics of the parental relationship have consistently been associated with the likelihood or frequency of contact between nonresident parents and their children. A number of studies have
found that the greater the cooperation between the
parents, the more contact there is and the more involved fathers are with their children (Ahrons &
Miller, 1993; Arditti & Bickley, 1996; Dunn, 2004;
Furstenberg & Nord, 1985; Pryor & Rodgers, 2001;
Simpson et al., 1995; Sobolewski & King, 2005;
Welsh, Buchanan, Flouri, & Lewis, 2004; Whiteside &
Becker, 2000). Trust and a positive view of nonresident fathers as parents were also associated with the
frequency of contact (Funder et al., 1993) and with the
likelihood of overnight stays in particular (Caruana &
Smyth, 2004; Maccoby & Mnookin, 1992). Maccoby
and Mnookin (1992) found, for example, that children
were less likely to stay overnight with their nonresident fathers if their mothers expressed misgivings
about the environment of the fathers' households than
if they did not (36% compared to 53%). In addition,
children were also more likely to stay overnight if
mothers rated the fathers as more involved before the
separation and less likely if the parents were not married prior to the separation or had not lived together
(Cooksey & Craig, 1998).

The picture in relation to interparental conflict is,
however, more mixed, with some studies indicating a
negative correlation between conflict and father-child

---

[2] The figures in the 1997 National Longitudinal Survey of
Youth in the United States were considerably lower; only
between a third and a quarter of 12- to 18-year-olds reported
any overnights with their nonresident fathers in the previous
12 months (Argys et al., 2007).

contact but others reporting little or no association (Dunn, 2004; Simpson et al., 1995; Sobolewski & King, 2005) or even a positive correlation (Amato & Rezac, 1994).

200   The physical distance between parents' homes has also been identified as a factor that makes contact and involvement more difficult and less likely for non-resident parents (Clarke-Stewart & Hayward, 1996; Cooksey & Craig, 1998). It is possible, however, that

205 when there are significant distances involved, over-night contact may be more likely and indeed a logisti-cally necessary part of contact following relocation (Pryor & Rodgers, 2001; Simpson et al., 1995). As Sobolewski and King (2005) point out, however, the

210 "direction of causality is particularly unclear with re-gard to distance" because uninvolved fathers may also be more likely to move farther away from their former partners and their children (p. 1200).

Other factors associated with overnight stays or

215 with overall contact include the father's employment status and level of education, the father's level of in-volvement with child rearing before the separation, and whether either parent has repartnered and has new children in the household (Maccoby & Mnookin,

220 1992). Being unemployed or having a low income means that nonresident parents may not be able to af-ford housing to accommodate their children, and hav-ing new children in the household increases the com-petition for time and space (Caruana & Smyth, 2004;

225 Parkinson & Smyth, 2003; Simpson et al., 1995). Both resident and nonresident parents in a large-scale Aus-tralian study cited lack of suitable accommodation and physical distance as reasons for children having day-only rather than overnight contact, but the more com-

230 monly cited factors were the child's age and choice and relational issues (conflict between the parents, concerns about the children's safety and well-being, and perceived obstruction or disinterest).

Association Between Overnight Stays and Quality of the Nonresident Parent-Child Relationship

A positive, but not necessarily strong, link be-

235 tween the frequency of contact and the quality of the relationship is expected on the basis of theories con-cerned with relationships and social capital in families (Berscheid & Peplau, 1983; Coleman, 1988; Day & Acock, 2004; Homans, 1951/1992). This association

240 has been confirmed by research findings, but the na-ture of the association and direction of effect is not clear (Amato & Gilbreth, 1999; Dunn, 2004). Al-though greater contact may foster greater emotional closeness and more involvement by nonresident par-

245 ents in the lives of their children, those who have closer relationships are also likely to seek more contact (Dunn, Cheng, O'Connor, & Bridges, 2004). Other factors may also underlie or mediate any association

between contact (in particular, overnight stays) and

250 children's relationships with their nonresident parents.

Evidence about the strength of the association is also somewhat mixed. On one hand, a number of stud-ies have reported strong correlations between the fre-quency of contact and the quality of the relationship

255 between nonresident fathers and their children (Clarke-Stewart & Hayward, 1996; Fabricius, 2003; King, 2006; Sobolewski & King, 2005). Others have found more modest correlations (Buchanan, Maccoby, & Dornbusch, 1996; Furstenberg & Nord, 1985; White-

260 side & Becker, 2000). But, as Sobolewski and King (2005) point out, these studies differ in terms of who reported (mother or child or a combination), using what measures, and whether they include or exclude from the analyses children who have had little or no

265 contact with their nonresident parents.[3]

More specifically, several studies that reported data on the relationship between overnight stays and the quality of the nonresident parent-child relationship found quite robust associations. Clarke-Stewart and

270 Hayward (1996) reported significantly more positive relationships with nonresident parents (based on a combination of resident parent and child measures) when children age 5 to 13 had more frequent and longer visits (on a scale from a few hours to longer

275 than a week), engaged in more activities, and spent holidays with their nonresident parents. Fabricius (2003) reported a dramatic increase in how close stu-dents felt to their fathers as the amount of time they spent living with them increased.

Association Between Contact and Overnight Stays and Quality of the Resident Parent-Child Relationship

280   The nonresident parent-child relationship is one of a number of coexisting relationships in the post-separation family network (Dunn, 2004; White & Gil-breth, 2001). It is therefore important to take account of any effect on or association with the child's other primary relationship—that with the resident parent.

285 The conclusion from several studies is that more con-tact and better nonresident parent-child relationships do not come at a cost to the resident parent-child rela-tionship (Fabricius, 2003; Furstenberg & Nord, 1985;

290 Maccoby, Buchanan, Mnookin, & Dornbusch, 1993). Indeed, children in one study reported having better relationships with both parents when they had contact that involved a wide range of activities and holidays

---

[3] Using mothers' reports of father-child contact ($r = .59$) resulted in a lower correlation than using the children's re-ports on both contact and relationship quality ($r = .78$); ex-cluding adolescents who had no contact with their nonresi-dent fathers also resulted in a lower correlation ($r = .55$; Sobolewski & King, 2005, p. 1203).

spent with their nonresident parents (Clarke-Stewart &
295 Hayward, 1996).

Although these studies do not indicate causality
or even any direction of effect, there are several reasons why more contact, and overnight stays, and a
better relationship between children and their nonresi-
300 dent parents might be beneficial for resident parents
and their own relationships with their children. First,
overnight stays allow resident parents to have a break
from the full-time care of their children (Clarke-
Stewart & Hayward, 1996) and require the other par-
305 ent to invest in more full-service parenting. In the absence of conflict over child-rearing issues, this might
avert the resident parent from feeling resentful that she
or he is left with the routine responsibilities of parenting while the nonresident parent can be the fun parent
310 (Warshak, 2000b).

Second, there is also ample evidence that children want more contact with their nonresident parents,
so facilitating this may make children happier with
their situations and with both parents. On the other
315 hand, one study found that resident mothers were more
satisfied with their relationships with their adolescent
children when the children had no contact and reported
being not at all close to their nonresident parents
(Menning, 2006). It is therefore useful to include re-
320 ports by both the children and their resident parents
about the quality of the relationship rather than rely on
one report only. In particular, there is good reason to
rely on children's reports of their relationships with
their parents rather than those of their parents (King,
325 2006; Maccoby et al., 1993; Sobolewski & King,
2005).

References

Ahrons, C. R., & Miller, R. B. (1993). The effect of the postdivorce relationship on paternal involvement: A longitudinal analysis. *American Journal of
Orthopsychiatry, 63*, 441–450.

Amato, P., & Gilbreth, J. (1999). Nonresident fathers and children's well-
being: A meta-analysis. *Journal of Marriage and Family, 61*, 557–573.

Amato, P. R., & Rezac, S. J. (1994). Contact with nonresident parents, interparental conflict, and children's behavior. *Journal of Family Issues, 15*,
191–207.

Aquilino, W. S. (2006). The noncustodial father-child relationship from adolescence into young adulthood. *Journal of Marriage and Family, 68*, 929–
946.

Arditti, J., & Bickley, P. (1996). Fathers' involvement in mothers' parenting
stress postdivorce. *Journal of Divorce and Remarriage, 26*, 1–23.

Argys, A., Peters, E., Cook, S., Garasky, S., Nepomnyaschy, L., & Sorensen,
E. (2007). Measuring contact between children and nonresident fathers. In
S. L. Hofferth & L. M. Casper (Eds.), *Handbook of measurement issues in
family research* (pp. 375–398). Mahwah, NJ: Lawrence Erlbaum.

Australian Bureau of Statistics. (2006). *Australian social trends, 2006*. Retrieved December 2006, from http://www.abs.gov.au/AUSSTATS/abs
@.nsf/DetailsPage/4102.02006?OpenDocument

Berscheid, E., & Peplau, L. A. (1983). The emerging science of relationships.
In H. H. Kelly et al. (Eds.), *Close relationships* (pp. 1–19). New York:
Freeman.

Biringen, Z., Greve-Spees, J., Howard, W., Leith, D., Tanner, L., Moore, S., et
al. (2002). Commentary and response to articles in previous issues: Commentary on Warshak's "Blanket restrictions: Overnight contact between
parents and young children." *Family and Conciliation Courts Review, 40*,
204–207.

Buchanan, C. M., Maccoby, E. E., & Dornbusch, S. M. (1996). *Adolescents
after divorce*. Cambridge, MA: Harvard University Press.

Caruana, C., & Smyth, B. (2004). Daytime-only contact. In B. Smyth (Ed.),
Parent-child contact and post separation and parenting arrangements (pp.
69–84). Melbourne: Australian Institute of Family Studies.

Clarke-Stewart, K. A., & Hayward, C. (1996). Advantages of father custody
and contact for the psychological well-being of school-age children. *Journal of Applied Developmental Psychology, 17*, 239–270.

Coleman, J. S. (1988). Social capital in the creation of human capital. *American Journal of Sociology, 94*(Suppl.), S95–S120.

Cooksey, E. C., & Craig, P. H. (1998). Parenting from a distance: The effects
of paternal characteristics on contact between the nonresidential fathers and
their children. *Demography, 35*, 187–200.

Day, R. D., & Acock, A. (2004). Youth ratings of family processes and father
role performance of resident and nonresident fathers. In R. D. Day & M. E.
Lamb (Eds.), *Conceptualizing and measuring father involvement* (pp. 273–
292). Mahwah, NJ: Lawrence Erlbaum.

Dubas, J. S., & Gerris, J. R. M. (2002). Longitudinal changes in time parents
spend in activities with their adolescent children as a function of child age,
paternal status, and gender. *Journal of Family Psychology, 16*, 415–427.

Dunn, J. (2004). Annotation: Children's relationships with their nonresident
fathers. *Journal of Child Psychology and Psychiatry, 45*, 659–671.

Dunn, J., Cheng, H., O'Connor, T. G., & Bridges, L. (2004). Children's perspectives on their relationships with their nonresident fathers: Influences,
outcomes and implications. *Journal of Child Psychology and Psychiatry,
45*, 553–566.

Fabricius, W. V. (2003). Listening to children of divorce: New findings that
diverge from Wallerstein, Lewis, and Blakeslee. *Family Relations, 52*, 385–
396.

Funder, K., Harrison, M., & Weston, R. (1993). *Settling down: Pathways of
parents after divorce*. Melbourne: Australian Institute of Family Studies.

Furstenberg, F., & Cherlin, A. (1991). *Divided families: What happens to
children when parents part*. Cambridge, MA: Harvard University Press.

Furstenberg, F., & Nord, C. W. (1985). Parenting apart: Patterns of childrear-
ing after marital disruption. *Journal of Marriage and Family, 47*, 893–904.

Gibson, J. (1992). *Non-custodial fathers and access patterns* (Research Report
No. 10). Canberra: Family Court of Australia.

Gould, J. W., & Stahl, P. M. (2001). Never paint by the numbers: A response
to Kelly & Lamb (2000), Solomon & Biringen (2001), and Lamb & Kelly
(2001). *Family and Conciliation Courts Review, 39*, 372–376.

Hawthorne, B. (2005, February). *Australian men's experience of nonresident
fathering*. Paper presented at the Australian Institute of Family Studies
Conference, Melbourne. Retrieved January 20, 2007, from http://www.
aifs.gov.au/institute/afrc9/hawthorne.pdf

Homans, G. (1992). *The human group*. New Brunswick, NJ: Transaction.
(Original work published 1951.)

King, V. (2006). The antecedents and consequences of adolescents' relationships with stepfathers and nonresident fathers. *Journal of Marriage and
Family, 68*, 910–928.

King, V., Harris, K. M., & Heard, H. E. (2004). Racial and ethnic diversity in
nonresident father involvement. *Journal of Marriage and Family, 66*, 1–21.

King, V., & Sobolewski, J. M. (2006). Nonresident fathers' contributions to
adolescent well-being. *Journal of Marriage and Family, 68*, 537–557.

Lamb, M. E., & Kelly, J. B. (2001). The continuing debate about overnight
visitation: Using the empirical literature to guide the development of parenting plans for young children: A rejoinder to Solomon & Biringen. *Family
and Conciliation Courts Review, 39*, 365–371.

Lamb, M. E., Sternberg, R., & Thompson, R. A. (1997). The effects of divorce
and custody arrangements on children's behavior, development, and adjustment. *Family and Conciliation Courts Review, 35*, 393–404.

Maccoby, E. E., Buchanan, C. M., Mnookin, R. H., & Dornbusch, S. M.
(1993). Postdivorce roles of mothers and fathers in the lives of their children. *Journal of Family Psychology, 7*, 24–38.

Maccoby, E. E., & Mnookin, R. H. (1992). *Dividing the child: Social and
legal terms of custody*. Cambridge, MA: Harvard University Press.

Manning, W., & Smock, P. (1999). New families and nonresident father-child
visitation. *Social Forces, 78*, 87–116.

Manning, W. D., & Lamb, K. A. (2003). Adolescent well-being in cohabiting,
married, and single-parent families. *Journal of Marriage and Family, 65*,
876–893.

Menning, C. L. (2006). Nonresident fathering and school failure. *Journal of
Family Issues, 27*, 1356–1382.

Parkinson, P., & Smyth, B. (2003). *When the difference is night and day:
Some empirical insights into patterns of parent-child contact after separation*. Paper given at 8th Australian Institute of Family Studies Conference,
Melbourne, Australia. Available at http://www.aifs.gov.au/institute/afrc8/
papers.html#p

Parkinson, P., & Smyth, B. (2004). Satisfaction and dissatisfaction with
father-child contact arrangements in Australia. *Child and Family Law
Quarterly, 16*, 289–304.

Pruett, M. K., Ebling, R., & Insabella, G. (2004). Parenting plans and visitation: Critical aspects of parenting plans for young children: Interjecting data into the debate about overnights. *Family Court Review, 42*, 39–59.

Pryor, J., & Rodgers, B. (2001). *Children in changing families: Life after parental separation*. Melbourne, Australia: Blackwell.

Seltzer, J. A., & Brandreth, Y. (1994). What fathers say about involvement with children after separation. *Journal of Family Issues, 15*, 49–77.

Simpson, B., McCarthy, P., & Walker, J. (1995). *Being there: Fathers after divorce*. Rugby, UK: Relate Centre for Family Studies.

Smyth, B. (2005). Time to rethink time? The experience of children after divorce. *Family Matters, 71*, 4–10.

Smyth, B., & Ferro, A. (2002). When the difference is night and day. *Family Matters, 63*, 54–59.

Sobolewski, J. M., & King, V. (2005). The importance of the co-parental relationship for non-resident fathers' ties to children. *Journal of Marriage and Family, 67*, 1196–1212.

Solomon, J., & Biringen, Z. (2001). The continuing debate about overnight visitation: Another look at the developmental research: Commentary on Kelly and Lamb's "Using child development research to make appropriate custody and access decisions for young children." *Family and Conciliation Courts Review, 39*, 355–364.

Solomon, J., & George, C. (1999). The development of attachment in separated and divorced families: Effects of overnight visitation, parent and couple variables. *Attachment and Human Development, 1*, 2–33.

Stewart, S. (2003). Nonresident parenting and adolescent adjustment: The quality of nonresident father-child interaction. *Journal of Family Issues, 24*, 217–244.

Stewart, S. D. (1999a). Disneyland dads, Disneyland moms? How nonresidential parents spend time with absent children. *Journal of Family Issues, 20*, 539–556.

Warshak, R. A. (2000b). Blanket restrictions: Overnight contact between parents and young children. *Family and Conciliation Courts Review, 38*, 422–445.

Warshak, R. A. (2002). Who will be there when I cry in the night? Revisiting overnights—A rejoinder to Biringen et al. *Family and Conciliation Courts Review, 40*, 208–218.

Welsh, E., Buchanan, A., Flouri, E., & Lewis, J. (2004). *"Involved" fathering and child well-being: Fathers' involvement with their secondary-school-aged children*. York, UK: National Children's Bureau and Joseph's Foundation.

White, L., & Gilbreth, J. (2001). When children have two fathers: Effects of relationships with stepfathers and noncustodial fathers on adolescent outcomes. *Journal of Marriage and Family, 63*, 155–167.

Whiteside, M. F., & Becker, B. J. (2000). Parental factors and the younger child's post divorce adjustment: A meta-analysis with implications for parenting arrangements. *Journal of Family Psychology, 14*, 5–26.

Authors' note: The original data are from the Australian Divorce Transitions Project (ADTP) conducted by the Australian Institute of Family Studies and are available from the Australian Social Sciences Data Archive, Study No. DI042 and Study No. DI043. The principal investigators on the ADTP adult project (No. DI042) were Kathleen Funder, Grania Sheehan, Bruce Smyth, and Belinda Fehlberg, and on the children's study (No. DI043), Kathleen Funder and Grania Sheehan. Although the principal investigators bear no responsibility for the further analysis or interpretation of the data presented in this article, we acknowledge their valuable role in the conceptualization and conduct of the study, without which this article would not have been possible.

Acknowledgments: We are grateful to Bruce Smyth, Jacqueline Goodnow, and the reviewers for their constructive comments and criticism on earlier drafts of this article.

Address correspondence to: Judy Cashmore, Faculty of Law, University of Sydney, 173-175 Phillip Street, Sydney 2000, Australia. E-mail: j.cashmore@usyd.edu.au

Notes

MODEL LITERATURE REVIEW I

Language Brokering: An Integrative Review of the Literature[1]

ABSTRACT. This article reviews the literature in the area of language brokering. Language brokers are children of immigrant families who translate and interpret for their parents and other individuals. Results suggest that language brokers possess unique characteristics that make them suitable for their role as the family's translator and interpreter. Parents select the child language broker based on certain personal qualities. Language brokers translate and interpret a variety of documents in a variety of settings. There is not a clear understanding of the influence of language brokering on children's academic performance. There is not a clear understanding of how language brokering experiences help or harm the parent-child relationship. Further research is needed to better understand the role that language brokering plays in the lives and well-being of children.

When immigrant families first arrive in the United States, they must adapt to their new environment, learn a new language, and to some extent, become familiar with the beliefs, values, and customs of
5   a new culture. Thus, the process of acculturation begins immediately. For many of these families, this process is stressful and difficult to handle (Baptise, 1987; Rumbaut, 1994). To help ease the burden of this transition, immigrant parents tend to rely on their chil-
10   dren or their extended family to function effectively in American society. For example, once children become familiar with the English language, they often serve as translators and interpreters for their nonfluent parents and extended family. These children, commonly re-
15   ferred to as *language brokers,* are expected to assist their parents in very complex, "adult-like" situations— situations that may or may not be developmentally appropriate (McQuillan & Tse, 1995; Tse, 1995a, 1995b, 1996a; Valenzuela, 1999).
20   Although children have served as language brokers for centuries, relatively little empirical attention has been given to them. Only recently, for example, have social and behavioral scientists begun to seriously consider and study this important phenomenon.
25   Reasons for this are only speculative. Perhaps it's because, historically speaking, psychological theorizing and research has focused primarily on individuals and groups of individuals from middle-class, European American families. Fortunately, however, many fields
30   in the social sciences (e.g., psychology) have become increasingly diverse and pluralistic and, as a result, increasingly sensitive to issues that relate directly to ethnically diverse individuals, families, and communities.

35   Although using children to serve as translators and interpreters has been widely accepted among immigrant communities, it is still a controversial issue. In the year 2002, California lawmakers introduced a bill to the state legislature prohibiting children from trans-
40   lating and interpreting in medical, legal, and social service settings (Coleman, 2003). They argue that (a) children are not translating information accurately, (b) translating legal and medical information may negatively affect the parent-child relationship, and (c) de-
45   livering information to a child about a serious medical condition may be traumatizing to the child. Dr. Anne Foster-Rosales, an obstetrician at the University of California–San Francisco Medical Center, explained, "I've been in a situation where I had to give a diagno-
50   sis of cervical cancer, and I have a 12-year-old boy in the room translating" (p. 19A). Clearly, there are multiple sides to this issue, and the extent to which language brokering should be legislated is debatable. What is less debatable, however, is the need for sound,
55   rigorous research on this understudied topic.
Researchers define language brokers as children of immigrant families who translate and interpret for their parents, members of the family, teachers, neighbors, or other adults (McQuillan & Tse, 1995). In
60   addition, these children also serve as mediators in a variety of situations (DeMent & Buriel, 1999; Tse, 1996a). It is important to note here the distinction between translating and interpreting. Although translating and interpreting are often considered to be syn-
65   onymous, or identical constructs, they are, in actuality, quite different. Translating is perhaps best associated with written work, where the translator is believed to possess exceptional understanding of multiple languages, thus having the ability and skill to translate
70   documents, materials, and the like. Interpretation, on the other hand, is best associated with verbal communication, where the interpreter is believed to possess exceptional understanding of potentially nuanced and circumscribed "meanings" that may be conveyed in
75   ordinary social interactions (Westermeyer, 1989).
Language brokering is not merely bilingualism. Bialystok (2001) conceptualizes bilingualism as the

---

ability to speak two or more languages. Others define it as absolute fluency in two languages (Bloomfield, 1933) or the ability to function in each language according to given needs (Grosjean, 1989). Clearly, bilingualism deals with the ability to learn, to understand, and to speak two or more languages, whereas language brokering deals with, as noted earlier, the practices of translating and interpreting. Bilingual individuals choose to learn a new language as part of their curriculum, whereas language brokers learn a language for their own and their family's survival. Thus, for these reasons, the literature on the area of bilingualism was not included in this review.

That said, it is also important to note here that Tse (1996b) was the first to review the literature on language brokering using 12 studies/articles. In her review, she focused on language brokering within the context of home-school communication. Tse proposed that a potential reason teachers and immigrant parents may not have good communication is that children serve as the family's interpreter and/or mediator. She suggested that the information being sent from the home to school may not be coming from the parent but the child. For example, the child may alter or select the information given by the parents to the teacher. Similarly, the information received from school may not be delivered accurately to parents, because the child may report selectively, reporting only information that he or she believes to be relevant. Finally, Tse proposed that language brokers may express their stress in different ways at school. For instance, child language brokers may feel overwhelmed by the different responsibilities (i.e., translating and interpreting) that they have at home, which in turn may affect their academic performance. Teachers and school administrators should make an attempt to be informed on how language brokers may experience stress differently from local, first language English-speaking students.

Little is known, at this point, about the process of language brokering and its effects on children and their families. It is imperative that social scientists, educators, and policy makers address this particular subgroup of children, especially considering the ongoing changes in demographics within the United States. Hence, the purpose of this article is to integratively review the literature in this area. It will expand on Tse's (1996b) review, primarily by highlighting additional dimensions about the area of language brokering. To help focus the article and to provide an organizing framework, the following research questions will be addressed: (a) What has been published on the topic of language brokering? (b) What are typical characteristics, or qualities, of the language broker? (c) How is a child's cognitive development affected by language brokering? (d) Does language brokering influence children's academic performance? (e) How does language brokering affect the parent-child relationship? To answer these questions, a comprehensive, in-depth search of the literature was conducted.

Method

Inclusion-Exclusion Criteria

Given that little research has been conducted in the area of language brokering, inclusion criteria were liberal, including journal articles, conference papers, unpublished manuscripts, newsletter reports, books, book chapters, and dissertations. Studies that contained the words *language broker* or *language brokering* were considered. A separate search including the words *translator, interpreter, children,* and *adolescents* was also conducted. Resources that did not address issues related to language brokers were excluded.

Literature Search

Upon entering the keywords *language broker* and *language brokering,* the *PsychInfo* and *ERIC* databases identified 38 matches. The outcome of this search led to 6 articles, 2 *ERIC* documents, 3 book chapters, and a dissertation. The remaining 26 resources were excluded because they did not meet the above criteria. After back-checking each article, the *ERIC* documents, and the dissertation to identify other pertinent resources, 6 additional articles were identified. The second search using the keywords *translator, interpreter, children,* and *adolescents* led to 19 matches, but none of them met the inclusion criteria.

As an added step, three preeminent language brokering researchers were contacted. These researchers identified 3 additional journal articles and 2 unpublished manuscripts that met the inclusion criteria. Also during the peer-review process of this article, the editor of the journal provided a copy of a recent article about the area of language brokering. Thus, the total number of resources used in this review was 24. Table 1 includes a listing and summary of each of them.

Results

What Has Been Published on the Topic of Language Brokering?

The literature in the area of language brokering is, generally speaking, scarce. Fifty-seven percent of the available research is published in peer-reviewed journals, 17% is published as book chapters, and 26% are conference papers, dissertations, or *ERIC* documents. Language brokering is a common phenomenon among children of immigrant parents (Orellana, 2003). For example, in a study by Tse (1995b), 100% of Latino/Hispanic children reported serving as language brokers for their parents and translated and interpreted in a variety of settings. Despite this common phenomenon in immigrant families, studies on language brokers or language brokering did not emerge in earnest in the literature until the mid-1990s. Early studies

Review I Language Brokering: An Integrative Review of the Literature

Table 1
List of Sources Included in Review

Authors	N	Methodology	Type	Purpose
Buriel, Perez, DeMent, Chavez, & Moran (1998)	122	qualitative	journal article	*To examine the relation of language brokering on biculturalism, self-efficacy, and academic performance. *This study focused on participants who spoke Spanish and English.

Summary of Major Findings

*Language brokering was more frequent among females. *Language brokering, language brokering feelings were associated with academic self-efficacy. *Academic self-efficacy was the strongest predictor of academic performance, followed by biculturalism, and total language brokering. *Places of brokering were the strongest predictor on performance.

| Chao (2002) | 307 | quantitative | conference paper | *To expand the research on the development of immigrant children by examining acculturation issues that are most central to their experiences as immigrants, that of language acculturation. *This study focused on participants who spoke Mandarin, Spanish, and English. |

Summary of Major Findings

*Translating is less likely to be performed by one child as family size increases, but it is less likely to be shared by all the siblings in the household. *Chinese parents are more likely to rely on one child for language brokering than are Mexican parents. *Translating is more frequent among the oldest and among those with higher levels of fluency in the native language and among children with prosocial behaviors. *Child's age was positively related to levels of translating in the past month. *Translation received in the past month was uncorrelated with any of the relationship variables.

| Cohen, Moran-Ellis, & Smaje (1999) | 38 | qualitative | journal article | *To explore the views of general practitioners about the appropriateness of children undertaking a task of interpretation between the general practitioners and an adult patient in primary care consultations. *This study focused on participants who spoke a variety of Asian (e.g., Mandarin), African languages (e.g., Swahili), and English. |

Summary of Major Findings

*Children were used as interpreters when professional interpreters were not available. *Children's interpretations were used when patient needed to describe signs and/or symptoms. *General practitioners felt children who serve as translators may not know the correct medical terminology when translating for their parents and/or general practitioner. *General practitioners stated that it was unsatisfactory to use children as translators, especially when discussing sensitive information (e.g., personal or intimate problems). *Children serving as translators could have an effect on the normal dynamics of the parent-child relationship. *Children may become extremely stressed when learning about parents' health and/or sexual activities.

| DeMent & Buriel (1999) | 13 | qualitative | unpublished manuscript | *To investigate in great depth the area of language brokering using college immigrants and children of immigrant parents who recall their experiences as language brokers. *This study focused on participants who spoke Mandarin, Vietnamese, Spanish, and English. |

Summary of Major Findings

*Children started brokering not very long after they arrived in the United States. They translated in different settings (e.g., making appointments with the doctor and paying bills). *Children reported that their parents stressed the importance of getting an education. *Children reported that they have a desire to help their parents. They also reported that, at times, they felt inadequate, frustrated, and upset because of brokering. *Children served as teachers. They introduced their parents to American holidays, culture, and values. *Language brokering was conceived as an obligation and as a form of not letting their parents down.

| Diaz-Lazaro (2002) | 159 | quantitative | dissertation | *To evaluate how language brokering, acculturation, and gender affect family authority structure, parental locus of control, and adolescents' perceptions of their solving abilities. *This study focused on participants who spoke Spanish and English. |

Summary of Major Findings

*There was no association between language brokering, family authority, and parental locus of control. *There was no association between language brokering and adolescents' problem-solving abilities. *There were no gender differences in language brokering. *There was no association between language brokering and adolescents' level of acculturation.

Note. In the original, this table contained a summary of all 24 studies. To save space, only the first five are shown.

investigated the prevalence of language brokering among children of immigrant families. Instruments to measure this construct were also developed during this timeframe (Buriel, Perez, DeMent, Chavez, & Moran, 1998; Tse, 1996a). These studies revealed the following:

1. The majority of immigrant children and adolescents perform as language brokers (McQuillan & Tse, 1995; Orellana, 2003; Tse, 1995a, 1995b, 1996a).

2. Children may start brokering within 1 to 5 years of their arrival in the United States and may start brokering as young as 8 or 9 years of age (McQuillan & Tse, 1995; Tse, 1995a, 1996b).

3. Language brokers translate in a variety of settings, such as school, home, and the streets and they translate and interpret for their parents, other members of their family, and sometimes for school administrators (DeMent & Buriel, 1999; Gullingsrud, 1998; McQuillan & Tse, 1995; Orellana, Dorner, & Pulido, 2003; Shannon, 1990; Tse, 1995a, 1995b, 1996a; Valenzuela, 1999; Weisskirch, 2005; Weisskirch & Alva, 2002).

4. Documents that language brokers usually translate and interpret include notes and letters from school, bank/credit card statements, immigration forms, and job applications (DeMent & Buriel, 1999; McQuillan & Tse, 1995; Orellana, 2003; Tse, 1995a, 1995b; Valenzuela, 1999; Weisskirch, 2005; Weisskirch & Alva, 2002).

It is apparent that language brokers encounter a variety of situations where they are required to take the role of an adult. Given that these children are taking on such roles, one question that comes to mind is, "How do these children feel about their role as the family's translator and interpreter?" Studies on the feelings children have about language brokering report mixed results. Some of the research reveals that brokers see translating as something normal, something they do. These studies have also shown that children enjoy translating because it gives them feelings of pride and allows them to learn more about their first and second languages, as well as their culture (Orellana, 2003; Santiago, 2003; Shannon, 1990; Tse, 1995a, 1996b; Valdes, Chavez, & Angelelli, 2003; Walinchowski, 2001; Weisskirch, 2005).

Other studies have reported findings that contradict those mentioned above. These studies have reported that language brokers experience feelings of frustration, embarrassment, or pressure to translate accurately (DeMent & Buriel, 1999; Love, 2003; McQuillan & Tse, 1995; Ng, 1998; Tse, 1995a; Valenzuela, 1999; Weisskirch & Alva, 2002). Consequently, some researchers argue that using children as translators and interpreters may affect the development of these children negatively. For example, Umaña-

Taylor (2003) argues that language brokers take on adult roles during their adolescence and these experiences could have negative implications for their identity development. Others argue that language brokers do not find their experiences helpful or enjoyable, and for the majority of the time, they did not feel good about translating and interpreting (Weisskirch & Alva, 2002).

The literature presented in this section provides an introductory discussion of the different situations children experience when they serve as the family's translator and interpreter. It is evident that these children help their parents and other adults to understand a great variety of written documents and social interactions. Although these practices may be considered by some researchers as very positive or as a normative part of what these children are expected to do, others do not. It appears, then, that the area of language brokering is divided into two different camps. One camp believes that children serving as language brokers find the experience enjoyable and that it helps them learn more about their first and second languages. The other camp believes, in contrast, that children serving as language brokers find translating and interpreting stressful and a burden.

It is too early to decide which camp is correct, given that the majority of the studies presented in this section were more descriptive and did not include a large number of children of diverse backgrounds. For example, Orellana (2003) used survey data and case studies, but all of the participants were Spanish-speaking children. Another example is Weisskirch and Alva (2002), who based their results on a sample of 36 children of Latino/Hispanic descent.

What Are Typical Characteristics, or Qualities, of the Language Broker?

There are very few published studies that have attempted to clearly or fully describe the typical language broker. Thus, this section will aim to highlight characteristics of the language broker. Recent studies have used quantitative, qualitative, and mixed methods to answer this question. These studies reveal that children of immigrant families start their role as translator and interpreter shortly after their arrival in the United States (DeMent & Buriel, 1999; Valdes et al., 2003) and that they broker regardless of their place of birth (Tse, 1995a). The research shows (a) that these children usually start brokering between the ages of 8 and 12 (McQuillan & Tse, 1995; Tse, 1995a, 1995b, 1996a), (b) that they are usually the oldest child (Chao, 2002; Valdes et al., 2003), and (c) that brokers are predominantly female (Buriel et al., 1998; Love, 2003; McQuillan & Tse, 1995; Valenzuela, 1999; Weisskirch, 2005). These studies provide useful information on the characteristics of the children, yet there may be

290 other qualities that language brokers have developed that influence their parents to choose them for this important role. The few studies that have investigated such qualities suggest that these children tend to be fluent in English and Spanish, confident, extroverted,
295 good-natured, friendly, sociable, good listeners, able to provide great detail, and able to emphasize feelings and emotions when translating (Chao, 2002; DeMent & Buriel, 1999; Valdes et al., 2003; Valenzuela, 1999).

300   In sum, the research presented in this section highlights the characteristics of children who play the role of their family's interpreter and translator. We may conclude, based on this research, that language brokers possess qualities that allow them to interact in
305 a variety of settings with different types of people. Still, discrepancies and limitations exist in this literature. For example, a number of studies argue that language brokering is a female-dominated activity, whereas other studies have not found gender differ-
310 ences (Diaz-Lazaro, 2002). Moreover, the few qualitative and mixed methods studies that have been conducted failed to include more representative samples of children of immigrant families. The majority of the studies have been conducted with Latino/Hispanic
315 children, and only a few studies have included Vietnamese and Chinese children, thus severely limiting the applicability of the findings to the larger immigrant population in the United States.

How Is a Child's Cognitive Development Affected by Brokering?

     Studies on translation have reported that children
320 who speak two or more languages may translate and interpret information accurately (Harris & Sharewood, 1978). Language brokers tend to translate documents that require a high level of understanding, such as notes and letters from school, bank/credit card state-
325 ments, job applications, and government and insurance forms (DeMent & Buriel, 1999; McQuillan & Tse, 1995). There are researchers who argue that language brokers may, as a result, develop a more sophisticated vocabulary that could help them build their lexicons
330 (Halgunseth, 2003). Furthermore, studies have shown that language brokers use higher cognitive abilities and problem-solving abilities to comprehend and interpret these types of documents (Walinchowski, 2001). Children not only translate documents but they also serve
335 as mediators in conversations between their parents and first-language English speakers, such as at parent-teacher conferences and when paying utility bills, making doctor's appointments, visiting hospitals, and making trips to the post office (DeMent & Buriel,
340 1999; Halgunseth, 2003; McQuillan & Tse, 1995; Tse, 1995a, 1996a). It is evident that language brokers act as translators and interpreters in a variety of settings—

345 settings in which they must switch from being a child to assuming the role of the adult in order to translate and interpret for their parents or elders.

     The research suggests that language brokers develop linguistic abilities that monolingual children do not acquire, which may potentially help the child in-
350 teract in a more mature and adult manner (Diaz-Lazaro, 2002; Shannon, 1990). The few qualitative studies that have been conducted report that language brokers feel that translating and interpreting for their parents has allowed them to be more mature and inde-
355 pendent, meet more people, and increase their proficiency in both languages (Halgunseth, 2003; Valdes et al., 2003). Given that language brokers are translating and interpreting a variety of documents in different settings, they may also develop higher decision-
360 making strategies. These children not only develop higher cognitive abilities, but their decision-making may be considered more adultlike. Several researchers argue that language brokers are considered the decision maker not only for their parents but also for the
365 entire family (Diaz-Lazaro, 2002; McQuillan & Tse, 1995; Tse, 1995b; Valenzuela, 1999).

     It is interesting that research has shown that language brokers may be selective about the information they translate, especially for their parents. For exam-
370 ple, a number of children who translated notes from school for their parents often omitted information that was negative (DeMent & Buriel, 1999). Although this finding may call into question the accuracy of language brokers, we can only speculate that children are
375 omitting this type of information because they do not want to hurt or cause shame to their parents. In certain communal cultures, children's poor behavior is often interpreted by parents as dishonorable (Comas-Diaz, 1993; Sue & Sue, 1990).

     The literature presented in this section highlights
380 how child language brokers may acquire higher cognitive and decision-making abilities due to their brokering experiences. Although these studies highlight the benefits of brokering, they are still far from being widely accepted or definitive. There is simply not
385 enough evidence to support the hypothesis that translating and interpreting enhances cognitive development and decision-making abilities. More of these studies are needed to determine the nature of the relationship between language brokering and cognitive
390 development and decision-making abilities.

Does Language Brokering Influence Children's Academic Performance?

     It is a common belief in the United States that children of immigrant families do not perform well in academia due to a lack of encouragement from parents
395 (Evans & Anderson, 1973). Researchers who have studied the academic performance of children of im-

migrants have reported that individual and institutional factors are the primary reasons for dropping out or performing poorly—not parents' lack of encouragement (Rumberger & Rodriguez, 2002). The literature in the area of language brokering and academic performance provides mixed results. Earlier studies suggest that language brokering is not significantly correlated with academic performance. For example, using a sample of 35 Latino/Hispanic students, Tse (1995a) reported that there was no association between academic performance and language brokering. Similarly, in other studies, children have stated that they did not associate their language brokering experiences with their academic performance. Furthermore, there are researchers who argue that language brokering may put children at risk for academic failure or may limit the child's academic and occupational opportunities because the family expects them to continue brokering (Umaña-Taylor, 2003).

Recently, mixed methods studies have been published with larger samples. These studies have started to look at the possible relationship between language brokering and academic performance. For example, Buriel et al. (1998) reported that language brokering was a strong predictor of academic performance. They also reported that language brokering scores and feelings about brokering were associated with academic self-efficacy. Similarly, in a study by Orellana (2003), children who have served as language brokers did significantly better on standardized tests of reading and math achievement. In another study by Walinchowski (2001), participants stated that although they felt frustrated about brokering, they used these experiences as tools for self-improvement.

In sum, the available literature informs us that there is no consensus on how language brokering experiences affect the academic performance of those who do it. Researchers are still debating about the positive or negative influences of language brokering on academic performance. The studies presented do provide important information that could be further investigated. A reliable approach for understanding this issue is to include mixed methodologies, as well as large and more diverse samples of children who are serving as language brokers.

How Does Language Brokering Affect the Parent–Child Relationship?

Research studies that have investigated the parent-child relationship of language brokers have been the sources of much controversy. Mental health professionals, social scientists, legislators, policy makers, professionals in the medical field, and educators have all been discussing how children who serve as translators and interpreters may be potentially harmed or benefited by these experiences. Currently, there are two persistent perspectives on this issue. The first are those who are against children serving as translators and interpreters, stating that this type of experience negatively affects the normal dynamics of the parent-child relationship. Cohen, Moran-Ellis, and Smaje (1999) conducted a study with general practitioners whose patients requested to have their children translate. In their study, the general practitioners reported being against using children in their consultations. The general practitioners strongly believed that having children serve as translators and interpreters when discussing their parents' health concerns could harm the parent-child relationship. Other researchers argue that having children translate and interpret for their parents led to unhealthy role reversals within the family, forcing the parents to become dependent on their children (Umaña-Taylor, 2003).

Earlier studies have shown that the experiences associated with language brokering help them develop a stronger bond to their parents. In a study by DeMent and Buriel (1999), (a) participants commented that brokering was a form of commitment to not disappoint their parents because they made a sacrifice in bringing the entire family to the United States, (b) other participants stated that they were concerned about finances and the health status of parents, (c) it was reported that parents developed a certain dependency on the language broker with regard to handling documents, and (d) the brokering experiences elicited feelings of compassion and helped them understand their parents' struggles. Language brokers are also considered active advocates of their parents' rights during complex situations (e.g., legal, financial). A qualitative study by Valenzuela (1999) reported that children inform their parents about their rights in the United States and educate them about the legal system. Some participants even helped their parents to hire a lawyer, if they believed that it was necessary.

More recent studies have revealed important information about how language brokers use their position of power to protect the welfare of their parents and other family members. Studies conducted by Orellana et al. (2003) and Valdes et al. (2003) reported that language brokers have stated that they use their position of power to protect their parents from embarrassment and humiliation. Some of the participants in their studies mentioned that they could not let employers, doctors, or other individuals embarrass their parents or other family members. These findings add new knowledge to this body of literature, where language brokers are now being considered the protectors or shields of the family.

In summary, there is no clear-cut answer to the question of whether language brokering has a positive or negative effect on the child-parent relationship. Furthermore, new research is suggesting how language

505 brokers use their power to protect the well-being of the family. The research presented in this section provides promising, albeit somewhat limited, insights concerning the characteristics and role of language brokers in the family. However, more research is still needed.

510 Past studies have not used participants of diverse backgrounds, which limits the generalizability of the results to larger groups of children. More studies are needed where more representative samples are used, as well as the inclusion of more sound, rigorous method-

515 ologies.

Discussion

In this article, information has been presented that describes the qualities of the language broker, the different situations language brokers experience, the types of documents they translate, the role language

520 brokering plays in the child's cognitive development, the association between language brokering and academic success, and the role language brokering plays within the parent-child relationship. Taken together, results of this review suggest the following:

525 1. Language brokering is very common among children of immigrant parents (Orellana, 2003). Children start brokering at an early age (8 to 9 years), regardless of their place of birth or order of birth (McQuillan & Tse, 1995; Tse, 1995a, 1996b). Lan-

530 guage brokering is often a female-dominated activity (Buriel et al., 1998; Love, 2003; McQuillan & Tse, 1995; Valenzuela, 1999; Weisskirch, 2005). The broker is not selected at random; parents base their selection on various qualities that language

535 brokers possess (Chao, 2002; DeMent & Buriel, 1999; Valdes et al., 2003; Valenzuela, 1999).

2. Brokers may develop higher levels of cognitive ability, given the types of documents (e.g., bank/credit card statements) they translate and in-

540 terpret for their parents. In addition, the situations where they translate or interpret (e.g., doctor's office, banks, government offices) highlight their adult-level cognitive capability (DeMent & Buriel, 1999; Halgunseth, 2003; McQuillan & Tse, 1995;

545 Tse, 1995a, 1996a; Walinchowski, 2001).

3. Although earlier studies reported that there was not a strong relationship between language brokering and academic performance (McQuillan & Tse, 1995; Tse, 1995a), recent research has started to de-

550 tect a positive relationship between these two constructs (Orellana, 2003).

4. There is insufficient evidence to conclude that language brokering has a positive or negative effect on the parent-child relationship. Scholars have not yet

555 reached consensus on this issue. There are those, for example, who believe language brokering has negative consequences on the parent-child relationship and, likewise, there are those who believe it plays a positive role.

560 Based on the literature presented, it is safe to conclude that language brokers are unique children with qualities and skills that help them interact in two different worlds. On one hand, these children interact with other children their age through play and other

565 types of activities. However, when necessary, language brokers assume their adultlike roles when they need to be the family's translator and interpreter. It is still unclear, though, whether children of immigrant families develop these qualities due to their brokering

570 experiences or other environmental or biological factors.

Children who serve as translators and interpreters are active participants in a number of demanding situations. The literature suggests that language brokers

575 develop higher cognitive abilities that allow them to be more knowledgeable of their first and second languages. Krashen (1985) stated that children who translate and interpret for their parents are being exposed to a variety of settings that, in the end, enhance their language acquisition. The literature reviewed demon-

580 strates that language brokers translate immediately on arrival in the United States. Cummins (1989) affirmed that it takes 5 to 7 years for immigrant students to develop academic level accuracy. As mentioned, this is not the case for language brokers, because some bro-

585 ker within 1 to 5 years of their arrival in the United States. It appears, then, that language brokers must try to learn English at a much faster rate.

Although there is not a clear-cut relationship between language brokering and academic performance,

590 researchers have argued that it is possible that the traditional educational assessment instruments used in school districts fail to capture the real abilities of language brokers. Oftentimes, the instruments used may

595 be potentially biased, given the characteristics of the samples in which they were normed. Tse (1995b) acknowledged that school districts should develop appropriate and more relevant assessment instruments for children who are language brokers.

600 Language brokering serves as a bridge of communication and understanding between parents and children. In some instances, translating and interpreting may help a child feel more connected to his or her parents. Children may then be seen as their parents'

605 "right hand," because they are required to make, or help make, decisions for the entire family. These activities allow the child to be more informed about different family concerns and to think and behave in a more adultlike manner. At the same time, this type of

610 experience may have negative implications for the parent-child relationship, causing the parents to become dependent on the child, and the child to possibly

feel overwhelmed by his or her role as the family's translator and interpreter.

615   As research in the area of language brokering grows, social scientists need to continue thinking critically about this topic. Some critical questions that remain unanswered include, Under what circumstances should children serve as interpreters and translators? 620 The literature suggests that language brokering happens in various settings (e.g., home, school, government, and medical), yet it is unclear whether these are acceptable settings to have a child serve as a translator or interpreter. It is possible that parents prefer their 625 child's assistance over that of a trained, adult interpreter because they feel more comfortable with them and trust them more. It is also possible that most service providers do not have the funds to hire trained interpreters and may believe that it is acceptable to 630 have a family member translate. Another critical question is, Who should be responsible for making this decision? The parents? The service provider? The child? In addition, should it be legislated, so as to standardize the process for people? To begin answer- 635 ing these questions, more research is clearly needed.

Limitations

One limitation of this review is the number of resources included. Although 24 resources including journal articles, newsletter reports, conference papers, book chapters, *ERIC* documents, and dissertations are 640 a fair amount of resources, more are needed to better understand the phenomenon of language brokering. It is imperative that further research be conducted to expand our knowledge base in this area. Another limitation is the type of studies used in this review. The 645 majority of them were merely descriptive.

Implications for Theory

Language brokering is a relatively new area of 700 study in the social sciences. This has caused those interested in it to use different theoretical frameworks to guide their work. Currently, there is no language bro- 650 kering theory per se, but researchers have used three widely accepted theories to conduct their research. 705 These theories include Acculturation theory, Family Systems theory, and contextual theories of cognitive development. These theoretical frameworks have 655 guided the different research conducted with language brokers. We believe that a grounded theory approach 710 is needed to develop a data-based theory that will better capture the experiences of language brokers and the nuances of the language brokering process.

Implications for Further Research

660   Language brokering is an open area that needs to 715 be further explored. The majority of research studies on language brokering have been descriptive in nature. This may be interpreted as a call to researchers, educa-

665 tors, and policy makers to pay attention to this neglected area of research. Some recommendations for further research include the following: (a) scale development studies, (b) developmental studies, (c) studies of psychosocial variables associated with language 670 brokering, (d) accuracy in translation, and (e) the characteristics of the language broker. No studies have evaluated the psychometric properties of the existing language brokering scales. This would be a good starting point, given that language brokering scales are already being used with children in different settings.

675   Developmental studies are needed given the lack of developmental data on language brokering. In this review, several of the studies were retrospective in nature, thus limiting our understanding of language brokering (Buriel et al., 1998; DeMent & Buriel, 1999; McQuillan & Tse, 1995). The results of such studies were based on participants' memories. A study by DeMent and Buriel (1999) suggests that language brokering happens in a developmental fashion. A number of researchers have proposed that developmental studies could provide answers to the many questions that currently remain unanswered. Furthermore, new research using mixed methods has provided insightful information about the language brokering phenomenon (Orellana, 2003; Orellana et al., 2003). Thus, further research should consider adopting such methodologies.

Psychosocial variables need to be included in further research. For example, variables such as ethnic identity have been associated with native language use with ethnic minority adolescents (Heller, 1987; Phinney, Romero, Nava, & Huang, 2001). Recently, Weisskirch (2005) studied this relationship among Latino adolescents. In his study, he found that feelings about language brokering predicted ethnic identity, and combined subscales of language brokering, gender, and acculturation predicted ethnic identity. Other variables, such as language preference, immigration status, psychological distress, and self-esteem, are important constructs to consider when conducting research with these groups of children. Researching the interaction of these variables with language brokering will provide a better understanding of how children who serve as translators and interpreters are being affected by these experiences.

A critically important issue that has not yet been investigated concerns the accuracy and proficiency of the language broker. Language brokers are playing important roles in society, and they are transferring delicate information that, if done inaccurately or incorrectly, could harm the well-being of the family and those around them. Yet, to date, no studies have examined how proficient a child must be to translate or interpret for their parents. This is perhaps the greatest weakness, or limitation, of the extant research. Further

720 research should, therefore, start to assess the accuracy and proficiency of these children and use this research to develop programs at the schools where children who 775 serve in these roles are instructed in how to master these two important skills. First, research needs to de-
725 velop methodologies that will allow us to investigate the accuracy and proficiency of language brokers. At this time, there is a deficiency in the availability of 780 psychometrically sound instruments that may help measure these two skills. The need for such instru-
730 ments is necessary, as we are not only dealing with children who come from different parts of the world but also children who will become part of mainstream U.S. society. These instruments need to consider worldview, family values, and acculturation. As the
735 number of language minority students is increasing, schools are trying new methods to help them become bilingual. Until we have empirical evidence that informs us on the proficiency and accuracy of language brokers, we will not be able to clearly understand this
740 phenomenon.

Language brokering is a common practice among children of immigrant families. The published studies suggest that parents carefully select the child who will serve as the language broker, yet these studies fail to
745 investigate the characteristics parents look for or what their process is for selecting the broker. It is recommended that more qualitative studies be conducted with immigrant parents to address this issue. It is also important to conduct developmental studies observing
750 how language brokers evolve to discover the specific qualities that best characterize the language broker.

Implications for Practice

Mental health researchers have argued that using children as translators and interpreters has negative consequences on the mental health of children
755 (Umaña-Taylor, 2003; Weisskirch & Alva, 2002). This is a call to those working in the mental health field to further investigate the implications of language brokering on children's mental health. Further research would also afford mental health professionals greater
760 insight into the unique issues they face. It is also important that mental health professionals be aware of the different roles children take and explore how language brokering experiences are affecting them.

Conclusion

This review presents the most current literature in
765 the area of language brokering and introduces the reader to some of the most salient issues in this area. It is evident that this line of research still has a long way to go. Many questions remain unanswered. Language brokering continues to be a form of adaptation and
770 survival among immigrant families. Research clearly needs to include language brokers from the full spectrum of immigrant families, as it is not a uniquely La-

tino phenomenon. This is a serious omission; children from all backgrounds engage in it. More research is needed to be able to answer the questions social scientists, educators, and policy makers have with regard to children who serve as translators and interpreters. Research of this nature will help social scientists and policy makers develop better, more appropriate services for those who need them.

References

References marked with an asterisk (*N* = 24) indicate studies summarized in Table 1.

Baptiste, D. (1987). Family therapy with Spanish heritage immigrant families in cultural transition. *Contemporary Family Therapy, 9,* 229–251.

Bialystok, E. (2001). *Bilingualism in development language, literacy, and cognition.* New York: Cambridge University Press.

Bloomfield, L. (1933). *Language.* New York: Holt.

*Buriel, R., Perez, W., DeMent, T. L., Chavez, D. V., & Moran, V. R. (1998). The relationship of language brokering to academic performance, biculturalism, and self-efficacy among Latino adolescents. *Hispanic Journal of Behavioral Sciences, 20*(3), 283–297.

*Chao, R. K. (April, 2002). The role of children's linguistic brokering among immigrant Chinese and Mexican families. In *Families of color: Developmental issues in contemporary sociohistorical contexts.* Symposium conducted at the biennial meeting of the Society for Research in Child Development, Minneapolis, Minnesota.

*Cohen, S., Moran-Ellis, J., & Smaje, C. (1999). Children as informal interpreters in GP consultations: Pragmatics and ideology. *Sociology of Health and Illness, 21*(2), 163–186.

Coleman, J. (2003, April 2). Bill would ban using children as interpreters. *The San Jose Mercury News,* p. 19A.

Comas-Diaz, L. (1993). Hispanic/Latino communities: Psychological implications. In D. R. Atkinson, G. Morten, & D. W. Sue (Eds.), *Counseling American minorities: A cross-cultural perspective* (4th ed., pp. 245–263). Madison, WI: Brown and Benchmark.

Cummins, J. (1989). *Empowering minority students.* Covina: California Association for Bilingual Education.

*DeMent, T., & Buriel, R. (1999, August). *Children as cultural brokers: Recollections of college students.* Paper presented at the SPSSI Conference on Immigrants and Immigration, Toronto, Canada.

*Diaz-Lazaro, C. M. (2002). *The effects of language brokering on perceptions of family authority structure, problem-solving abilities, and parental locus of control in Latino adolescents and their parents.* Unpublished doctoral dissertation, State University of New York at Buffalo.

Evans, F. B., & Anderson, J. G. (1973). The psychocultural origins of achievement and achievement motivation: The Mexican-American family. *Sociology of Education, 46,* 396–416.

Grosjean, F. (1989). Neurolinguistics, beware! The bilingual is not two monolinguals in one person. *Brain and Language, 36,* 3–15.

*Gullingsrud, M. (1998). I am the immigrant in my classroom. *Voices From the Middle, 6*(1), 3037.

*Halgunseth, L. (2003). Language brokering: Positive developmental outcomes. In M. Coleman & L. Ganong (Eds.), *Points and counterpoints: Controversial relationships and family issues in the 21st century: An anthology* (pp. 154–157). Los Angeles, CA: Roxbury.

Harris, B., & Sherwood, B. (1978). Translating as an innate skill. In D. Gerver & H. W. Sinaiko (Eds.), *Language interpretation and communication* (pp. 155–170). New York: Plenum.

Heller, M. (1987). The role of language in the formation of ethnic identity. In J. S. Phinney & M. Rotheram (Eds.), *Children's ethnic socialization* (pp. 180–200). Newbury Park, CA: Sage.

Krashen, S. (1985). *The input hypothesis: Issues and implications.* Torrance, CA: Laredo.

*Love, J. A. (2003, April). *Language brokering, autonomy, parent-child bonding, and depression.* Paper presented at the 2003 Conference of the Society on the Research of Child Development, Miami, Florida.

*McQuillan, J., & Tse, L. (1995). Child language brokering in linguistic minority communities: Effects on cultural interaction, cognition and literacy. *Language and Education, 9*(3), 195–215.

*Ng, J. (1998). From kitchen to classroom: Reflections of a language broker. *Voices From the Middle, 6*(1), 38–40.

*Orellana, M. F. (2003). Responsibilities of children in Latino immigrant homes. *New Directions for Youth Development, 100,* 25–39.

*Orellana, M. F., Dorner, L., & Pulido, L. (2003). Accessing assets: Immigrant youth's work as family translators or "para-phrasers." *Social Problems, 50*(4), 505–524.

Phinney, J. S., Romero, I., Nava, M., & Huang, D. (2001). The role of language, parents, and peers in ethnic identity among adolescents in immigrant families. *Journal of Youth and Adolescence, 30*(2), 135–153.

Rumbaut, R. G. (1994). The crucible within: Ethnic identity, self-esteem, and segmented assimilation among children of immigrants. *International Migration Review, 28,* 748–795.

Rumberger, R. W., & Rodriguez, G. M. (2002). Chicano dropouts: An update of research and policy issues. In R. Valencia (Ed.), *Chicano school failure and success past, present, and future* (2nd ed., pp. 114–146). New York: RoutledgeFalmer.

*Santiago, S. (2003). Language brokering: A personal experience. In M. Coleman & L. Ganong (Eds.), *Points and counterpoints: Controversial relationship and family issues in the 21st century: An anthology* (pp. 160–161). Los Angeles, CA: Roxbury.

*Shannon, S. M. (1990). English in the barrio: The quality of contact among immigrant children. *Hispanic Journal of Behavioral Sciences, 12*(3), 256–276.

Sue, D. W., & Sue, D. (1990). *Counseling the culturally different: Theory and practice* (2nd ed.). New York: Wiley.

*Tse, L. (1995a). Language brokering among Latino adolescents: Prevalence, attitudes, and school performance. *Hispanic Journal of Behavioral Sciences, 17*(2), 180–193.

*Tse, L. (1995b). When students translate for parents: Effects of language brokering. *CABE Newsletter, 17*(4), 16–17.

*Tse, L. (1996a). Language brokering in linguistic minority communities: The case of Chinese- and Vietnamese-American students. *Bilingual Research Journal, 20*(3–4), 485–498.

*Tse, L. (1996b). Who decides? The effects of language brokering on home-school communication. *Journal of Educational Issues of Language Minority Students, 16,* 225–234.

*Umaña-Taylor, A. J. (2003). Language brokering as a stressor for immigrant children and their families. In M. Coleman & L. Ganong (Eds.), *Points and counterpoints: Controversial relationship and family issues in the 21st century: An anthology* (pp. 157–159). Los Angeles, CA: Roxbury.

*Valdes, G., Chavez, C., & Angelelli, C. (2003). A performance team: Young interpreters and their parents. In G. Valdes (Ed.), *Expanding definitions of giftedness: The case of young interpreters from immigrant countries* (pp. 63–97). Mahwah, NJ: Lawrence Erlbaum.

*Valenzuela, A. (1999). Gender roles and settlement activities among children and their immigrant families. *American Behavioral Scientist, 42*(4), 720–742.

*Walinchowski, M. (2001). Language brokering: Laying the foundation for success and bilingualism. In R. Lara-Alecio (Chair), *Research in bilingual education.* Symposium conducted at the Annual Educational Research Exchange, College Station, Texas.

*Weisskirch, R. S. (2005). The relationship of language brokering to ethnic identity for Latino adolescents. *Hispanic Journal of Behavioral Sciences, 27*(3), 286–299.

*Weisskirch, R. S., & Alva, S. A. (2002). Language brokering and the acculturation of Latino children. *Hispanic Journal of Behavioral Sciences, 24*(3), 369–378.

Westermeyer, J. (1989). *Psychiatric care of immigrants: A clinical guide.* Washington, DC: American Psychiatric Press.

About the authors: *Alejandro Morales* is a doctoral student in counseling psychology at the University of Nebraska–Lincoln. He holds a bachelor's degree in psychology from California State University, Dominguez Hills, and a master's degree in counseling psychology from the University of Nebraska–Lincoln. His areas of research interest are language brokering, Latino ethnic/racial identity development, acculturation, Latino families, and Latino mental health. He enjoys reading Latin American literature, Harry Potter, and books about self-care and well-being, and listening to Spanish rock. *William E. Hanson*, Ph.D., earned his doctorate in counseling psychology from Arizona State University and his master's from the University of Minnesota. He completed his predoctoral internship at the Duke/Durham VA Medical Center in 1996–1997. Between 1998 and 2005, he was an assistant professor in the Department of Educational Psychology at the University of Nebraska–Lincoln. Currently, he is a faculty member in the Department of Educational Studies at Purdue University, where he teaches in the APA accredited Counseling Psychology Program. He conducts and publishes research on the counseling process, in particular, the process of sharing psychological test results with clients; mixed methods; and problematic gambling among college students. For fun, he enjoys reading books by Carl Hiaasen, traveling, listening to live blues/jazz, and playing sports.

Authors' Note: An earlier version of this article was presented at the annual convention of the National Latina/o Psychological Association. Thanks to Drs. L. Mark Carrier and Silvia Santos for their many helpful editorial comments.

Address correspondence to: Alejandro Morales, Department of Educational Psychology, 114 TEAC, University of Nebraska–Lincoln, Lincoln, NE 68588-0345; E-mail: moralesl@bigred.unl.edu

APPENDIX A

Sample *ERIC* Search

1. *Title*: Alliances and Arguments: A Case Study of a Child With Persisting Speech Difficulties in Peer Play
   Abstract: The ability to argue and to create alliances with peers are important social competencies for all children, including those who have speech, language, and communication needs. In this study, we investigated the management of arguments and alliances by a group of 5-year-old male friends, one of whom has a persisting speech....

2. *Title*: A Statistical Model of the Grammatical Choices in Child Production of Dative Sentences
   Abstract: Focusing on children's production of the dative alternation in English, we examine whether children's choices are influenced by the same factors that influence adults' choices, and whether, like adults, they are sensitive to multiple factors simultaneously. We do so by using mixed-effect regression models to analyse child....

3. *Title*: Maternal Functional Speech to Children: A Comparison of Autism Spectrum Disorder, Down Syndrome, and Typical Development
   Abstract: Children with developmental disabilities benefit from their language environment as much as, or even more than, typically developing (TD) children, but maternal language directed to developmentally delayed children is an underinvestigated topic. The purposes of the present study were to compare maternal functional language....

4. *Title*: Promising Strategies for Collaborating With Hispanic Parents During Family-Centered Speech-Language Intervention
   Abstract: Early intervention programs are developed on the premise that parents or primary caregivers generalize treatment strategies within naturalistic environments. The diverse characteristics of children within early language intervention reinforce the urgency for services that consider the needs of each child within his or her broader....

5. *Title*: Regular/Irregular is Not the Whole Story: The Role of Frequency and Generalization in the Acquisition of German Past Participle Inflection
   Abstract: The acquisition of German participle inflection was investigated using spontaneous speech samples from six children between 1; 4 and 3; 8 and ten children between 1; 4 and 2; 10 recorded longitudinally at regular intervals. Child-directed speech was also....

6. *Title*: Lexical and Phonological Development in Children With Childhood Apraxia of Speech—A Commentary on Stoel-Gammon's "Relationships Between Lexical and Phonological Development in Young Children"
   Abstract: Although not the focus of her article, phonological development in young children with speech sound disorders of various types is highly germane to Stoel-Gammon's discussion (this issue) for at least two primary reasons. Most obvious is that typical processes and milestones of phonological development are the standards and benchmarks against which we measure....

7. *Title*: Increasing the Odds: Applying Emergentist Theory in Language Intervention
   Abstract: Purpose: This review introduces emergentism, which is a leading theory of language development that states that language ability is the product of interactions between the child's language environment and his or her learning capabilities. The review suggests....

8. *Title*: Learning to Liaise and Elide "Comme il Faut": Evidence From Bilingual Children
   Abstract: Liaison and elision in French are phonological phenomena that apply across word boundaries. French-speaking children make errors in contexts where liaison/elision typically occurs in adult speech. In this study, we asked if acquisition of French liaison/elision can be explained in a constructivist framework. We tested if....

9. *Title*: Stepping Backwards in Development: Integrating Developmental Speech Perception With Lexical and Phonological Development—A Commentary on Stoel-Gammon's "Relationships Between Lexical and Phonological Development in Young Children"
   Abstract: Within the subfields of linguistics, traditional approaches tend to examine different phenomena in isolation. As Stoel-Gammon (this issue) correctly states, there is little interaction between the subfields. However, for a more comprehensive understanding of language acquisition in general and, more specifically, lexical and....

10. *Title*: Mechanisms Linking Phonological Development to Lexical Development—A Commentary on Stoel-Gammon's "Relationships Between Lexical and Phonological Development in Young Children"
Abstract: When Roger Brown selected Adam, Eve, and Sarah to be the first three participants in the modern study of child language, one of the criteria was the intelligibility of their speech (Brown, 1973). According to the prevailing view at the time, accuracy of pronunciation was a peripheral phenomenon....

11. *Title*: Do Newly Formed Word Representations Encode Non-Criterial Information?
Abstract: Lexical stress is useful for a number of language learning tasks. In particular, it helps infants segment the speech stream and identify phonetic contrasts. Recent work has demonstrated that infants aged 1; 0 can learn two novel words differing only in their stress pattern. In the current study, we ask whether infants aged....

12. *Title*: Parental Numeric Language Input to Mandarin Chinese and English Speaking Preschool Children
Abstract: The present study examined the number-specific parental language input to Mandarin- and English-speaking preschool-aged children. Mandarin and English transcripts from the CHILDES database were examined for amount of numeric speech, specific types of numeric speech, and syntactic frames in....

13. *Title*: The Input Ambiguity Hypothesis and Case Blindness: An Account of Cross-Linguistic and Intra-Linguistic Differences in Case Errors
Abstract: English-acquiring children frequently make pronoun case errors, while German-acquiring children rarely do. Nonetheless, German-acquiring children frequently make article case errors. It is proposed that when child-directed speech contains a high percentage of case-ambiguous forms, case errors are common in child....

14. *Title*: Relationships Between Lexical and Phonological Development: A Look at Bilingual Children—A Commentary on Stoel-Gammon's "Relationships Between Lexical and Phonological Development in Young Children"
Abstract: Stoel-Gammon (this issue) highlights the close and symbiotic association that exists between the lexical and phonological domains in early linguistic development. Her comprehensive review considers two bodies of literature: (1) child-centred studies; and (2) studies based on adult psycholinguistic research. Within the child....

15. *Title*: Interrelations Between Communicative Behaviors at the Outset of Speech: Parents as Observers
Abstract: The Hebrew Parent Questionnaire for Communication and Early Language (HPQ-CEL) was administered by 154 parents of Hebrew-speaking toddlers aged 1; 0 to 1; 3 (77 boys, 77 girls). The questionnaire guided parents in observing and rating their toddlers in six contexts at home. The study aimed to identify inter-correlations between toddlers' non-linguistic behaviors....

16. *Title*: When Parent Perceptions of the Language Development of Toddlers With Developmental Delays Before and After Participation in Parent-Coached Language Interventions
Abstract: Purpose: This study examined parent perception of early communication development before and after participation in language intervention. Method: Fifty-three parents of toddlers with developmental delays and fewer than 10 spoken words completed the Parent Perception of Language Development, an experimental measure, before and....

17. *Title*: Imitation Therapy for Non-Verbal Toddlers
Abstract: When imitation skills are not present in young children, speech and language skills typically fail to emerge. There is little information on practices that foster the emergence of imitation skills in general and verbal imitation skills in particular. The present study attempted to add to our limited evidence base regarding....

18. *Title*: Gender-Marked Determiners Help Dutch Learners' Word Recognition When Gender Information Itself Does Not
Abstract: Dutch, unlike English, contains two gender-marked forms of the definite article. Does the presence of multiple definite article forms lead Dutch learners to be delayed relative to English learners in the acquisition of their determiner system? Using the Preferential Looking Procedure, we found that Dutch-learning children aged 1; 7 to 2; 0 use articles during....

19. *Title*: Successive Single-Word Utterances and Use of Conversational Input: A Pre-Syntactic Route to Multiword Utterances
Abstract: In the period between sole use of single words and majority use of multiword utterances, children draw from their existing productive capability and conversational input to facilitate the eventual outcome of majority use of multiword utterances. During this period, children use word combinations that are not yet mature multiword utterances, termed "successive single-word utterances" (SSWUs)....

20. *Title*: Baby Talk Home Visits: Development and Initial Evaluations of a Primary Prevention Service
Abstract: Language delay is a common developmental difficulty. Research indicates that it is influenced by environmental factors, particularly social deprivation, but that a parent's interaction protects children's language development against these factors. It is hypothesized that by supporting parents' interaction, language....

21.   *Title*: Phonological Development of Word-Initial Korean Obstruents in Young Korean Children
      Abstract: This study investigates the acquisition of word-initial Korean obstruents (i.e., stops, affricates, and fricatives). Korean obstruents are characterized by a three-way contrast among stops and affricates (i.e., fortis, aspirated, and lenis) and a two-way fricative contrast (i.e., fortis and lenis). All these obstruents are voiceless word-initially. Cross-sectional....

22.   *Title*: On the Interaction of Deaffrication and Consonant Harmony
      Abstract: Error patterns in children's phonological development are often described as simplifying processes that can interact with one another with different consequences. Some interactions limit the applicability of an error pattern, and others extend it to more words. Theories predict that error patterns interact to their full potential. While specific interactions have been documented for certain pairs....

23.   *Title*: Children's Command of Plural and Possessive Marking on Hebrew Nouns: A Comparison of Obligatory Versus Optional Inflections
      Abstract: We compare learning of two inflection types—obligatory noun plurals and optional noun possessives. We tested 107 Hebrew-speaking children aged 6–7 on the same tasks at the beginning and end of first grade. Performance on both constructions improved during this short period, but plurals scored higher from the start, with improvement only in changing stems. The main remaining challenge in mastering....

24.   *Title*: Education Practitioner-Led Intervention to Facilitate Language Learning in Young Children: An Effectiveness Study
      Abstract: In the UK there is much concern about the educational progress of children from areas of significant social disadvantage entering primary school with impoverished language skills. These children are not routinely referred to speech and language therapy services and therefore education....

25.   *Title*: Sources of Variability in Children's Language Growth
      Abstract: The present longitudinal study examines the role of caregiver speech in language development, especially syntactic development, using 47 parent-child pairs of diverse SES background from 14 to 46 months. We assess the diversity (variety) of words and syntactic structures produced by caregivers....

26.   *Title*: Children's Knowledge of the Quantifier "Dou" in Mandarin Chinese
      Abstract: The quantifier "dou" (roughly corresponding to English "all") in Mandarin Chinese has been the topic of much discussion in the theoretical literature. This study investigated children's knowledge of this quantifier using a new methodological technique, which we dubbed the Question-Statement Task. Three questions were addressed: (i) whether young Mandarin-speaking children know that "dou" is a....

27.   *Title*: Early Verb Learning in 20-Month-Old Japanese-Speaking Children
      Abstract: The present study investigated whether children's representations of morphosyntactic information are abstract enough to guide early verb learning. Using an infant-controlled habituation paradigm with a switch design, Japanese-speaking children aged 1; 8 were habituated to two different events in which an object was engaging in an action. Each event was paired with a novel word embedded in a single....

28.   *Title*: An Empirical Generative Framework for Computational Modeling of Language Acquisition
      Abstract: This paper reports progress in developing a computer model of language acquisition in the form of (1) a generative grammar that is (2) algorithmically learnable from realistic corpus data, (3) viable in its large-scale quantitative performance and (4) psychologically real. First, we describe new algorithmic methods for unsupervised....

29.   *Title*: Out of the Mouth of Babes: First-Time Disadvantaged Mothers and Their Perceptions of Infant Communication
      Abstract: An increasing emphasis is being placed on the importance of speech, language, and communication (SLC) development during the first two years of life, since this contributes to cognitive ability and to later educational outcomes. This article explores what disadvantaged, first-time mothers know and understand about three key....

30.   *Title*: Early and Late Talkers: School-Age Language, Literacy, and Neurolinguistic Differences
      Abstract: Early language development sets the stage for a lifetime of competence in language and literacy. However, the neural mechanisms associated with the relative advantages of early communication success, or the disadvantages of having delayed language development, are not well explored. In this....

31.   *Title*: Learning Grammatical Categories from Distributional Cues: Flexible Frames for Language Acquisition
      Abstract: Numerous distributional cues in the child's environment may potentially assist in language learning, but what cues are useful to the child and when are these cues utilised? We propose that the most useful source of distributional cue is a flexible frame surrounding the word, where the language....

32.   *Title*: Segmental Distribution Patterns of English Infant- and Adult-Directed Speech
      Abstract: This study compared segmental distribution patterns for consonants and vowels in English infant-directed speech (IDS) and adult-directed speech (ADS). A previous study of Korean indicated that segmental patterns of IDS differed from ADS patterns (Lee, Davis, & MacNeilage, 2008). The aim of the current study was to determine whether....

33.   *Title*: Development or Impairment?
      Abstract: Joanne Paradis' Keynote Article on bilingualism and specific language impairment (SLI) is an impressive overview of research in language acquisition and language impairment. Studying different populations is crucial both for theorizing about language....

34.   *Title*: Simplified and Expanded Input in a Focused Stimulation Program for a Child With Expressive Language Delay (ELD)
      Abstract: There is considerable debate regarding the simplification of adults' language when talking to young children with expressive language delays (ELD). While simplified input, also called telegraphic speech, is used by many parents and clinicians working with young children, its use has been discouraged....

35.   *Title*: Now You Hear It, Now You Don't: Vowel Devoicing in Japanese Infant-Directed Speech
      Abstract: In this work, we examine a context in which a conflict arises between two roles that infant-directed speech (IDS) plays: making language structure salient and modeling the adult form of a language. Vowel devoicing in fluent adult Japanese creates violations of the canonical Japanese consonant....

36.   *Title*: Words in Puddles of Sound: Modelling Psycholinguistic Effects in Speech Segmentation
      Abstract: There are numerous models of how speech segmentation may proceed in infants acquiring their first language. We present a framework for considering the relative merits and limitations of these various approaches. We then present a model of speech segmentation that aims to reveal important sources....

37.   *Title*: Modeling the Contribution of Phonotactic Cues to the Problem of Word Segmentation
      Abstract: How do infants find the words in the speech stream? Computational models help us understand this feat by revealing the advantages and disadvantages of different strategies that infants might use. Here, we outline a computational model of word segmentation that aims both to incorporate cues proposed by language acquisition....

38.   *Title*: Segmenting Words From Natural Speech: Subsegmental Variation in Segmental Cues
      Abstract: Most computational models of word segmentation are trained and tested on transcripts of speech, rather than the speech itself, and assume that speech is converted into a sequence of symbols prior to word segmentation. We present a way of representing speech....

39.   *Title*: Semantic Bias in the Acquisition of Relative Clauses in Japanese
      Abstract: This study analyzes the acquisition of relative clauses in Japanese to determine the semantic and functional characteristics of children's relative clauses in spontaneous speech. Longitudinal data from five Japanese children are analyzed and compared with English data (Diessel & Tomasello, 2000). The results show that the relative....

40.   *Title*: Cognitive Architectures and Language Acquisition: A Case Study in Pronoun Comprehension
      Abstract: In this paper we discuss a computational cognitive model of children's poor performance on pronoun interpretation (the so-called Delay of Principle B Effect, or DPBE). This cognitive model is based on a theoretical account that attributes the DPBE to children's inability as hearers to also take into account the speaker's perspective. The cognitive model predicts that child....

41.   *Title*: The Growth of Tense Productivity
      Abstract: Purpose: This study tests empirical predictions of a maturational model for the growth of tense in children younger than 36 months using a type-based productivity measure. Method: Caregiver-child language samples were collected from 20 typically developing children every 3 months from 21 to 33 months of age. Growth in the....

42.   *Title*: Segmental Production in Mandarin-Learning Infants
      Abstract: The early development of vocalic and consonantal production in Mandarin-learning infants was studied at the transition from babbling to producing first words. Spontaneous vocalizations were recorded for 24 infants grouped by age: G1 (0; 7 to 1; 0) and G2 (1; 1 to 1; 6). Additionally, the infant-directed speech of 24 caregivers was recorded during natural....

43. *Title*: Universal Production Patterns and Ambient Language Influences in Babbling: A Cross-Linguistic Study of Korean- and English-Learning Infants
Abstract: The phonetic characteristics of canonical babbling produced by Korean- and English-learning infants were compared with consonant and vowel frequencies observed in infant-directed speech produced by Korean- and English-speaking mothers. For infant output, babbling samples from six Korean-learning infants were compared with an existing English babbling database....

44. *Title*: Talking About Writing: What We Can Learn From Conversations Between Parents and Their Young Children
Abstract: In six analyses using the Child Language Data Exchange System known as CHILDES, we explored whether and how parents and their 1.5- to 5-year-old children talk about writing. Parent speech might include information about the similarity between print and speech....

45. *Title*: Syntax at Age Two: Cross-Linguistic Differences
Abstract: The 1990s witnessed a major expansion in research on children's morphosyntactic development, due largely to the availability of computer-searchable corpora of spontaneous speech in the CHILDES database. This led to a rapid emergence of parallel findings in different languages, with much attention devoted to the widely attested difficulties in inflectional....

46. *Title*: Sharing Spoken Language: Sounds, Conversations, and Told Stories
Abstract: Infants and toddlers encounter numerous spoken story experiences early in their lives: conversations, oral stories, and language games such as songs and rhymes. Many adults are even surprised to learn that children this young need these kinds of natural language experiences at all. Adults help very young children take a step....

47. *Title*: Development of Children's Ability to Distinguish Sarcasm and Verbal Irony
Abstract: Adults distinguish between ironic remarks directed at targets (sarcasm) and ironic remarks not directed at specific targets. We investigated the development of children's appreciation for this distinction by presenting these speech acts to 71 five- to six-year-olds and 71 nine- to ten-year-olds. Five- to six-year-olds were beginning to understand the non-literal....

48. *Title*: Cross-Linguistic Relations Between Quantifiers and Numerals in Language Acquisition: Evidence From Japanese
Abstract: A study of 104 Japanese-speaking 2- to 5-year-olds tested the relation between numeral and quantifier acquisition. A first study assessed Japanese children's comprehension of quantifiers, numerals, and classifiers. Relative to English-speaking counterparts, Japanese children were delayed in numeral comprehension at 2 years of age but showed no difference at 3....

49. *Title*: Self-Repair of Speech by Four-Year-Old Finnish Children
Abstract: The aim of this study was to examine what four-year-old children repair in their speech. For this purpose, conversational self-repairs (N = 316) made by two typically developing Finnish-speaking children (aged 4; 8 and 4; 11) were examined. The data comprised eight hours of natural interactions videotaped at the children's homes. The tapes were analyzed using....

50. *Title*: The Development of Aspectual Marking in Child Mandarin Chinese
Abstract: Cross-linguistic research on the development of tense-aspect marking has revealed a strong effect of lexical aspect. But the degree of this effect varies across languages. Explanation for this universal tendency and language-specific variation is still an open issue. This study investigates the early emergence and subsequent development of four grammatical....

51. *Title*: Two-Year-Olds Compute Syntactic Structure On-Line
Abstract: Syntax allows human beings to build an infinite number of new sentences from a finite stock of words. Because toddlers typically utter only one or two words at a time, they have been thought to have no syntax. Using event-related potentials (ERPs), we demonstrated that 2-year-olds do compute syntactic structure when listening to spoken sentences. We observed an early left-lateralized brain....

52. *Title*: Feasibility and Benefit of Parent Participation in a Program Emphasizing Preschool Child Language Development While Homeless
Abstract: Purpose: This exploratory study examined the feasibility of homeless parents' participation in an intervention to increase use of facilitating language strategies during interactions with their preschool children while residing in family homeless shelters. This study also examined the intervention's impact on the parents' use of facilitating language....

53. *Title*: Abstract Categories or Limited-Scope Formulae? The Case of Children's Determiners
     Abstract: Six tests of the spontaneous speech of twenty-one English-speaking children (1; 10 to 2; 8; MLUs 1[middle dot]53 to 4[middle dot]38) demonstrate the presence of the syntactic category determiner from the start of combinatorial speech, supporting nativist accounts. Children use multiple determiners before a noun to the same....

54. *Title*: Grammaticality Judgments in Autism: Deviance or Delay
     Abstract: Language in autism has been the subject of intense interest because communication deficits are central to the disorder, and because autism serves as an arena for testing theories of language acquisition. High-functioning older children with autism are often considered to have intact grammatical....

55. *Title*: Teachers Talking to Young Children: Invitations to Negotiate Meaning in Everyday Conversations
     Abstract: The purpose of the study reported in this article was to investigate conversations involving dialogue and negotiation of meaning, through which children will learn to talk and talk to learn. In kindergarten, children will learn both to listen to language and to use language, but we have few studies of what characterizes the....

56. *Title*: Language Delay in Severely Neglected Children: A Cumulative or Specific Effect of Risk Factors?
     Abstract: Objectives: This research sought to determine if the language delay (LD) of severely neglected children under 3 years old was better explained by a cumulative risk model or by the specificity of risk factors. The objective was also to identify the risk factors with the strongest impact on LD among various biological, psychological, and environmental factors....

57. *Title*: Object Clitic Omission: Two Language Types
     Abstract: The literature generally assumes that object clitic omission is equally allowed in all child languages. In this paper we challenge this claim by means of an elicitation experiment carried out with children acquiring two closely related languages, Catalan and Spanish. Our results show that while omission is high in young Catalan-speaking children, it is very low....

58. *Title*: Knowing More than One Can Say: The Early Regular Plural
     Abstract: This paper reports on partial knowledge in two-year-old children's learning of the regular English plural. In Experiments 1 and 2, children were presented with one kind and its label and then were either presented with two of that same kind (A[right arrow]AA) or the initial picture next to a very different thing (A[right arrow]AB). The children in A[right arrow]AA rarely produced the plural....

59. *Title*: Emerging Temporality: Past Tense and Temporal/Aspectual Markers in Spanish-Speaking Children's Intra-Conversational Narratives
     Abstract: This study describes how young Spanish-speaking children become gradually more adept at encoding temporality using grammar and discourse skills in intra-conversational narratives. The research involved parallel case studies of two Spanish-speaking children followed longitudinally from ages two to three. Type/token frequencies of verb tense, temporal/aspectual markers and narrative components were....

60. *Title*: How to Measure Development in Corpora? An Association Strength Approach
     Abstract: In this paper we propose a method for characterizing development in large longitudinal corpora. The method has the following three features: (i) it suggests how to represent development without assuming predefined stages; (ii) it includes caregiver speech/child-directed speech; (iii) it uses....

61. *Title*: The Relationship of Audibility and the Development of Canonical Babbling in Young Children With Hearing Impairment
     Abstract: This article investigated the relationship between age at onset of canonical babbling and audibility of amplified speech in children with hearing impairment. Thirteen children with severe-profound hearing impairment and two children with normal hearing participated in a longitudinal investigation of vocalization development. A nonconcurrent multiple baseline....

62. *Title*: The Emergence of Dutch Connectives; How Cumulative Cognitive Complexity Explains the Order of Acquisition
     Abstract: Before they are three years old, most children have started to build coherent discourse. This article focuses on one important linguistic device children have to learn: connectives. The main questions are: Do connectives emerge in a fixed order? And if so, how can this order be explained? In line with Bloom "et al." (1980) we propose to explain similarities in the development in terms of cumulative....

63. *Title*: The Structure and Nature of Phonological Neighbourhoods in Children's Early Lexicons
     Abstract: This research examines phonological neighbourhoods in the lexicons of children acquiring English. Analyses of neighbourhood densities were done on children's earliest words and on a corpus of spontaneous speech, used to measure neighbours in the target language. Neighbourhood densities were analyzed for words created by changing....

64.   *Title*: Children's Use of Gesture to Resolve Lexical Ambiguity
      Abstract: We report on a study investigating 3- to 5-year-old children's use of gesture to resolve lexical
      ambiguity. Children were told three short stories that contained two homonym senses; for example, "bat" (flying
      mammal) and "bat" (sports equipment). They were then asked to re-tell these stories to a second experimenter.
      The data were coded for the means that children used during attempts at....

65.   *Title*: Defining Spoken Language Benchmarks and Selecting Measures of Expressive Language Development for
      Young Children With Autism Spectrum Disorders
      Abstract: Purpose: The aims of this article are twofold: (a) to offer a set of recommended measures that can be
      used for evaluating the efficacy of interventions that target spoken language acquisition as part of treatment
      research studies or for use in applied settings and (b) to propose and define a common terminology for
      describing....

66.   *Title*: Slowed Speech Input Has a Differential Impact on On-Line and Off-Line Processing in Children's
      Comprehension of Pronouns
      Abstract: The central question underlying this study revolves around how children process co-reference
      relationships—such as those evidenced by pronouns ("him") and reflexives ("himself")—and how a slowed rate
      of speech input may critically affect this process. Previous studies of child language....

67.   *Title*: Parents' Views on Changes in Their Child's Communication and Linguistic and Socioemotional
      Development After Cochlear Implantation
      Abstract: Our aim was to obtain versatile information on the communication and socioemotional development of
      implanted children in their everyday environment. We studied 18 children implanted unilaterally at the mean age
      of 3 years 4 months. All had normal nonverbal intelligence, but 8 (44%) had concomitant problems. Their
      parents filled out semistructured questionnaires at 6 months and then annually....

68.   *Title*: Development in Children's Comprehension of Linguistic Register
      Abstract: For socially appropriate communication, speakers must command a variety of linguistic styles, or
      "registers," that vary according to social context and social relationships. This study examined preschool
      children's ability to use a speaker's register choice to infer the identity of their addressee. Four-year-olds could
      draw correct inferences based on Spanish and formal speech....

69.   *Title*: The Longitudinal Development of Clusters in French
      Abstract: Studies of English and German find that children tend to acquire word-final consonant clusters before
      word-initial consonant clusters. This order of acquisition is generally attributed to articulatory, frequency and/or
      morphological factors. This contrasts with recent experimental findings from French, where two-year-olds were
      better at producing word-initial....

70.   *Title*: Temporal Cognition and Temporal Language the First and Second Times Around. Commentary on
      McCormack and Hoerl
      Abstract: McCormack and Hoerl's state-of-the-art review of the development of temporal concepts from the end
      of infancy to the end of the fifth year shows that young children's conception of time is quite different from that
      of adults. Adults and 5-year-old children can construe an event from a range of temporal perspectives and can
      describe it from a variety of reference times (RTs) that may not coincide....

71.   *Title*: Verb Focus Particles in Children's Language: Production and Comprehension of "Auch" "Also" in
      German Learners from 1 Year to 4 Years of Age
      Abstract: This article investigates the acquisition of the focus particle "auch" "also" by German-learning
      children. We report data from spontaneous and elicited production of utterances with the focus particle "auch" by
      1- to 4-year-olds complementing earlier findings of a delayed production of the unaccented "auch" compared to
      the accented one. But in contrast to....

72.   *Title*: Development of Prosodic Patterns in Mandarin-Learning Infants
      Abstract: Early prosodic development (f_0 variation) was systematically measured in Mandarin-learning infants at
      the transition from babbling to producing first words. Spontaneous vocalizations of twenty-four infants aged 0;7
      to 1;6 were recorded in 45-minute sessions. The speech production of twenty-four caregivers was also audio-
      recorded during caregiver....

73.   *Title*: An Independent Psychometric Evaluation of a Speech and Language Tool for Two-Year-Old Children
      from a Sure Start Trailblazer Site in the West Midlands
      Abstract: Speech and language difficulties can be indicative of other cognitive, social and developmental
      problems. Tools used in the UK have not (1) targeted two-year-old children, (2) included both parents' reports
      and independent observations, and (3) simultaneously evaluated expression, understanding and speech....

74. *Title*: Connecting Cues: Overlapping Regularities Support Cue Discovery in Infancy
     Abstract: The present work examined the discovery of linguistic cues during a word segmentation task. Whereas previous studies have focused on sensitivity to individual cues, this study addresses how individual cues may be used to discover additional, correlated cues. Twenty-four 9-month-old infants were familiarized with a speech stream in which syllable-level transition....

75. *Title*: Basic Parameters of Spontaneous Speech as a Sensitive Method for Measuring Change during the Course of Aphasia
     Abstract: Background: Spontaneous speech of aphasic persons is often scored on rating scales assessing aphasic symptoms. Rating scales have the advantage of an easy and fast scoring system, but might lack sensitivity. Quantitative analysis of either aphasic symptoms or basic parameters provides a useful alternative. Basic parameters are essential units of language....

76. *Title*: Liaison Acquisition, Word Segmentation, and Construction in French: A Usage-Based Account
     Abstract: In the linguistics field, liaison in French is interpreted as an indicator of interactions between the various levels of language organization. The current study examines the same issue while adopting a developmental perspective. Five experiments involving children aged two to six years provide evidence for a developmental scenario which interrelates a number of....

77. *Title*: Language Skills in Shy and Non-Shy Preschoolers and the Effects of Assessment Context
     Abstract: Nineteen shy, twenty-three middle and twenty-five non-shy junior kindergarten children were assessed at school by an unfamiliar examiner, and at home where their parents administered a parallel form of the expressive and receptive vocabulary tests given at school. A speech sample between the child and parent was also collected....

78. *Title*: What's in a Name? Coming to Terms With the Child's Linguistic Environment
     Abstract: This article reviews the proliferation of terms that have been coined to denote the language environment of the young child. It is argued that terms are often deployed by researchers without due consideration of their appropriateness for particular empirical studies. It is further suggested that just three of the dozen or more....

79. *Title*: Home Literacy Environment: Characteristics of Children With Cerebral Palsy
     Abstract: Background: Various aspects of the home literacy environment are considered to stimulate the emergent literacy development in children without disabilities. It is important to gain insight into the home literacy environment of children with cerebral palsy given that they have been shown to have difficulty acquiring literacy skills. Aims: The aims of the present study were to investigate whether....

80. *Title*: Segmental Properties of Input to Infants: A Study of Korean
     Abstract: Segmental distributions of Korean infant-directed speech (IDS) and adult-directed speech (ADS) were compared. Significant differences were found in both consonant and vowel patterns. Korean-speaking mothers using IDS displayed more frequent labial consonantal place and less frequent coronal and glottal place and fricative....

81. *Title*: Evaluation of Core Vocabulary Intervention for Treatment of Inconsistent Phonological Disorder: Three Treatment Case Studies
     Abstract: Children with unintelligible speech differ in severity, underlying deficit, type of surface error patterns and response to treatment. Detailed treatment case studies, evaluating specific intervention protocols for particular diagnostic groups, can identify best practice for children with speech disorder. Three treatment case....

82. *Title*: Acoustical Cues and Grammatical Units in Speech to Two Preverbal Infants
     Abstract: The current study examines the syntactic and prosodic characteristics of the maternal speech to two infants between six and ten months. Consistent with previous work, we find infant-directed speech to be characterized by generally short utterances, isolated words and phrases, and large numbers of questions, but longer utterance....

83. *Title*: Development of Communication Skills in Finnish Pre-School Children Examined by the Children's Communication Checklist (CCC)
     Abstract: The communication skills of typically developing Finnish-speaking children between three and six years of age were examined using the Children's Communication Checklist (CCC). The differences between the boys and girls were also investigated. Results showed that the performance of the three-year-old children differed on the Speech subscale of the CCC compared to....

84.   *Title*: Morphological Cues vs. Number of Nominals in Learning Verb Types in Turkish: The Syntactic Bootstrapping Mechanism Revisited
       Abstract: The syntactic bootstrapping mechanism of verb learning was evaluated against child-directed speech in Turkish, a language with rich morphology, nominal ellipsis and free word order. Machine-learning algorithms were run on transcribed caregiver speech directed....

85.   *Title*: The Value of Vocalizing: Five-Month-Old Infants Associate Their Own Noncry Vocalizations With Responses From Caregivers
       Abstract: The early noncry vocalizations of infants are salient social signals. Caregivers spontaneously respond to 30%–50% of these sounds, and their responsiveness to infants' prelinguistic noncry vocalizations facilitates the development of phonology and speech. Have infants learned that their vocalizations influence the behavior of social partners? If they have....

86.   *Title*: Boundary Alignment Enables 11-Month-Olds to Segment Vowel Initial Words From Speech
       Abstract: Past research has indicated that English-learning infants begin segmenting words from speech by 7.5 months of age (Jusczyk & Aslin, 1995). More recent work has demonstrated, however, that 7.5-month-olds' segmentation abilities are severely limited. For example, the ability to segment vowel-initial words from speech reportedly....

87.   *Title*: Explaining Errors in Children's Questions
       Abstract: The ability to explain the occurrence of errors in children's speech is an essential component of successful theories of language acquisition. The present study tested some generativist and constructivist predictions about error on the questions produced by 10 English-learning children....

88.   *Title*: Prosodic Structure in Early Word Segmentation: ERP Evidence From Dutch Ten-Month-Olds
       Abstract: Recognizing word boundaries in continuous speech requires detailed knowledge of the native language. In the first year of life, infants acquire considerable word segmentation abilities. Infants at this early stage in word segmentation rely to a large extent on the metrical pattern of their native language....

89.   *Title*: Measuring Growth in Bilingual and Monolingual Children's English Productive Vocabulary Development: The Utility of Combining Parent and Teacher Report
       Abstract: This longitudinal study examined growth in the English productive vocabularies of bilingual and monolingual children between ages 24 and 36 months and explored the utility and validity of supplementing parent reports with teacher reports to improve the estimation of children's vocabulary. Low-income, English-speaking and English/Spanish-speaking parents and Early Head Start and Head Start program....

90.   *Title*: Measuring Phonological Development: A Follow-Up Study of Five Children Acquiring Finnish
       Abstract: This study applies the Phonological Mean Length of Utterance measurement (PMLU; Ingram & Ingram, 2001; Ingram, 2002) to the data of five children acquiring Finnish and evaluates their phonological development longitudinally at four different age points: 2;0, 2;6, 3;0, and 3;6. The children's results on PMLU and related measures are discussed together with remarks on individual differences....

91.   *Title*: The Acquisition of "Ser," "Estar" (and "Be") by a Spanish-English Bilingual Child: The Early Stages
       Abstract: This article studies the acquisition of copulas by a Spanish-English bilingual between the ages of 1;6 and 3;0, examines the possibility of interlanguage influence, and considers the distributional frequencies of copular constructions in the speech of the child and in the language....

92.   *Title*: Canonical and Epenthetic Plural Marking in Spanish-Speaking Children With Specific Language Impairment
       Abstract: In this study, we investigate whether specific language impairment (SLI) manifests itself grammatically in the same way in Spanish and English with respect to nominal plural marking. English-speaking children with SLI are very proficient at marking plural on nouns. Spanish has two main nominal plural allomorphs: /s/ and /es/. The /es/ allomorph has received....

93.   *Title*: Children's Interpretation of Indefinites in Sentences Containing Negation: A Reassessment of the Cross-Linguistic Picture
       Abstract: Previous research suggests that children's behavior with respect to the interpretation of indefinite objects in negative sentences may differ depending on the target language: whereas young English-speaking children tend to select a surface scope interpretation (e.g., Musolino [1998]), young Dutch-speaking children consistently prefer an inverse scope....

94.   *Title*: The Influence of Discourse Context on Children's Provision of Auxiliary BE
       Abstract: Children pass through a stage in development when they produce utterances that contain auxiliary BE ("he's playing") and utterances where auxiliary BE is omitted ("he playing"). One explanation that has been put forward to explain this phenomenon is the presence of questions in the input that model S-V word order (Theakston, Lieven, & Tomasello, 2003). The current paper reports two studies that....

95.   *Title*: A Qualitative Examination of Current Guidelines for Evidence-Based Practice in Child Language Intervention
        Abstract: Purpose: The present investigation examines the time, effort, and resources that evidence-based practice (EBP) requires, and looks at what types of results are obtained. Method: Principles of EBP as outlined by the American Speech-Language-Hearing Association were applied to 3 treatment case studies. Results: The cases took....

96.   *Title*: Noun Grammaticalization and Determiner use in French Children's Speech: A Gradual Development With Prosodic and Lexical Influences
        Abstract: This study investigates when and how French-learning children acquire the main grammatical constraint on the noun category (i.e. the obligatory use of a preceding determiner). Spontaneous speech samples coming from the corpora of 20 children in each of three age groups, 1; 8, 2; 6, 3; 3, were transcribed and coded with respect to morphosyntactic, lexical....

97.   *Title*: Child-Directed Speech: Relation to Socioeconomic Status, Knowledge of Child Development, and Child Vocabulary Skill
        Abstract: This study sought to determine why American parents from different socioeconomic backgrounds communicate in different ways with their children. Forty-seven parent-child dyads were videotaped engaging in naturalistic interactions in the home for 90 minutes at child age 2; 6. Transcripts of these interactions provided....

98.   *Title*: Opportunities for the Development of Communicative Competence for Children in an Orphanage in South Africa
        Abstract: Orphanage life places children at risk of developmental delay, particularly with regard to speech and language acquisition. The aim of this study was to evaluate opportunities for children in an orphanage in South Africa to acquire communicative competence, by examining adult-child....

99.   *Title*: The Acquisition of German Relative Clauses: A Case Study
        Abstract: This paper investigates the development of relative clauses in the speech of one German-speaking child aged 2; 0 to 5; 0. The earliest relative clauses we found in the data occur in topicalization constructions that are only a little different from simple sentences: they contain a single proposition, express the actor prior....

100.   *Title*: Speech and Language Development in Cri Du Chat Syndrome: A Critical Review
        Abstract: This article reviews research on speech and language abilities in people with cri du chat syndrome (CCS). CCS is a rare genetic disorder, with an estimated incidence between 1 in 15,000 and 1 in 50,000 births, resulting from a deletion on the short arm of chromosome 5. In general, individuals have delayed speech....

101.   *Title*: Pronouns and Verbs in Adult Speech to Children: A Corpus Analysis
        Abstract: Assessing whether domain-general mechanisms could account for language acquisition requires determining whether statistical regularities among surface cues in child directed speech (CDS) are sufficient for inducing deep syntactic and semantic structure. This....

102.   *Title*: Prosodically Conditioned Variability in Children's Production of French Determiners
        Abstract: Researchers have long noted that children's grammatical morphemes are variably produced, raising questions about when and how grammatical competence is acquired. This study examined the spontaneous production of determiners by two French-speaking children aged 1; 5–2; 5. It found that determiners were produced earlier with monosyllabic words, and later with disyllabic and trisyllabic words....

103.   *Title*: Retrospective Parent Report of Early Vocal Behaviours in Children With Suspected Childhood Apraxia of Speech (sCAS)
        Abstract: Parents of children with suspected Childhood Apraxia of Speech (sCAS, n = 20), Specific Language Impairment (SLI, n = 20), and typically developing speech and language skills (TD, n = 20) participated in this study, which aimed to quantify and compare reports....

104.   *Title*: The Acquisition of Gender Marking by Young German-Speaking Children: Evidence for Learning Guided by Phonological Regularities
        Abstract: The acquisition of noun gender on articles was studied in a sample of 21 young German-speaking children. Longitudinal spontaneous speech data were used. Data analysis is based on 22 two-hourly speech samples per child from six children between 1; 4 and 3; 8....

105.   *Title*: Evaluation of Core Vocabulary Intervention for Treatment of Inconsistent Phonological Disorder: Three Treatment Case Studies
        Abstract: Children with unintelligible speech differ in severity, underlying deficit, type of surface error patterns and response to treatment. Detailed treatment case studies, evaluating specific intervention protocols for particular diagnostic groups, can identify best practice for children with speech disorder. Three treatment....

106.   *Title*: The Interpretation of Disjunction in Universal Grammar
       Abstract: Child and adult speakers of English have different ideas of what "or" means in ordinary statements of the form "A or B." Even more far-reaching differences between children and adults are found in other languages. This tells us that young children do not learn what "or" means by watching how adults use "or." An alternative is to suppose that children draw upon....

107.   *Title*: Babbling and First Words in Children With Slow Expressive Development
       Abstract: This study examined early vocal production to assess whether it is possible to identify predictors of vocabulary development prior to the age point at which lexical delay is usually identified. Characteristics of babbling and first words in 12 Italian children with slow expressive development (late talkers; LT) were compared with those of 12 typically developing (TD) peers. Syllable structure and....

108.   *Title*: Morphosyntactic Learning and the Development of Tense
       Abstract: In this article, we propose that the Root Infinitive (RI) phenomenon in child language is best viewed and explained as the interaction between morphological learning and syntactic development. We make the following specific suggestions: The optionality in RI reflects the presence of a grammar such as Chinese which does not....

109.   *Title*: Bootstrapping Lexical and Syntactic Acquisition
       Abstract: This paper focuses on how phrasal prosody and function words may interact during early language acquisition. Experimental results show that infants have access to intermediate prosodic phrases (phonological phrases) during the first year of life, and use these to constrain lexical segmentation. These same intermediate prosodic....

110.   *Title*: Listening to Language at Birth: Evidence for a Bias for Speech in Neonates
       Abstract: The nature and origin of the human capacity for acquiring language is not yet fully understood. Here we uncover early roots of this capacity by demonstrating that humans are born with a preference for listening to speech. Human neonates adjusted their high amplitude sucking to preferentially listen to speech....

111.   *Title*: Understanding the Developmental Dynamics of Subject Omission: The Role of Processing Limitations in Learning
       Abstract: P. Bloom's (1990) data on subject omission are often taken as strong support for the view that child language can be explained in terms of full competence coupled with processing limitations in production. This paper examines whether processing limitations in learning may provide a more parsimonious explanation of the data with....

112.   *Title*: Compensatory Vowel Lengthening for Omitted Coda Consonants: A Phonetic Investigation of Children's Early Representations of Prosodic Words
       Abstract: Children's early word productions often differ from the target form, sometimes exhibiting vowel lengthening when word-final coda consonants are omitted (e.g., "dog" /d[open o]g/ [arrow right] [d[open o]:]). It has typically been assumed that such lengthening compensates for a missing prosodic unit (a mora). However, this study raises the alternative hypothesis that vowel lengthening in early....

113.   *Title*: On the Robustness of Vocal Development: An Examination of Infants with Moderate-to-Severe Hearing Loss and Additional Risk Factors
       Abstract: Purpose: Onset of canonical babbling by 10 months of age is surprisingly robust in infancy, suggesting that there must be deep biological forces that keep the development of this key vocal capability on course. This study further evaluated the robustness of canonical babbling and other aspects of prelinguistic vocal development. Method: Longitudinal observation was conducted on four infants who were....

114.   *Title*: Parent-Child Interaction in Nigerian Families: Conversation Analysis, Context, and Culture
       Abstract: This paper uses a conversation analysis (CA) approach to explore parent-child interaction (PCI) within Nigerian families. We illustrate how speech and language therapists (SLTs), by using CA, can tailor recommendations according to the interactional style of each individual family that are....

115.   *Title*: Linguistic Constraints on Children's Ability to Isolate Phonemes in Arabic
       Abstract: The study tested the effect of three factors on Arab children's (N = 256) phoneme isolation: "phoneme's linguistic affiliation" (standard phonemes vs. spoken phonemes), phoneme position (initial vs. final), and linguistic context (singleton vs. cluster). Two groups of children speaking two different vernaculars were tested. The two vernaculars differed with respect to whether they included four....

116.   *Title*: A Toddler's Treatment of "Mm" and "Mm Hm" in Talk With a Parent
       Abstract: The study to be reported in this paper examined the work accomplished by "mm" and "mm hm" in the interactions of a parent and his daughter aged 0;10–2;0. Using the findings of Gardner (2001) for adults, the analysis shows that "mm" accomplished a range of functions based on its sequential placement and prosodic features, whereas "mm hm" was much more restricted to its use as a continuer. The....

117.   *Title*: Predicting Language Outcomes for Internationally Adopted Children
       Abstract: Purpose: Language and speech are difficult to assess in newly arrived internationally adopted children. The purpose of this study was to determine if assessments completed when toddlers were first adopted could predict language outcomes at age 2. Local norms were used to develop early....

118.   *Title*: Crosslinguistic Evidence for the Diminutive Advantage: Gender Agreement in Russian and Serbian Children
       Abstract: Our previous research showed that Russian children commit fewer gender-agreement errors with diminutive nouns than with their simplex counterparts. Experiment 1 replicates this finding with Russian children (N = 24, mean 3;7, range 2;10–4;6). Gender agreement was recorded from adjective usage as children described animal pictures given just their names, varying in derivational status....

119.   *Title*: Spoken Word Recognition by Latino Children Learning Spanish as Their First Language
       Abstract: Research on the development of efficiency in spoken language understanding has focused largely on middle-class children learning English. Here we extend this research to Spanish-learning children (n = 49; M = 2;0; range = 1;3–3;1) living in the USA in Latino families from primarily low socioeconomic backgrounds. Children looked at pictures of familiar objects while....

120.   *Title*: Auditory Sensitivity and the Prelinguistic Vocalizations of Early-Amplified Infants
       Abstract: Purpose: Vocalization development has not been studied thoroughly in infants with early-identified hearing loss who receive hearing aids in the first year of life. This study sought to evaluate the relationship between auditory sensitivity and prelinguistic vocalization patterns in infants during the babbling stage. Method: Spontaneous vocalizations of 15 early-identified infants with varying....

121.   *Title*: Language Acquisition is Language Change
       Abstract: According to the theory of Universal Grammar, the primary linguistic data guides children through an innately specified space of hypotheses. On this view, similarities between child-English and adult-German are as unsurprising as similarities between cousins who have never met. By contrast, experience-based approaches to language....

122.   *Title*: Community-Based Caregiver Training: A Rationale and Model for Early Interventionists Who Work With Low-Income Families
       Abstract: Speech language pathologists have recently begun to provide community-based education programs to help prevent speech and language problems. These training opportunities can be particularly useful to programs that serve low-income families. The authors....

123.   *Title*: Interactional Style, Elicitation Strategies, and Language Production in Professional Language Intervention
       Abstract: This paper explores language intervention for children with specific language impairment in Sweden. The elicitation strategies, style of interaction, and language production used by speech and language pathologists (SLPs)....

124.   *Title*: Prelinguistic Predictors of Language Outcome at 3 Years of Age
       Abstract: Purpose: The purpose of this study was to examine the predictive validity of a collection of prelinguistic skills measured longitudinally in the second year of life to language outcome in the third year in children with typical language development. Method: A collection of prelinguistic skills was assessed in 160 children early....

125.   *Title*: Clinical Implications of the Effects of Lexical Aspect and Phonology on Children's Production of the Regular Past Tense
       Abstract: This study examined the effect of lexical aspect and phonology on regular past-tense production. Data are presented from a group of 31 children, mean age 33 months, with typical language development. A case study of a 50-month-old child with Specific Language Impairment (SLI) is also presented....

126.   *Title*: Infant Word Segmentation Revisited: Edge Alignment Facilitates Target Extraction
       Abstract: In a landmark study, Jusczyk and Aslin (1995) demonstrated that English-learning infants are able to segment words from continuous speech at 7.5 months of age. In the current study, we explored the possibility that infants segment words from the edges of utterances more readily than the middle of utterances. The same procedure was used as in Jusczyk and....

127.   *Title*: Assessing Linguistic Competence: Verbal Inflection in Child Tamil
       Abstract: Within child language acquisition research, there has been a fair amount of controversy regarding children's knowledge of the grammatical properties associated with verbal inflection (e.g., tense, agreement, and aspect). Some researchers have proposed that the child's....

128.   *Title*: Direct Object Predictability: Effects on Young Children's Imitation of Sentences
Abstract: We hypothesize that the conceptual relation between a verb and its direct object can make a sentence easier ("The cat is eating some food.") or harder ("The cat is eating a sock.") to parse and understand. If children's limited performance systems contribute to the ungrammatical brevity of their speech, they should perform better on sentences that require fewer....

129.   *Title*: Patterns of Intra-Word Phonological Variability During the Second Year of Life
Abstract: Phonological representation for adult speakers is generally assumed to include sublexical information at the level of the phoneme. Some have suggested, however, that young children operate with more holistic lexical representations. If young children use whole-word representation and adults employ phonemic representation, then a component of phonological development includes a transition from....

130.   *Title*: Grammar and Frequency Effects in the Acquisition of Prosodic Words in European Portuguese
Abstract: This paper investigates the acquisition of prosodic words in European Portuguese (EP) through analysis of grammatical and statistical properties of the target language and child speech. The analysis of grammatical properties shows that there are solid cues to....

131.   *Title*: Clinical Implications of Research on Language Development and Disorders in Bilingual Children
Abstract: Assessing and treating bilingual children with speech and language disorders is difficult given the relative paucity of data on the speech and language skills of typically developing bilingual children and those with speech....

132.   *Title*: Prelinguistic Pitch Patterns Expressing "Communication" and "Apprehension"
Abstract: This study examined whether pitch patterns of prelinguistic vocalizations could discriminate between social vocalizations, uttered apparently with the intention to communicate, and "private" speech, related to solitary activities as an expression of "thinking." Four healthy 10-month-old English-speaking infants (two boys and two girls) were simultaneously video....

133.   *Title*: The Input-Output Relationship in First Language Acquisition
Abstract: This study provides an account of the distributional information and the production rates in a particularly rich corpus of German child and adult language. Three structural domains are analysed: the parts-of-speech distribution for a coded corpus of circa one million words as well as the....

134.   *Title*: Development of Displaced Speech in Early Mother-Child Conversations
Abstract: This study documents the development of symbolic, spatial, and temporal displacement of toddlers' speech. Fifty-six children and their mothers were observed longitudinally five times from 18 to 30 months of age during a staged communication play while they engaged in scenes that encouraged interacting, requesting, and commenting and scenes that explicitly focused....

135.   *Title*: Lexical Learning in Sung and Spoken Story Script Contexts
Abstract: Although most children seem to love music, our understanding of the role it plays in facilitating speech and language learning is limited, as is research validating its efficacy in the clinical setting. The purpose of this study was to examine how singing affects children's quick incidental learning (QUIL) of novel vocabulary....

136.   *Title*: Mothers Provide Differential Feedback to Infants' Prelinguistic Sounds
Abstract: Few studies have focused on mechanisms of developmental change during the prelinguistic period. The lack of focus on early vocal development is surprising given that maternal responsiveness to infants during the first two years has been found to influence later language development. In addition, in a variety of species, social feedback is essential for vocal....

137.   *Title*: Language Socialization of the Child Through Caretaker-Child Personal Narratives: A Comparison of Thai and English
Abstract: The present study reports preliminary findings on the elicitation strategies used by Thai and English caretakers when eliciting past event narratives from preschoolers. Ten Thai and 10 English-speaking caretaker-child dyads were recruited from Bangkok, Thailand, and from Sydney, Australia. Caretakers were asked to elicit past event narratives from their children....

Notes

INDEX

Notes

Notes

Notes

Notes

Notes